THE LANGUAGE AND IMAGERY
OF THE BIBLE

The Language and Imagery of the Bible

G. B. CAIRD

*Dean Ireland's Professor of Exegesis of Holy Scripture
in the University of Oxford*

'Like apples of gold set in silver filigree
is a word spoken in season'

(Prov. 25:11)

DUCKWORTH

First published in 1980 by
Gerald Duckworth & Co. Ltd.
The Old Piano Factory
43 Gloucester Crescent, London NW1

British Library Cataloguing in Publication Data

Caird, George Bradford
    The language and imagery of the Bible.
    1. Bible – Language, style
    I. Title
    220'.01'4   BS537

ISBN 0-7156-1444-4

Printed in Great Britain
by Ebenezer Baylis & Son Limited
The Trinity Press, Worcester, and London

CONTENTS

PREFACE

This is a book by an amateur, written for amateurs. Only an amateur could undertake to write on such a subject, since one lifetime is too short for anyone to become expert on more than one of the qualifying disciplines. For language is not the concern of the linguist alone, but of the literary critic, the psychologist, the anthropologist, the lawyer, the philosopher and the theologian as well. A prudent expert cultivates his own garden, not wasting time in looking over the fence at what his neighbours are doing. The amateur accepts cuttings from everyone, hoping that they will take in his own soil. I have tried to find out what writers in all these fields have been saying, and I have made use of their ideas when they have caught my fancy. But it is not my intention to trespass on the grounds of any of them. I am content to leave the Semitic philologist to grapple with the origins and affinities of Hebrew, the psychologist to discourse on the relation of words and mind, and the philosopher to investigate the truth of propositions and the mystical bond between words and the objects they denote. I am, if I may be allowed to readjust my metaphor, a walker on the common out of which they have carved their allotments. I offer to other wayfarers on the same paths this guide to the things that may catch their eye or their ear.

I have done my best in the footnotes to acknowledge the range and variety of my debts to others, but some must be accorded a special mention. Above all my wife has been to me at all times both Muse and critic, and she and our children have opened for me doors into worlds that were new to me. The initial impulse to write this book came from my dear friend and teacher, Nathaniel Micklem. I owe an obvious debt to my friends James Barr and Stephen Ullmann and to my former pupil Donald Evans. I learnt much from supervising the doctoral dissertations of Brian Wrenn on the prophets of the Old Testament and of Walter Houston on the prophets of the New. Finally, I owe a less direct debt of gratitude to those with whom I have disagreed, since they have compelled me to think out the reasons for my disagreement. They also serve who have the courage to be mistaken.

G.B.C.

INTRODUCTION

> Even with inanimate things that produce sounds—a flute,
> say, or a lyre—unless their notes mark definite intervals, how
> can you tell what tune is being played? Or again, if the
> trumpet-call is not clear, who will prepare for battle?
>
> (1 Cor. 14:7–8).

Our concern is with the Bible. What are the exact melodies, harmony
and counterpoint of its haunting music? To what battles do its
trumpet fanfares summon us? It has been the common conviction
of all Christians that their life must be lived under the authority of
the word of God, and that this word is spoken in Scripture; but how
may the ordinary reader be sure that he is allowing Scripture to
speak to him with its own authentic and authoritative voice? The
essence of Protestantism has been that the word of God is not
bound, and that, above all the choirs of ecclesiastical dogma,
tradition or fashion, without benefit of clergy, Scripture is capable
of making itself heard 'with most miraculous organ'. 'All things in
Scripture are not alike plain in themselves, nor alike clear unto all:
yet those things which are necessary to be known, believed, and
observed for salvation, are so clearly propounded and opened in
some place of Scripture or other, that not only the learned, but the
unlearned, in a due use of the ordinary means, may attain unto a
sufficient understanding of them.'[1] But since it has become evident
that for four and a half centuries the denominations of divided
Christendom have all appealed to the authority of Scripture in
support of their divergent doctrines and practices, we cannot
evade the question whether we have correctly understood 'the
ordinary means' and correctly discriminated between passages which
are clear and those which are opaque.

In an obvious and superficial sense this is a question about
translation. The student of the Scriptures can never for long be

---

[1] *The Westminster Confession* I. vii.

allowed to forget that the Old Testament is written in Hebrew (and Aramaic) and the New Testament in Greek; and in this book, written for those who read the Bible in English, we shall be unable to avoid some reference to those inexorable facts. But a translator of the Bible, or indeed of any other ancient text, cannot succeed in his task merely by a transference from one language to another; he must also undertake the transfer from the thought forms and pre-suppositions of the ancient world, from all its mental furnishings, to those of the present day. In this larger task of translation he runs the double risk either of modernising or of archaising: to modernise is to ignore the culture gap of many centuries and to read the Bible as though it were contemporary literature; and to archaise is to exaggerate the culture gap and to ignore the similarities between the biblical world and our own. Yet not even in this wider sense is translation our primary business. We shall be addressing ourselves not to the languages of the Bible, but to its language; not to the fact that it stands written in ancient and foreign tongues, the speech of ancient and alien cultures, but to the more fundamental fact that it is written in words.

In many of its branches the science of language is a long established discipline. Etymology, morphology, grammar, syntax and rhetoric have engaged the minds of scholars at least since Plato and Aristotle, and lexicography is almost as old. But it is only in the last hundred years that the new branch of semantics has developed, which is concerned with meaning; and it is only in the last twenty years that theologians have begun to take any notice of it.[2] This book might well be described as a text book of elementary semantics with illustrations from the Old and New Testaments.

In the ranks of biblical scholars there have indeed always been competent philologists whose training enabled them to practise semantics with an instinctive accuracy, long before it had been turned into a scientific study; but the dominant schools of theological interpretation have not normally looked to them for leadership. Instead, as James Barr has demonstrated, there has been a

---

[2] For an outline of the subject and a summary of the pioneer work of Michel Bréal in France, Ferdinand de Saussure in Switzerland, Gustav Stern in Sweden, Otto Jespersen in Norway, and C. K. Ogden and I. A. Richards in Britain, see S. Ullmann, *Semantics: an Introduction to the Science of Meaning*; and for the application of their principles to biblical study see James Barr, *The Semantics of Biblical Language*.

tendency to rely on pseudolinguistic evidence and argument. It is not, however, the purpose of this book to argue, as he has eloquently done, against those who have committed linguistic blunders. Instead, I have tried to set out systematically for the ordinary reader the questions he needs to ask if he is to enhance his understanding of the Bible and his delight in its inexhaustible treasures.

Wherever it seemed necessary, I have indicated the version of the Bible from which I have quoted. Elsewhere I have often used my own translation. But as often as not I have relied on the New English Bible, which, notwithstanding the 'chorus of indolent reviewers', is incomparably the best of the modern translations.[3]

[3] Quotations from the New English Bible, second edition (c) 1970, are used by permission of the Oxford and Cambridge University Presses.

Part One

GENERAL

Chapter One

The Uses and Abuses of Language

When we use words, we do not commonly pause to consider the purposes that underlie this piece of human behaviour, any more than we are conscious of the grammar of our native tongue. These purposes are many and complex, but they may all be classified under five heads. We use words: (1) to talk about people, things and ideas (Informative); (2) to think (Cognitive); (3) to do things and to get things done (Performative and Causative); (4) to display or elicit attitudes and feelings (Expressive and Evocative); and (5) to provide a means of communal solidarity (Cohesive). The first two clearly belong together, since much of our talking to others is thinking aloud, and thinking may be described as talking to oneself.[1] For reasons which will become apparent in a moment we shall call these two uses Referential. Similarly the third and fourth uses belong together under the general heading Commissive,[2] since we involve ourselves in or commit ourselves to the actions, attitudes and feelings to which we give utterance.

Each of these proper uses of language has its corresponding abuse. We may use words to misinform, to come to erroneous conclusions, to commit ourselves to actions we either cannot or do not intend to perform, attitudes we do not hold or feelings we have never experienced, and to make social intercourse difficult, unpleasant or impossible. We arrive therefore at the following table of language uses with their concomitant virtues and vices.

---

[1] The Hebrew for 'to think' is 'to say in one's heart', and the simple verb '*mr* (say) is sometimes so used. See, e.g., 1 Sam. 16:6, where the AV 'said' makes nonsense of the story, and the NEB correctly translates 'thought' (cf. 2 Kings 5:11). Similarly in Greek *logos* means both speech and reason (see C. H. Dodd, *The Johannine Epistles*, pp. 3-4).

[2] For a detailed exposition of this term see D. D. Evans, *The Language of Self-Involvement*, pp. 52-5.

		Use	*Virtue*	*Vice*
Referential	{ 1.	Informative	Truth	Falsehood
	2.	Cognitive	Rationality	Fallacy
Commissive	{ 3.	Performative	Validity	Invalidity
	4.	Expressive	Sincerity	Insincerity
	5.	Cohesive	Rapport	Discord

The various uses and abuses of language operate sometimes in isolation, but far more often in combination. 'In actual discussion terms are used at least as much for the sake of their suasory and emotive effects as for their strictly symbolic value.'[3] If then we are to understand what other people are saying to us, it is important for us to be able to recognise which use we are dealing with or, where more than one is involved, which is dominant. In our reading of the Bible we cannot escape such questions. The Old Testament historians for example had an obvious interest in sound theological attitudes, but to what extent did this impair the accuracy of their reporting? When Paul in his letters refers to his opponents, are these passages descriptive or evaluative, i.e. do they provide an adequate basis for the reconstruction of the views he is attacking, or do they merely or mainly depict his reaction to these views (see e.g. Phil. 3:19; Col. 2:18)?

1. Informative.

Of all linguistic acts the simplest and the most fundamental is naming things. To name is to give identity and character, in some sense even to create. Because we now recognise this, it is no longer fashionable to dismiss as naive or primitive the treatment of names in the Bible. Adam gives a name to every living creature, and that name constitutes its place in the scheme of things (Gen. 2:19). When God calls the heavenly bodies by name, this guarantees that 'not one is missing' (Isa. 40:26). 'The Lord's word made the heavens; for he spoke and it was' (Ps. 33:6, 9). Language imposes a

---

[3] C. K. Ogden and I. A. Richards, *The Meaning of Meaning*, p. 123. See also W. Empson, *The Structure of Complex Words*; and cf. this remark of Sir William Petty, quoted by Samuel Pepys: 'Much ye greatest part of all humane understanding is lost by our discoursing and writing of matters nonsensically, that is in words subject to more sences than one, to ye rendering disputations Infinite upon every Proposition that can be made in any Science whether divinity, law, etc.'

shape on the chaos of the world. There is an outside world of brute fact, but it impinges upon us in a welter of impressions which, even in the process of perception, we reduce to order by receiving them through a linguistic screen.

Yet even this simplest of acts is compounded of two elements: a name both identifies and describes. In the terminology made popular by J. S. Mill, a name denotes a person or thing having certain qualities and connotes the qualities which all such persons or things have in common (*A System of Logic*, p. 20). Modern linguists draw the same distinction by means of the terms sense and referent: the sense is what we are saying, the referent what we are saying it about.

Proper nouns are an exception, since they only identify: they have denotation, but no connotation. There is indeed a common human tendency to endow proper names with connotation by punning or fanciful etymology (see pp. 45–6). We shall also find that words may change their status, so that a proper noun may become common (and connotative) and a common noun may become proper (and merely identifying).[4] Ordinary words may also be used without much regard to their connotation, but simply as identifying or mnemonic symbols. Thus when 'Ezra' has a vision of a man 'flying with the clouds of heaven' (2 Esdr. 13:1), the clouds have no other linguistic function except to identify this figure with the similar visionary figure of Dan. 7:13, and it would be over-interpretation if we attempted to suck any further sense out of them. Similarly a title is a word or phrase which has some connotative value, indicating status (King of Israel), achievement (Saviour of the World), office (Governor of Syria), or role (the Lamb), but which may be used mainly for identification (e.g. Acts 26:26; 2 Tim. 1:10; Rev. 19:7). If then we wish to discuss whether the phrase 'Son of man' was or was not used as a title in the time of Jesus, it is essential to determine what it is that we are being asked to affirm or deny.[5]

The attachment of a name to a referent is known as predication. Here already we come across a source of ambiguity, which is a possible cause of misunderstanding, but also one of the main

[4] See below, pp. 63–4, and on metonymy pp. 136–7.
[5] See G. Vermes, *Jesus the Jew*, pp. 160 ff.

growing points of language; and to it we shall return again and again. Is a sentence a statement about the subject or about the predicate? If I say 'X is a gentleman', this may be an answer to the question, 'What sort of a person is X?', or to the question, 'What do you mean by the word gentleman?'. Similarly, in the New Testament, when Peter says to Jesus, 'You are the Messiah', this is superficially an answer to the question, 'Who do you say that I am?'. Peter appears to be assigning Jesus to a well recognised role. But what is really happening is that the shadowy figure of the Messiah, hitherto glimpsed only from afar, around which conflicting expectations have gathered, is now identified with the clearly defined characteristics and attitudes of Jesus.

In interpreting the words of others the first task is the identification of the referent, and it is not always as easy as it sounds. 'Normally, whenever we hear anything said we spring spontaneously to an immediate conclusion, namely, that the speaker is referring to what we should be referring to were we speaking the words ourselves. In some cases this interpretation may be correct: this will prove to be what he has referred to. But in most discussions which attempt greater subtleties than could be handled in a gesture language this will not be so.'[6] If this is felt to be a difficulty between contemporaries, who share a language and have the supplementary aid of gesture available to them, how much greater must the difficulty be when we are reaching across a gap of centuries to a culture in which some of the common objects of daily life are unfamiliar to us! What, for example, were *teraphim*, if they could be small enough for Rachel to put them in her camel-bag and sit on them (Gen. 31:34) and large enough to give the illusion of a sleeping man when concealed in David's bed (1 Sam. 19:13)?

Even within the Bible instances occur of ignorance of the referent. In early times, as we know from the stories of Samuel and David, there was a priestly garment called ephod (1 Sam. 2:18; 2 Sam. 6:14). But ephod was also the name given to a totally different object carried by a priest, a container holding the Urim and Thummim, used in divination (1 Sam. 21:9; 22:18; 30:7). When the Priestly Code was compiled over five centuries later, all memory of the diviner's ephod had disappeared, and the instruction is given

[6] Ogden and Richards, op. cit., p. 15.

that the Urim and Thummim be placed in the breast-piece of Aaron's elaborate gold vestment, the ephod (Exod. 28:30). The ark described in the same document (Exod. 25:10–22; 37:1–9) can bear little or no resemblance to the ark which Hophni and Phineas carried into the battle of Aphek (1 Sam. 4:4), and which David subsequently installed in the newly captured Jerusalem (2 Sam. 6:2). That ark seems to have been a plain wooden box, probably with cherubim carved on the corners, the empty throne of 'Yahweh of hosts who is enthroned upon the cherubim'. It vanished in 587 B.C. when Jerusalem was sacked, if indeed it had not already been taken away by Shishak (1 Kings 14:25–26). In the Priestly Code, Solomon's enormous gold cherubim, fifteen feet high and each with a fifteen-foot wing-span (1 Kings 6:23–28), have been incorporated into the ark, and so have become an implausible part of the portable talisman which the levites were supposed to carry ahead of Israel's marching column, constructed all of a piece with the *kapporeth* or mercy-seat.

At many points archaeology can help us by the recovery of arte-facts. An eighteenth-century artist's reconstruction of the temple of Solomon looked very much like Blenheim Palace; and if today we know better than this, it is because the ground-plans of several other ancient temples have in the meantime been excavated.

A quite different complication of the problem of identifying the referent is presented by letters, which frequently contain allusions to previous correspondence or conversations, clear enough to the original readers, but obscure to us (e.g. 1 Cor. 5:9; 7:1). In one of his most tantalising sentences Paul uses no fewer than five opaque terms—'the rebellion', 'the man of lawlessness', 'the mystery of lawlessness', 'the restraining power', 'the restraining person'—and adds the comment that he explained all this to his readers the last time he was with them (2 Thess. 2:3–7).

But these are only aggravations of the general problem posed by Ogden and Richards, from which there is no escape when we are dealing with any of the central religious teachings of the Bible. To what, for instance, did Jesus refer when he used the phrase 'the kingdom of God'? We shall return to this question later, and for our immediate purpose it is enough to note three illustrative points. (a) It is an unwarrantable assumption that the phrase has exactly the same reference each time it is used. (b) The history of the

use of the phrase in the Old Testament and the intertesta-
mental literature serves to clarify the question, not to answer it;
Jesus would scarcely have devoted so many of his parables to
explaining what he meant by the kingdom of God if he understood
by it exactly what everybody else did. (c) The debate between those
who hold that Jesus declared the kingdom of God to have arrived
and those who hold that he declared it to be imminent is reducible
to its simplest terms when we recognise that the parties to the
debate have differently identified the referent. If Jesus was referring to the final vindication of God's purposes in the reign of justice
and peace, where the righteous are to banquet with Abraham,
Isaac and Jacob (Matt. 8:11; Luke 13:28–29), it is mere nonsense
even to suggest that this was present on earth when Caiaphas was
High Priest and Pilate Governor of Judaea. On the other hand, if
Jesus was referring to the redemptive sovereignty of God let loose
into the world for the destruction of Satan and all his works (Matt.
12:28; Luke 11:20), it makes nonsense of the whole record of his
ministry to argue that for him this lay still in the future. And we
have only so to state the matter to see that on various occasions
Jesus referred to both.

2. *Cognitive.*

Outside of those sciences whose language is mathematics, most of
our thinking, and all our rational thinking, is done with words.
There are, indeed, many other forms of mental activity, some of
them requiring a high degree of intelligence and coherence, which
do not call for verbal articulation, such as the processes which
control the daily activities of craftsman and housewife, of athlete
and dancer, of artist and musician; but none of these is what we
commonly designate as thought. It is by means of language that we
organise our past experience and present perceptions, and to some
extent also determine our future behaviour; and the three basic
tools of thought which it provides are naming, classification and
comparison.

Even our capacity for observation is closely related to the avail-
ability of names for what we perceive. We do not accurately observe
anything to the point of distinguishing it from all similar objects
until we can give it a name of its own. It has been remarked that

classical Hebrew is deficient in words for colour, and there can be little doubt that this betokens a corresponding deficiency in discrimination, at least on the part of those who wrote the books of the Old Testament, probably also among the population at large. We must beware, however, of generalising from one example. The vocabulary of the Old Testament is poor in words denoting birds, trees and flowers; yet it would be rash to assume from this that no words existed among country people. If Aristophanes' play *The Birds* had not been preserved, with its muster of over a hundred species, we might have been disposed to make a similarly erroneous assumption about classical Greek. The priests who compiled Leviticus were well aware of the names of species which the laws of ritual purity required them to distinguish (Lev. 11:1–30).

In the realm of ideas there may be cultural reasons why important distinctions are not reflected in vocabulary. In English we can distinguish between revenge and vengeance on the one hand, which are close but not exact synonyms, and retribution on the other. But Hebrew has only one word (*neqamah*) to cover all three. The reason for this is that in Hebrew law there was no public prosecution; even a charge of murder had to be brought to court by the next of kin, the redeemer of blood (*gôel haddam*). There was thus no occasion to separate personal vengeance from retributive justice, even when these ideas were applied by analogy to God. Thus in the lofty prophecies of the later chapters of Isaiah, God is regarded as the avenging kinsman who comes to vindicate his wronged people (e.g. Isa. 43:14; 61:2). Once we have come to terms with the limitations which language can impose upon thought, we better appreciate those embarrassing passages which appear on the surface to be gloat songs over a fallen enemy, but which are intended as psalms of thanksgiving that divine justice does not for ever allow tyranny to prosper. Yet it would be unfair to imply that, for lack of a word, the distinction between vengeance and retribution was wholly unrecognised. A. T. Hanson (*The Wrath of the Lamb*, pp. 21 ff.) has drawn attention to an important development in the concept of the wrath of God. At first the phrase signified a personal attitude of God towards wrong-doers, but it came in the course of time to be used in an impersonal style, suggesting rather a principle of retribution: 'there came great wrath for this upon Israel' (1 Chron. 27:24). Without such a development it would be difficult to make much of

Paul's statement that Jesus 'delivers us from the coming wrath' (1 Thess. 1:10). The wrath is no doubt in some sense God's wrath; yet we cannot set the angry God and the merciful Jesus on opposite sides at the Judgment. Mercy and wrath are not on the same level as expressions of God's attitude to man.[7]

Classification is the way of defining objects of our experience by arranging them in groups according to their affinities, in such a way that general statements may be made which apply to every member of the class. The most obvious affinities are species and genus, but there are also affinities of space, time, cause and effect. Generalisations that we frame in this way are working hypotheses by which we seek to make sense of our environment and experience and to render life practical; but they need to be checked in the light of fresh experience and sometimes modified, altered or discarded. Thus the class name mammal enables us to propound the generalisation that all mammals are viviparous; and this serves well enough as a working hypothesis until we are introduced to the egg-laying platypus.

The creation narrative in Genesis shows that its author was aware of classification by genus and species. But the ancient Israelite was on the whole more interested in generalisations about human life and conduct, and his proverbial literature is full of them. The Bible could well be regarded as the text book of his working hypotheses, revised in the light of subsequent experience and insight. The Deuteronomic editors of the Book of Judges, for example, detected a recurring pattern in the history of the period they were recording, and so they conceived a cyclic theory of the providential ordering of history which was to have a profound influence on later thought (Judg. 2:16–23).

Another illustration of this theme is provided by the biblical treatment of the relation between behaviour classified as sin and experience classified as suffering. The sages of Israel observed that certain aberrations of conduct were followed by disagreeable consequences: 'idle hands make a man poor'; 'a cruel man makes trouble for his kin'; 'tale-bearing breaks up friendship'; 'bread got by fraud tastes good, but afterwards it fills the mouth with grit';

---

[7] For the various ways in which this disparity has been expressed by Jewish and Christian thinkers, see G. B. Caird, *Principalities and Powers*, pp. 37 ff.

'wine and women rob the wise of their wits, and a frequenter of prostitutes becomes more and more reckless, until sores and worms take possession of him' (Prov. 10:4; 11:17; 16:28; 20:17; Ecclus. 19:2–3). They therefore formed the working hypothesis, which was to become the orthodoxy of many generations, that all sin causes suffering; and it was only too easy for them to commit the logical fallacy of reversing the proposition and arguing that all suffering is caused by sin. Before we hasten to probe the inadequacies of this thesis in its two variant forms, we should pause long enough to acknowledge that it was a major factor in the education of a people's conscience. The Israelite did not start with a ready-made list of sins and perversely explore the consequences. He started with the consequences and explored the causes, and so developed his moral sense, by asking, 'What did I do wrong?'[8]

There can be little doubt that this orthodox theory was the source of much unnecessary anguish, as indeed it still is today, notwithstanding the drastic modification of it by Jesus. Jesus accepted the view that sin brings suffering, and therefore that some suffering is caused by sin (Mark 2:5). But he repudiated the reversal of the generalisation, refusing to accept it as an explanation of the massacre of Galileans by Pilate or of the accidental deaths brought about by the collapse of a tower (Luke 13:1–5). If a man was born blind, it was futile to ask whether he or his parents had sinned; he was rather to be regarded as an opportunity for doing God's work of healing (John 9:1–3).

The most eloquent protest against the Old Testament orthodoxy is the Book of Job. We miss the point of the triple cycle of debates between Job and his friends unless we recognise that he shares with them the major premiss that God rewards the good and punishes the wicked: their minor premiss is that Job has suffered greatly, from which they conclude that he has sinned greatly; his minor premiss is that he is innocent, and his conclusion that something has gone badly astray in the divine dispensation of justice. The resolution comes when the voice from the whirlwind sets before Job a panorama of mystery in the natural world, which cannot be fitted into his tidy anthropocentric world-view, and so enables him

---

[8] 'It is frequently difficult to distinguish between the Psalmist's sense of guilt because of his consciousness of sin, and his sense of guilt as the consciousness of calamity.' C. Montefiore, *Lectures on the Origin and Growth of Religion*, p. 515.

to break out of his religious orthodoxy into a new vision of God beside which his old religion appears second-hand. 'I knew of you only by report, but now I see you with my own eyes' (42:5). In the course of the debate Job gives vent to one of the earliest recorded pleas for intellectual integrity: 'Is it on God's behalf that you argue dishonestly, or in his defence that you allege what is false?' (13:7). The hypothesis must be altered to fit the facts, not the facts wrested to fit the hypothesis.

Job's protest against false generalisation makes a direct and understandable appeal to the modern reader,[9] but it was never in the main line of biblical development. That lay through the discovery that the innocent often suffer with the guilty, sometimes even in their stead, and that the voluntary acceptance of vicarious suffering may be redemptive. 'He was pierced for our transgressions, tortured for our iniquities; the chastisement he bore is health for us and by his scourging we are healed' (Isa. 53:5).

The third contribution of language to thought is comparison, the illumination of the unknown by the known; and the parables of Jesus are the most obvious biblical example of it. 'How shall we picture the kingdom of God, or by what parable shall we describe it? It is like the mustard-seed' (Mark 4:30-31). What is perhaps less obvious is that a high proportion of the vocabulary of daily speech consists of the comparisons we call metaphor (see Part II). We have only to think of the immense range of objects which we describe by the metaphorical use of words which literally refer to a part of the human body: head, crown, eye, nose, mouth, teeth, neck, shoulder, breast, heart, arm, elbow, finger (dactyl), belly, leg, knee, foot.[10]

In one respect comparison is very like classification. Both processes depend on our ability to isolate significant resemblances and to ignore other irrelevant characteristics. When we classify certain animals as mammals, we are excluding from consideration that some

---

[9] We have of course plenty of false generalisations of our own. We speak of newspapers, radio and television as 'the media', though they are sufficiently different in their operation and effects that any statement about 'the media' is likely to be false. Biblical scholars are not immune from this tyranny of words: we shall see later that such words as 'eschatology' and 'apocalyptic' are also false generalisations.

[10] Owen Barfield (*Poetic Diction*, pp. 70 ff.) points out that, although logically the literal precedes the metaphorical, if we look at the actual history of language, the further we go back the more figurative it becomes.

are carnivores and some herbivores, that some go on four feet, some on two and some on none, that some are gregarious, some nocturnal, some aquatic, etc. Similarly our understanding of a metaphor depends on our ability to detect and concentrate on the point or points of comparison, to the exclusion of all else. The neck of a bottle is not so called because it supports a head of beer, nor do children (if they are well brought up) point with chocolate fingers. So when the psalmist pictures the sun coming out 'like a bridegroom from his wedding canopy' (Ps. 19:5), we are not expected to enquire after the bride; and when Jesus declares that 'the Son of man came . . . to give his life as a ransom for many' (Mark 10:45), it is wise not to ask to whom the ransom was paid.

In its simplest form metaphor is the transfer of a name from its original referent to another; but this is commonly accompanied by a corresponding transference of feeling or attitude, and it is the second part of the process that makes metaphor such a potent influence in the emergence of moral ideas. Deep in the heart of mankind there is an instinctive aversion to dirt, disease and death; and in almost every language the words which convey this abhorrence are used metaphorically to express and evoke a similar loathing for sin, and especially for sins of fraud, sensuality and violence. The transference of this instinctive repugnance from the physical to the moral sphere is an important part of ethical education, for there is no deterrent so powerful as the horror of being unclean. The Jewish laws of cleanness and uncleanness, though they may have hindered the full concentration of this instinct upon moral offences, served nevertheless to keep it vividly alive, so that biblical language is rich in terms expressing a sense of contamination and a need for cleansing, which awaited only the clear moral insight of Jesus to direct them to their proper usage (Mark 7:18–23). The unclean in Old Testament law was that which disqualified a person from participation in worship, so that in effect he was debarred from the presence of God; and the institution of sacrifice, at least in the later Judaism, was largely concerned with the removal of this barrier. It is for this reason that the New Testament so constantly employs the language of sacrifice to declare the benefits of the Cross. A sense of pollution, whether of body or of spirit, implies an essential sanctity, and the imperative need of those whom sin has defiled is that which can cleanse the conscience from dead works (Heb. 9:14).

A similar transference of attitude was effected by the use of metaphors drawn from warfare. In the earliest period of Old Testament history God was thought to be literally a God of battle. 'Yahweh is a warrior: Yahweh is his name. The chariots of Pharaoh and his army he has cast into the sea' (Exod. 15:3-4). One of the collections of ballads which preserved the memory of Israel's wilderness campaigns was entitled 'The Book of the Wars of Yahweh' (Num. 21:14). With the growth of moral sensitivity, however, it came to be recognised that war between nations is an offence against the gracious intentions of God, who uses it, as he uses other human wrongdoing, to further his own beneficent purposes, but without approving of it. 'From end to end of the earth he stamps out war: he breaks the bow, he snaps the spear and burns the shield in the fire' (Ps. 46:9). But this did not lead to the disuse of martial imagery, for there is a different kind of warfare to be waged against the forces of chaos and wickedness, requiring a different type of weapon.

> Have you visited the storehouse of the snow
> or seen the arsenal where rain is stored,
> which I have kept ready for the day of calamity,
> for war and the hour of battle?   (Job 38:22).

By the time we come to the New Testament the transference of pugnacity, loyalty and courage from the literal to the metaphorical war is complete. 'Our fight is not against human foes, but against cosmic powers, against the authorities and potentates of this dark world, against the superhuman forces of evil in the heavens' (Eph. 6:12).

There are many today who would prefer to dispense altogether with the language of sacrifice and of warfare, the first because of squeamishness and unfamiliarity, the second because it is all too familiar and demonstrably too easy to take with a literalness which negates its true intention. But religion and morality are not best served by those who play safe, particularly when playing safe entails the disregard of powerful human impulses which by a bold use of metaphor may be tamed and harnessed.

All, or almost all, of the language used by the Bible to refer to God is metaphor (the one possible exception is the word 'holy').

But the metaphors derived from human relationships have a special interest and importance, because they lend themselves to a two-way traffic in ideas. When the Bible calls God judge, king, father or husband it is, in the first instance, using the human known to throw light on the divine unknown, and particularly on God's attitude to his worshippers. But no sooner has the metaphor travelled from earth to heaven than it begins the return journey to earth, bearing with it an ideal standard by which the conduct of human judges, kings, fathers and husbands is to be assessed. Because 'the father of the fatherless, the widow's champion is God in his holy dwelling-place' (Ps. 68:5), God's human counterpart must 'give the orphan his rights, plead the widow's cause' (Isa. 1:17). The human king must be endowed with the insight of God (Isa. 11:3; cf. 1 Sam. 16:7). Husbands must love their wives as Christ loved the church (Eph. 5:25). This phenomenon is a further illustration of the benefits that can accrue from the ambiguity of predication mentioned above.

If language is the indispensable vehicle of thought, it follows that its breakdown must bring thought to a standstill. The servant all too readily becomes the master, and we submit to the revolution when we allow words to do our thinking for us. We shall be exploring the ways in which this can happen in the rest of this chapter and in succeeding chapters. Here it is enough for us to note that some at least of the biblical writers were alive to the tyranny of words. Jeremiah accused his contemporaries of blinding themselves to the truth with the incantatory catchword, 'the temple of the Lord, the temple of the Lord, the temple of the Lord', and reminded them that even the attachment of the name of God to a shrine provided no insurance policy against the wickedness of its worshippers (Jer. 7:4–15). His prophecy of the new covenant engraved on the heart contains an implicit criticism of the fixity, superficiality and externalism of a covenant engraved on tablets of stone. We have already seen the author of the Book of Job grappling with the dangers of overgeneralisation, and another example of this is found in Paul's argument on justification. He has laid down the principle that man's acceptance by God depends on his faith, not on his success in obeying the moral law; and his critics, real or imaginary, take this to mean that, according to Paul, God is not interested in morality (Rom. 6:1, 15). It is to Paul, too, that we owe the gnomic summary of Jeremiah's insight: 'the written word kills, but the Spirit gives life' (2 Cor. 3:6).

This is not to say that either Jeremiah or Paul objected to the Decalogue, provided that it was not treated as a dead and deadening code. The Decalogue itself contains, in the second commandment, a warning against the idolatrous use of symbols which would restrict and domesticate the concept of God. It has frequently been remarked that, for all its vigorous denunciation of idolatry, the Old Testament has singularly little to say about the application of the principle to verbal symbolism.[11] If this is true, then one reason may be that visual symbols have a higher and more obvious degree of fixity than verbal ones. But Deutero–Isaiah at least seems to be immune from this criticism: 'To whom then will you liken me, whom set up as my equal? asks the Holy One' (Isa. 40:25). So too is the author of the Wisdom of Solomon, whose diagnosis that 'the invention of idols is the root of immorality' has its ground in the observation that 'in their devotion to idols they have thought wrongly about God' (Wisd. 14:12, 30).

3. *Performative.*

A legal deed and an act of Parliament both consist entirely of words. There are occasions when it is essential to draw a distinction between actions and words, as when John reminds his readers that love must not be a matter of words or talk but must show itself in action (1 John 3:18). But this familiar contrast must not be allowed to disguise from us that in daily life we use words almost as often to do things as to talk about things. When Pharaoh says to Joseph, 'I hereby give you authority over the whole land of Egypt' (Gen. 41:41); when Judah says to Jacob, 'I will go surety for Benjamin' (Gen. 43:9); when Tobias says, 'I now take this my beloved to wife' (Tob. 8:7); when Jesus says, 'Now I vest in you the kingship which my Father vested in me' (Luke 22:29); when Pilate says, 'I find no case for this man to answer' (Luke 23:4); when Paul says,

---

[11] 'Even words are in some sense idols, and any use of symbols implies a possible misuse through the confusion of the spirit with the letter—of a meaning with its casual vehicle.' R. R. Marett, *Sacraments of Simple Folk*, p. 121. 'We are all struggling under the weight of sackloads of the holy soil of Israel.' S. I. Hayakawa, *Symbol, Status and Personality*, p.153 (on 2 Kings 5:17).

'I appeal to you', 'I give my judgment', 'I commend you' (1 Cor. 1:10; 7:25; 11:2); they are none of them reporting an action which has been accomplished by non-verbal means, but doing with words exactly what they say they are doing. To such utterances J. L. Austin gave the name performatives,[12] since their purpose is not to inform but to perform. They are not, like those we have been discussing hitherto, referential statements which can be true or false, though for a variety of reasons which Austin called 'infelicities', they may turn out to be null. Herod Antipas had no right to marry Herodias (Mark 6:18). Joab and Abiathar proclaimed Adonijah king at Enrogel, but had no authority to do so (1 Kings 1:5–40). Elimelech's next-of-kin contracted to redeem his property, but had to back down because he had overlooked the legal requirement of marriage with the widow of Elimelech's childless son (Ruth 4:1–6). Under Israelite law a vow made by a daughter or a wife could be annulled by father or husband, but remained valid if he kept silence on first hearing it (Num. 30:3–8). Among the marrying branch of Essenes annulment was restricted to vows 'which should never have been made' (CD 16:10–12).

Performatives commit the speaker to stand by his words. The heir's blessing cannot be revoked, even if obtained by subterfuge (Gen. 27:33, 35). The vow must be performed, however rash (Judg. 11:35). A royal decree may not be changed at the king's discretion (Dan. 6:15). If a father settles his estate on his sons during his own lifetime, he forgoes the right of subsequently altering the terms of the bequest (Luke 15:31). 'What I have written, I have written' (John 19:22). Frequently the vivid poetic style of the Bible envisages words as having a substantive existence of their own, issuing from the speaker's mouth somewhat after the fashion of a balloon from the mouth of a character in a cartoon. Slander wounds like an arrow, gossip like a sword (Ps. 52:2; Prov. 12:18). The judge strikes down the ruthless with the rod of his mouth (Isa. 11:4). Words, in fact, are like servants dispatched to do the bidding of their master. 'By the blessing of the upright a city is built up; the words of the wicked tear it down' (Prov. 11:11). And like human servants, words may be active or idle according as their task is performed or neglected. The idle words of which account must be given

12 *How To Do Things With Words*, pp. 4 ff.

on the day of judgment (Matt. 12:36) are not, as the NEB would
have it, 'thoughtless' words, such as a carefree joke, but deedless
ones, loafers which ought to be up and busy about what they say,
the broken promise, the unpaid vow, words which said, 'I go, sir'
and never went (Matt. 21:29).

The word of God is envisaged with the same concreteness as the
words of men, but with this difference that God's word is always
active and alive (Heb. 4:12), always performative without infelicities. 'For he spoke, and it was; he commanded, and it stood firm'
(Ps. 33:9). 'God said, "Let there be light", and there was light'
(Gen. 1:3). 'I have sworn by myself, my mouth has uttered victory,
a word that shall not be recalled' (Isa. 45:23). 'So shall the word
which comes from my mouth prevail; it shall not return to me
empty-handed without accomplishing my purpose or succeeding in
the task I gave it' (Isa. 55:11). 'All things were lying in peace and
silence, and night in her swift course was half spent, when your
almighty word leapt from your royal throne in heaven into the
midst of that doomed land like a relentless warrior, bearing the
sharp sword of your inflexible decree' (Wisd. 18:14–16).

Many performatives depend for their effectiveness (but not for
their validity) on a response. An order does not produce the intended
result unless it is obeyed; otherwise it will only have the unintended,
though possibly foreseen, effect of rendering its recipient disobedient
(cf. Rom. 5:20).[13] For this reason Austin distinguished between
what he called illocutionary and perlocutionary force, subsequently
renamed by Evans (op. cit., pp. 69–74) performative force and
causal power. An invitation to dinner has illocutionary or performative force if it is a genuine invitation to a real dinner, and not to a
barmecide's feast; but it has perlocutionary or causal power only
if it persuades the guests to come (Luke 14:16–20).

Frequently the performative force of words is corroborated by a
symbolic act, as a greeting or a compact is reinforced by a handshake (Gal. 2:9). When Jeremiah smashed his pitcher in the valley
of Hinnom, what he did was more than a sermon illustration or a
publicity stunt; it was the promulgation of a divine warrant for the

---

[13] In a hyperbolic style, however, the foreseen result may be treated as though it
were intended. It is predictable that prophetic preaching will either elicit national
repentance or harden the nation in its recalcitrance. Accordingly the hardening process
is incorporated into Isaiah's commission (Isa. 6:10; cf. Mark 4:12).

destruction of Jerusalem. When Jesus broke bread in token of his forthcoming death and handed it to his disciples, he was making over to them the benefits of his passion. Actions speak louder than words, though not always as clearly. Yet only a believer in magic would suppose that the overt act had a performative force not to be found in equal measure in the accompanying words.

The distinction between performative force and causal power enables us to draw an illuminating parallel between the stories of David and Jesus. As a boy David was anointed king by Samuel in a ceremony which his father and brothers witnessed, but without appreciating its significance. But David's acclamation as king, first by Judah and later by all Israel, came a long time afterwards, when he had spent many years as a servant at the court of Saul and as an outlaw from it. To the secular historian it might seem unreasonable to treat the public enthronement as a national response to the private anointing, since one can respond only to that of which one is aware. Yet to the courtly narrator of the biblical story the connexion was obvious enough. The immediate consequence of the anointing by Samuel was that 'the Spirit of the Lord came upon David' (1 Sam. 16:13), and so heightened his natural gifts and graces that he became a distinguished military leader and popular hero; and it was to this proved worth that the tribes of Israel made their response.

The baptism of Jesus was a public event, but it was the occasion of a private experience of which, according to our earliest account, not even the Baptist was cognisant (Mark 1:10–11). In the tradition of the early church this experience was quickly identified as Jesus' anointing to messianic kingship, though at the same time it was firmly held that his enthronement at God's right hand had come about as a sequel to his crucifixion and resurrection, and that his acclamation by Israel was still incomplete. 'Let all Israel then accept as certain that God has made this Jesus, whom you crucified, both Lord and Messiah' (Acts 2:36). Here too the link is established by the Spirit, for 'God anointed him with the Holy Spirit and with power' (Acts 10:38); and Israel was being asked to respond to the presence of that Spirit, both in the ministry of Jesus and in his Pentecostal gift to his church.

Once it is acknowledged that God's performative utterances may long antedate their implementation, it is but a short step to see them *sub specie aeternitatis*. 'Before I formed you in the womb I knew you for my own; before you were born I consecrated you, I appointed you a prophet to the nations' (Jer. 1:5). 'In his good pleasure God, who had set me apart from birth and called me through his grace, chose to reveal his Son to me, in order that I might proclaim him among the nations' (Gal. 1:15–16). In the second of these quotations Paul is clearly making a deliberate allusion to the call of Jeremiah, notwithstanding that in his case there was this immense difference, that God's commission had come when he was in full cry as a persecutor of the church and as the enemy of what he came to recognise as the true purpose of God. In the Bible, predestination is never confused with determinism. God's appointments have absolute performative force, but their causal power never dispenses with human response. With Jeremiah there was diffidence to be overcome, with Paul fanatical resistance; and Paul at least never had any doubt that the power to which he surrendered was the constraint of love (2 Cor. 5:14; Gal. 2:20).

Verbal acts may, of course, be performed by delegation. A servant may be commissioned to contract a marriage for his master's son (Gen. 24:3–4). The comptroller of the royal household carries on his shoulder the key of the house of David, so that 'what he opens no man shall shut, and what he shuts no man shall open' (Isa. 22:22; cf. Rev. 3:7). When Paul is on trial before Caesar's representative, it is at Caesar's tribunal that he stands (Acts 25:10). One of the distinctions between a true prophet and a false one is that the false prophet has not been sent (Jer. 23:21; 28:15); whereas the true prophet has been given 'authority over nations and over kingdoms, to pull down and to uproot, to destroy and to demolish, to build and to plant', by letting loose into the world that word of God which is 'like a hammer that splinters rock' (Jer. 1:10; 23:29). Only God has the right to forgive sins, but he may delegate that right to the Son of man (Mark 2:10; cf. Dan. 7:13). Jesus in turn delegates his authority to his disciples: 'to receive you is to receive me, and to receive me is to receive the one who sent me' (Matt. 10:40; cf. Luke 10:16). Ezra can even address the angel Uriel as though he were God himself (2 Esdr. 5:43 ff.).

It does not necessarily follow that a delegate will carry out his task to the satisfaction of his principal; but, until he has been deprived of his office, his abuse of authority does not detract from the validity of his commission. The steward who is under threat of dismissal for incompetence is still within his rights in cancelling the exorbitant interest which, in disregard of the law against usury, he had charged his master's debtors (Luke 16:1–8).[14] The scribes who occupy the chair of Moses are the recognised administrators of the civil and criminal code of the Jewish nation, and their rulings must be accepted, even if they are personally unfit for their position of trust (Matt. 23:2). Pilate connives at a miscarriage of justice, but that alters neither his status as Caesar's accredited viceroy nor the more important fact that his authority has been given to him from above (John 19:11).

Just as performative force may operate through delegation, so the response it requires in order to have causal power may operate through representation. When Nebuchadnezzar promulgated a decree in the presence of satraps, prefects, viceroys, counsellors, treasurers, judges, chief constables, and all governors of provinces, we are told that 'all the peoples and nations of every language prostrated themselves' i.e. in the persons of their official representatives (Dan. 3:7). There is a close parallel to this in the story of the acceptance of the covenant at Sinai. 'Moses came and summoned the elders of the people and set before them all these commands which the Lord had laid upon him. The people all answered together, "Whatever the Lord has said we will do" ' (Exod. 19:7–8). In some instances an opportunity is provided for a person to ratify what has been done on his behalf. Thus annually at the Passover the head of the household, in reply to his son's question, identifies himself with the Exodus generation and their response to God: 'this commemorates what the Lord did for me when I came out of Egypt' (Exod. 13:8). In the same way the Christian is invited to identify himself with Christ's obedient self-surrender to the declared will of God: 'the love of Christ leaves us no choice, when once we have reached the conclusion that one man has died for all and therefore all mankind has died' (2 Cor. 5:14).

4. Expressive

Whereas the object of referential language is to clarify and convey

[14] See J. D. M. Derrett, *Law in the New Testament*, pp. 48–71; and *Studies in the New Testament* I, pp. 1–3.

2

an idea, the object of expressive language is to capture and communicate or to respond to an experience. It is the language of the imagination, of poetry and of worship. In ordinary speech these two styles of use contrive to coexist, so that most, if not all, of our daily utterances are neither wholly referential nor wholly expressive, but a mixture in varying proportions. On the one hand, few things ever impinge upon our notice about which our feelings are entirely neutral; even the apparent objectivity of scientific statements arises out of an interest in the subject and its method which is a sort of emotional involvement. On the other hand, only a handful of words like 'good' and 'bad' are so totally evaluative as to have no descriptive element whatever. Nevertheless, if we are to understand what someone else is saying, and in particular if we are to understand what the Bible is saying, it is important for us to recognise which of these two emphases is uppermost is any given item of speech.

The kind of ambiguity that can arise is well illustrated by an allusion which Paul makes to 'angel-worship' in his rebuttal of the so-called 'heresy' at Colossae (Col. 2:18). One commentator after another has assumed that there was active in Colossae a theosophical clique who were encouraging members of the church to join in the worship of hierarchies of angels, somewhat after the fashion of the Gnostic groups of a hundred years later. They may be correct in this reading of an obscure passage. But it is at least as likely that 'angel-worship' was Paul's pejorative and emotive term for a practice he wished to ridicule, and that the 'heretics' themselves would have resented and repudiated it.

Some feelings betray themselves by symptoms: embarrassment by a blush, fear by pallor or an unsteady hand, pain by a wince and pleasure by a smile. But a great variety of feelings remain private to ourselves until we give ourselves away by putting them into words: bodily states, such as fatigue, hunger or excitement; sensations of heat, cold or discomfort, responses such as wonder, disgust, horror or surprise; and moods such as joy, hope, sorrow, despair or contentment. When we are prompted to give vent to any of these, we have three kinds of linguistic device at our disposal: the subtle emotive association which clings to most words and is one of the means whereby we distinguish between synonyms and choose the *mot juste*; the sound of the words themselves; and a wide range of terms which exist to describe, express and evoke feeling. Our immediate concern is with the third of these, since the first two and the part they play in determining meaning will be dealt with in the next chapter. But something must be said at this point about sound.

The expressive quality of mere sound is most obvious in those otherwise meaningless ejaculations by which we signify pleasure or pain, sorrow or joy. By far the commonest of these in the Bible are the Hebrew *hoi* and the Greek *ouai*, both of which the AV translated by 'woe to' and interpreted as terms of imprecation, whereas the NEB normally renders the one by 'shame on' and the other by 'alas for', understanding them as exclamations respectively of abhorrence and of regret. But the power to evoke feeling simply by the bright ring of words, together with the joy we take in it, is also a quality of all poetry, and notoriously the hardest quality to reproduce in translation. Yet a sensitive ear can make a difference, as may be seen from a comparison of the various renderings of Isaiah's vision. When the RSV tells us 'each had six wings: with two he covered his face, and with two he covered his feet, and with two he flew' (Isa. 6:2), we know that these seraphim could only have landed flat on their faces if they had attempted to take off; whereas the seraphim in the AV and NEB are capable of being airborne.

It is one of the curiosities of language that many of the words expressive of feeling are bivocal, i.e. capable of signifying both stimulus and response, while some words which are their partial synonyms can signify only the one or the other. The following brief list of English words will illustrate the point.

Stimulus and response	Stimulus only	Response only
Love	Darling	Affection
Honour	Worth	Esteem
Wonder	Prodigy	Awe
Curiosity	Oddity	Inquisitiveness
Horror	Bugbear	Disgust
Delight	Treat	Zest

Hebrew and Greek have such words, no less than English; but one of the problems of translation is that the range of bivocal words in different languages never exactly coincides. Thus 'fear' is bivocal in Hebrew but not in English.[15] When Jacob takes an oath by the fear of Isaac, he is not swearing by his father's timidity, but by the God of whom Isaac went in awe (Gen. 31:53; cf. Isa. 8:13). 'Praise' in Hebrew can refer to the object or ground of praise; the NEB in Deut. 10:21 has wisely retained 'He is your praise', but in Ps. 148:14 has resorted to paraphrase in order to cope with 'the praise of all his saints', which means 'those qualities in the holy people which entitle them to praise'.

For biblical theology by far the most important of these bivocal words is 'glory'. The underlying Hebrew word (*kabod*) is derived from a root meaning 'heavy'; it connotes primarily the weight a person carries, his dignity, worth, status, majesty, and only in a derivative sense the honour or esteem due to his greatness. The two senses, however, lie so closely together that in many contexts it is unprofitable to attempt to separate them. When the psalmist calls God 'my glory' (Ps. 3:3), he may mean 'the one whose presence gives me standing', or 'the one in whom I exult'; or he may mean both! Certainly it is fruitless to enquire whether in the phrase 'Glory to God' the missing verb is indicative or imperative, since a doxology is by its very nature both an affirmation and a call to worship. But can we be so easily satisfied that the Paul of Ephesians is indulging in liturgical ambiguity when he says of his own sufferings that 'they are your glory' (Eph. 3:13)? Is he reminding his Gentile readers that they ought to take pride in what he has undergone on their behalf, or assuring them that the hardships he has endured in the cause of Gentile–Jewish unity and their share in the glory of the new humanity are obverse and reverse of the one coin?

The bivocal character of expressive nouns extends in Hebrew into the verbal system in a way which has only rare parallels in Greek and none in English; and this phenomenon has in the past been the cause of serious misunderstandings which are not yet wholly dispersed. The Hebrew verb ramifies into a number of stems (intensive, declarative, causative, reflexive etc.), one of which, the niphal, may be either reflexive or passive. The two niphal forms which are of relevance to our present theme are those derived from the same roots as the nouns 'glory' and 'holiness'. The first of these

---

[15] Except in the one expression, 'That is my fear', = 'That is what I am afraid of'.

(*nikbad*) can mean either 'to manifest one's glory' or 'to be glorified' (i.e. invested with honour or held in high esteem). The second (*niqdash*) can mean either 'to manifest one's holiness' or 'to be regarded as holy'. It is admittedly hard to distinguish between these senses, because the one implies the other; but context usually determines which is uppermost. Ezekiel used both words reflexively of God's manifesting his own glory or holiness, and so did later writers who were influenced by him.[16] But when the Old Testament came to be translated into Greek, the Septuagint translators uniformly rendered these words by the Greek passive, which, though it can be taken reflexively or intransitively, nevertheless was liable to give the impression that true passives were intended. The result is that the AV got Ezek. 38:23 right, Exod. 14:4, 17,18 nearly right, and all the other examples wrong, and even the best modern translations are strangely inconsistent. There is a particularly important example of this usage at Isa. 5:16, where the correct rendering is:

> But the Lord of Hosts displays his majesty in justice,
> and by righteousness the holy God shows himself holy.

The prophet, whose career began with a vision of God exalted in his holiness, has become convinced that what exalts God above his creatures and separates him from them is his transcendent justice and righteousness.

All this has an effect on the way in which we read the New Testament too. We can now see that the first clause of the Lord's Prayer, 'hallowed be your name', is not a petition to be answered by the human response of revering the name of God, but one to be answered by divine action, in fulfilment of the promise made through Ezekiel: 'when they see that I reveal my holiness through you, the nations will know that I am the Lord' (Ezek. 36:23). The proof of this, if further proof is needed, is to be found in the prayer with which in the Fourth Gospel Jesus responds to the coming of the Greeks: 'Father, glorify your name' (John 12:28). In the next chapter of John we have another case in point. 'Now the Son of man is glorified, and in him God is glorified. If God is glorified in

---

[16] For *nikbad* see Ezek. 28:22; 39:13; Exod. 14:4, 17, 18; Lev. 10:3; Isa. 44:23; 49:3; 60:21; 61:3; and for *niqdash* see Ezek. 20:41; 28:22, 25; 36:23; 38:23; Lev. 10:3.

him, God will also glorify him in himself, and he will glorify him now' (John 13:31). It will be obvious that, in this fivefold repetition of a single verb, the first instance cannot be equal in all respects to the second and third. The first is a true passive: the Son of man is to be glorified by God in the bestowal of a new access of glory which he is to share with those who will be united with him through his death (cf. 12:32; 17:22). But God is glorified by his own act of manifesting his glory through Jesus, just as the glory of Jesus is thereafter to be manifested through his disciples (14:13; 17:10).[17]

There are a few words in the Bible which exercise a peculiarly powerful emotional appeal because they are symbols that have directly engaged the writer's and the nation's affections. 'If I forget you, Jerusalem, let my right hand wither away' (Ps. 137:5). 'Fair and lofty, the joy of the whole earth, is Zion's hill' (Ps. 48:2). 'O how I love your law' (Ps. 119:97). It is not easy to determine how far the attachment is to the name and how far it is to what the name signifies; but in such instances there is always an element of both, and the higher the degree of idealisation, the greater the danger that the word will become an idol supplanting the reality, a 'trigger symbol' stimulating the expected emotion. Bonds of affection can become fetters, as Paul discovered when, from being a passionate Pharisee, he became an equally passionate Christian. He had believed that in the law he possessed 'the very shape of knowledge and truth' (Rom. 2:20). The ambivalence towards the law which gives so much trouble to readers of his epistles arises out of the shock he experienced when he saw that his very devotion to the holy law had blinded him to the glory of God in the person of Christ (2 Cor. 4:4–6). He contrived to break the old ties, partly by allowing Christ to fill the place in his thinking and his loyalty previously occupied by the law, partly by some vigorous language of repudiation. When he calls the Jews by the offensive name, 'the Mutilation' (*katatomê*), using a deliberate corruption of the proud self-designation, 'the Circumcision' (*peritomê*), by which the Jews distinguished themselves from Gentiles, he is, as the context clearly indicates, combatting the residual Pharisee in his own heart and the poignant memories of a beloved past he can never quite disown (Phil. 3:2).

---

[17] See G. B. Caird, 'The Glory of God in the Fourth Gospel: an exercise in biblical semantics', in *New Testament Studies 15* (1969), pp. 265–77.

The power and the peril of affective words is further illustrated by the disputes in the Gospels about the sabbath. Although the sabbath law was only one of the 613 commandments of the Torah, to the Pharisee living in a world dominated by Gentiles it had a unique importance. Other commandments could be observed or disregarded in private, but the weekly keeping of the sabbath was a public gesture of allegiance, a manifesto placarded before the world. The very word 'sabbath', therefore, tended to evoke feelings in which religion and patriotism were explosively mingled, and any disrespect to the sabbath, real or imagined, would be regarded much as a modern patriot might regard disrespect towards the flag. To Jesus, on the other hand, this use of the word 'sabbath' as a nationalist banner merely obscured the purpose of mercy which the sabbath was designed to serve (Mark 3:1–6; Luke 13:10–16; 14:1–6).

If words may be used as banners, they may also be used as bludgeons, to batter one's opponent and discredit his cause. We have just observed one instance of this in Paul's caricature of circumcision as mutilation, which was meant to suggest that the rite of initiation was in fact a disqualification for God's service (Lev. 21:16–20). But this was a trick which Paul no doubt learnt from the Old Testament itself. Saul had a son called Ishbaal and Jonathan a son called Meribbaal (1 Chr. 8:33–34); but when the word *ba'al* (lord) came to be suspect as a title for the God of Israel because of its association with foreign cults (Hos. 2:16), the one name was corrupted into Ishbosheth and the other into Mephibosheth, by the use of words signifying shame (2 Sam. 2:8; 9:6). The Philistines of Ekron had a god whom they addressed as Baal-zebul (lord of the house), and the Israelites expressed their contempt of foreign deities by renaming him Baal-zebub (lord of the flies) (2 Kings 1:3).[18]

When we reach the point at which words are used as weapons, it is inevitable that there should be a clash between the referential use of language, whose object is truth, and the emotive use, whose

[18] In later Jewish tradition both words became names of Satan, and both occur as variant readings in manuscripts of Mark 3:22, where Jesus is accused of casting out evil spirits by the power of Satan. It is probable that Beelzebul is the original, since the name suggested to Jesus the parable of the lord of the house who keeps his property intact until overpowered by someone stronger than he.

object is victory. But a conflict between use and abuse must not be confused with the deeper and more fruitful tension which exists between the referential and the expressive in their reputable and legitimate use, which bears some relation to the tension between philosophy and poetry, or between morality and worship, a tension lying at the heart of any religion that is worthy of the name. For one half of the religious mind is utilitarian and regards all things, including life itself, as raw material to be used in the service of a purpose, while the other half is experiential, looking on all things as gifts to be enjoyed, objects of delight and wonder, signposts to the greater wonder of their Creator. 'What born fools all men were who lived in ignorance of God, who from the good things before their eyes could not learn to know him who really is, and failed to recognise the artificer though they observed his works! . . . If it was through delight in the beauty of these things that men supposed them gods, they ought to have understood how much better is the Lord and Master of it all; for it was by the prime author of all beauty that they were created' (Wisd. 13:1, 3).

5. Cohesive

Much of the small talk of our daily exchange consists of what B. Malinowski called the language of 'phatic communion', by which he meant any linguistic behaviour designed primarily to establish rapport, to set another person at his ease, to create a sense of mutual trust and common ethos. Such behaviour has roughly the same status among human beings as non-aggression signals and mutual grooming do among certain species of animals and birds. Under this head Malinowski included most forms of social inter-course: formulae of greeting, approach and reassurance; comments on the obvious (e.g. the weather); gossip and competitive anecdote; and even those types of disagreement which establish a bond of antipathy.

Being on the whole a serious book, the Bible contains few instances of such talk, but it provides ample evidence that small talk played as large a part in the life of ancient Israel as in any other society, not least in the reiterated warnings of the sages against casual verbal indiscretions. 'When men talk too much, sin is never far away; common sense holds its tongue.' 'Stupid men talk nonsense.' 'Folly may amuse the empty-headed; a man of understanding makes straight for his goal.' 'An ill-mannered man is like an unseasonable story, continually on the lips of the ill-bred. A proverb will fall flat when uttered by a fool, for he will produce it at the wrong time.' 'Speak, if you are old—it is your privilege—but come to the point and do not interrupt the music. Where entertainment is provided, do not keep up a stream of talk' (Prov. 10:19; 15:2, 21; Ecclus. 20:19; 32:3-4). Above all, the oriental has never been sparing with his greetings. When Jesus sent his disciples out in twos to proclaim the arrival of the kingdom of God, one of the many indications of the urgent haste of their mission is that they were instructed to 'exchange no greetings on the road' (Luke 10:4); for the interminable interchange of eastern etiquette might delay them for as much as half a day.

There are occasions when a steady flood of words has its uses, quite apart from the significance of anything that may actually be said. When David was leader of a gang of outlawed freebooters, engaged in what today would be called the protection racket, one of the farmers who had accepted his services refused to pay; and his loyal wife, Abigail, managed to stop David in his tracks and divert him from his punitive intentions by setting up a solid roadblock of talk (1 Sam. 25).

The cohesive use of language is not, however, necessarily trivial. Phatic communion may tap deep springs of conduct, reminding us of early influences and first loves. Consider the allusive use of the word 'cross' in the letters of Paul. Much of the use of the Old Testament in the New is of this allusive kind, establishing rapport between author and reader and giving confidence in a background of shared assumptions. A quotation may be the basis of an appeal to authority, but an allusion is always a reminder of what is held in common.

There is a strong element of phatic communion in all forms of worship, but especially in the more stylised forms, where oft-repeated words slip from the lips without passing through the mind, and what matters is the fact of their communal use. We do not know very much about the worship of temple and synagogue in Old Testament times, but it appears that the main singing of the psalms was carried out by the levitical choir (Ecclus. 50:18), and that the congregation participated only with a stereotyped response

2*

(2 Chr. 7:3; cf. Ps. 118 and 136). Israel was well aware of the dangers of psittacism, the automatic response to words without regard to sense or reference, but the general assumption was that this was a characteristic of heathen cults (1 Kings 18:26; Acts 19:34), and this point of view gains some support from the teaching of Jesus (Matt. 6:7).

Phatic communion is tolerant of unintelligibility,[19] and a striking example of this is provided by the early Christian experience of glossolalia or speaking with tongues. From Paul's description of this phenomenon (1 Cor. 12–14) it is clear that it was normally unintelligible both to speaker and to hearer. He does not deny that it is one of the gifts of the Spirit or that it comprises some sort of communion with God. But even as a communal bond he rates it low: it does not build up the church. His advice, therefore, is that anyone whose overwhelming new experience can find no better expression than this incoherent, ecstatic speech should pray for the additional gift of articulate utterance, and that such people should not speak with tongues in church unless at least one of them can talk sense.[20]

There is, however, a more general way in which language makes for social cohesion. All those who share a common language together make up a speech community; and speech communities, as Leonard Bloomfield has pointed out,[21] rarely coincide exactly with groupings based on economic, political, cultural or religious ties. Throughout the Old Testament period Israel had cultural links both with Egypt and with Mesopotamia, where different languages were spoken. After the conquests of Alexander the Great (334–323 B.C.), Greek became the lingua franca of the eastern Mediterranean, including many independent states. The titulum over the cross, written in Hebrew, Greek and Latin (John 19:20), gives only a hint of the multiplicity of languages within the Roman Empire. And among the Jews there were Hebrews and Hellenists, i.e. some whose native language was Aramaic and some whose native language was Greek.

[19] Cf. S. Brock, 'The phenomenon of the LXX' in *Oudtestamentische Studien* XVII, p. 32: '. . . especially in the case of religious translations there tends to be a high degree of tolerance on the part of the reader towards unintelligibility.'

[20] See A. E. Thisleton, 'The "Interpretation" of Tongues' in *Journal of Theologica Studies*, n.s. XXX (1979), pp. 15–36.

[21] *Language*, ch. 3.

It is natural for us to think of Hebrew as the language of Israel, but this is an oversimplification. The language of Haran, whence Abraham is said to have come, was Aramaic, as can be seen from Jacob's treaty with his uncle Laban (Gen. 31:48). Hebrew was the language of Canaan (Isa. 19:18), and was taken over by Israel from the Canaanites, along with their knowledge of agriculture and the pertinent sacrificial rites. Israel and her immediate neighbours thus formed a speech-community which the prophets, in face of the baleful effect of Canaanite fertility cults on Israelite morality, found it necessary to break down. When during the last three centuries B.C. Hebrew fell gradually into disuse and was supplanted by Aramaic as the vernacular of Palestinian Jews, this was reversion rather than innovation. These facts ought to have deterred those writers, ancient and modern, who have held that Hebrew was a unique language, specially designed by the Holy Spirit for conveying theological truth.[22] Even within Israel, Hebrew was the language of the false prophet as well as of the true.

Within any large speech-community there may be numerous subgroups, created by dialect, class or the jargon of a trade or profession. The Greek of the New Testament is part of the *koinê*, the vernacular of the eastern empire, which was spoken even in Rome itself.[23] But it is *koinê* Greek spoken with a Jewish accent. A Gentile Greek would have understood it, but he would have thought it somewhat barbaric, and he would probably have had the same kinds of difficulty with it as a Londoner might have with the English spoken in Glasgow, New York, Calcutta or Tonga. For the Palestinian Jew Greek was a second language, and even the Jews of the Dispersion, for whom Greek was the first or only language, lived in close enclaves, associating mainly with one another, and

---

[22] The earliest use of this argument is in the Testament of Naphtali, 1.8:4–6. 'For at that time the Lord, blessed be he, came down from his highest heavens and brought down with him seventy ministering angels, Michael at their head. He commanded them to teach the seventy families which sprang from the loins of Noah seventy languages. Forthwith the angels descended and did according to the command of their Creator. But the holy language, the Hebrew language, remained only in the house of Shem and Eber, and in the house of Abraham our father, who is one of their descendants.'

[23] Paul's letter to Rome was written in Greek. Juvenal complains (3. 58) that he cannot bear the Greek take-over of the capital ('non possum ferre, Quirites, Graecam urbem') and inveighs (6. 187) against Roman women who think it fashionable to talk nothing but Greek. According to Quintilian (1.1.12), Roman children were taught Greek before Latin.

hearing week by week the Scriptures read in the Greek version we know as the Septuagint.[24] Early in the third century B.C., less than fifty years after Greek became the official language of Egypt, the Jews of Alexandria began translating their Hebrew Scriptures into Greek: first came the Pentateuch, then other books followed, until by New Testament times the process was almost complete. Many hands were involved in the work, with many different styles of translation. But all of these are what we should call literal, i.e. translated word by word and retaining a good deal of the syntax, idiom and general flavour of the Hebrew original. Many of the Greek words used were not exact equivalents of the Hebrew, and so came to acquire new shades of meaning; and of this we shall examine a number of examples later in this book.[25] The existence of translation Greek in a sacred book does not of course in itself prove the existence of a corresponding Greek dialect. It might be a purely literary phenomenon. But the Greek of the New Testament strongly suggests that this was not so. It contains Semitic turns of phrase (Semitisms) which are of three kinds: those showing the influence of Aramaic (Aramaisms); those showing the direct influence of Hebrew (Hebraisms); and those showing the indirect influence of Hebrew through the Septuagint (Septuagintalisms). If these occurred in isolation from one another, we should suspect them to be the results of translation from documentary sources. But since they regularly occur in close juxtaposition, the only reasonable explanation is that the authors spoke Greek exactly as they wrote it.[26]

---

[24] G. la Piana ('Foreign groups in Rome during the first centuries of the Empire', in *The Harvard Theological Review* xx (1927)) has shown that immigrants in the capital tended, as we might have guessed, to live in tightly knit social groups according to the country of their origin. Such groups are usually tenacious of their language and culture. Dr C. P. Thompson tells me that the Spanish Jewish community in Istanbul still retains the forms of fourteenth- and fifteenth-century Spanish (the time when their ancestors left Spain), long since obsolete in the peninsula.

[25] See also C. H. Dodd, *The Bible and the Greeks*.

[26] See N. Turner, *A Grammar of New Testament Greek: IV Style*.

Chapter Two

The Meaning of Meaning

Before we ask what the Bible means, it is essential that we ask ourselves what we mean by the word 'means'. For meaning is a highly ambiguous term, and the only safe way of handling it is to identify by indexing the various senses in which it is commonly used. We have already made a good start in the previous chapter by the vital distinction between meaning^R (referent) and meaning^S (sense), i.e. between what is being spoken about and what is being said about it. To these we must shortly add a third legitimate partner. But first we must set about the exclusion of a pair of intruders.

Let us begin with meaning^V (value). Consider the statement: 'the Fourth Gospel means more to me than all the letters of Paul.' This does not necessarily imply a greater understanding of the one than of the other; it is an expression of preference, which might even be made by someone who in fact understood Paul better than John. Meaning^V threatens to usurp the throne which belongs by right to meaning^S, and its spurious claims attract two ill-assorted classes of adherent: the very devout, whom it encourages to concentrate on what moves them deeply, instead of listening to what the Bible actually has to say; and the mildly religious who rise up in defence of familiar cadences whenever a modern translation of the Bible is brought to their notice.

A more subtle hazard is presented by meaning^E (entailment). If I say that nationalism means war, I am not asking anybody to believe that the two words are interchangeable synonyms, but that the one phenomenon leads inexorably to the other. When the author of Hebrews says of Jesus that 'he learned obedience in the school of suffering' (5:8), he is not telling us that Jesus learned how to obey, and certainly not that he learned the dictionary definition of the word 'obedience', but rather that he learned what obedience entails: the world being what it is, obedience for him meant suffering.

Meaning[E] sets a trap into which theologians are prone to fall. Many volumes have been written, for example, about justification by faith, whose authors, ignoring the fact that 'justify' (whether in Hebrew, Greek or English) means 'to declare or prove somebody to be in the right', have tried to pack into the meaning[S] of the word all that is entailed for faith and conduct in being justified by God. Some of them then compound their error by claiming that Paul has broken free of the forensic metaphor with which he began.[1]

After this cautionary digression, we return to the main highway opened up by F. de Saussure with his distinction between *la langue* (language) and *la parole* (speech), which marked the birth of the modern science of linguistics.[2] By language Saussure meant the whole stock of words, idioms and syntax available, the potential, the common property of all users. By speech he meant any particular and actual use of language by a speaker or writer.[3] Some scholars have since suggested that there is need for an intermediate term, idiolect or lexis, to designate the range of language within the competence and command of each individual user; but this is a refinement we shall not require. What we do need to note is that each user has complete control over speech but very little control over language.

Before Saussure this point had already been made less scientifically but more imaginatively by Lewis Carroll.

'There's glory for you!' 'I don't know what you mean by "glory",' Alice said. Humpty Dumpty smiled contemptuously. 'Of course you don't—till I tell you. I meant 'there's a nice knockdown argument for you!' 'But "glory" doesn't mean "a nice knockdown argument",' Alice objected. 'When I use a word,' Humpty Dumpty said, in a rather scornful tone, 'it means just what I choose it to mean—neither more nor less.' 'The question is,' said Alice, 'whether you can *make* words mean so many different things.' 'The question is,' said Humpty Dumpty, 'which is to be master—that's all.'

---

[1] For a noble example, see J. Jeremias, *The Central Message of the New Testament*, p. 64: 'Although it is quite certain that justification is and remains a forensic notion, God's amnesty, nevertheless the forensic image is shattered.' If a word 'is and remains' a forensic metaphor, then the imagery of the lawcourt from which the metaphor is drawn must be intact. See Chapter Eight, below, on metaphor.

[2] *Cours de linguistique générale*, pp. 25 ff.

[3] From now on I shall use 'speak' and 'speaker' to cover both the spoken and the written word, except where a distinction between the two is necessary.

Then, having explained the meaning of 'impenetrability', Humpty Dumpty goes on: 'When I make a word do a lot of work like that . . . I always pay it extra.' Our sympathies are enlisted on both sides, since each is standing for a valid principle, Alice, somewhat pedantically, maintaining the intractability of language, and Humpty Dumpty, somewhat cavalierly, asserting his mastery over speech.

In our attempt to analyse the meaning of meaning, we shall have to discriminate between the public meaning which is characteristic of language and the user's meaning which is characteristic of speech. One of the obvious differences between language and speech is that language consists of words (along with the syntax which holds them together), whereas speech consists of sentences. We need, therefore, one definition of meaning^S for words and another for sentences. The meaning^S of a word is the contribution it is capable of making to any sentence in which it stands. The meaning^S of a sentence is what the speaker intends to convey by it.

Here then is the promised third partner, meaning^I (intention). In the firm this partner has three functions, two of which very nearly coincide with those of the other partners: the sense and the referent of any act of speech are those which the speaker intends. The third function is connected with the uses of language enumerated in the last chapter. Does the speaker intend what he says to be referential, commissive or merely social? The answer to 'What did he mean?' might be 'He meant you to go', or 'He meant to make you angry'; but neither answer would necessarily give any clue to what the speaker in fact said. To understand why a speaker says what he does is not the same thing as understanding what he is saying.[4]

This emphasis on intention raises a question whether there is not yet a further type of meaning which we have overlooked—hearer's meaning. We are not at this point concerned with the obvious fact that in speaking each of us involuntarily gives away information, as the Ephraimites gave themselves away to the enemy by their inability to pronounce 'shibboleth' (Judg. 12:6), and as Peter's accent betrayed his Galilean origin (Matt. 26:73). Nor are we concerned with the equally obvious and important fact that there are qualifications for accurate hearing: the hearer must know the speaker's language, both literally and figuratively, and he must in

---

[4] On the intentional fallacy, see below, p. 61.

many instances have that commitment to self-involvement without which most commissive utterances are unintelligible. What does concern us is that words have associations of memory and experience which differ for different people; everybody knows how hard it is to be sure that what is received is exactly what is transmitted, without interference or distortion. That people habitually attach a meaning of their own to what they hear or read is beyond doubt, but it does not follow that this kind of hearer's meaning is in any sense a part of the meaning of what is spoken or written. The purpose of speech is communication; and when user's meaning and hearer's meaning do not coincide, this is nothing more or less than a failure of understanding, a breakdown of communication. This has an obvious importance for our reading of the Bible. It is possible to read the Bible, or indeed any other book, in a meditative fashion so that it becomes a stimulus to our own thinking. But when that happens, the thoughts are our own and are not to be confused with the meaning of what we have read. The most we are entitled to say is that any speaker who wishes to be intelligible will take account of the capacity of his audience, so that our judgment about what they are likely to have made of his words provides one possible clue to his intention.

If however we redraft our question and ask whether an utterance cannot have more meaning in it than the original speaker or writer intended or understood at the time, that is another matter. We shall return to this at the end of the chapter when we have acquired more tools to deal with it.

1. Public meaning

Language as a means of communication depends on what Otto Jespersen has called a 'latitude of correctness'. Humpty Dumpty is justified in insisting that a user is free to do what he likes with words, including paying them overtime. But if we do not know what 'glory' or 'impenetrability' mean until he explains, how can we be sure that we know the meaning of the words he uses in his explanations? Within broad limits, there is such a thing as correct speech. Otherwise we should all be shut up in the prisons of our private languages.

The public meaning of words is the business of the lexicographer, and it is compounded of most of the types of information which a good dictionary supplies: definition, etymology, sound and feeling. The rest of the information given in a dictionary relates to changes of meaning which are the subject of the next chapter.

(a) *Definition*

Even a casual glance at a dictionary ought to disclose two facts about the words it contains: that most of them have more than one meaning, and that their range of meaning is defined, wherever possible, by a list of words of similar or overlapping meaning (synonyms). The simplest test to show whether we have understood a word is the substitution of a synonym, the test we have already been using in the indexing of the word 'meaning'; and one excellent form of it is translation.

Polysemy (multiple meaning) and synonymy are the co-ordinates which enable us to tabulate the entire word-stock of a language as a series of words grids. The Greek word *cosmos* will serve well as an example. Except in places where it means adornment or beauty (e.g. 1 Pet. 3:3), the normal English translation of *cosmos* is 'world'. But 'world' in English is a word of notorious ambiguity, and some of this ambiguity is derived from its Greek counterpart.[5] In the New Testament *cosmos* (world) has five clearly distinguishable senses, though a good many finer distinctions might no doubt be drawn. It can mean the created universe (John 17:5; 1 Cor. 2:7). More often it is the world of mankind: in some contexts it simply means everyone, usually with some degree of hyperbole (John 12:19; cf. Acts 19:27); in others it means this present life (Rom. 5:12; 1 Tim. 6:7; Tit. 2:12); and in others again the existing world order, past or present (2 Pet. 2:5; 3:6). But in the great majority of passages, and especially where it is qualified as 'this world', it has a pejorative tone: it means the existing world order, organised in ignorance of God and in resistance to him, the object both of God's judgment and of his redemptive love, all that is signified by the adjective 'worldly' (Gal. 6:14; Eph. 6:12; 1 John 2:15; 5:19).

Each of these five senses has a different set of synonyms, a small illustrative selection of which is shown in the following table.

[5] See C. S. Lewis, *Studies in Words*, pp. 214–68.

1. Creation   *gê* (earth), *oikoumenê* (world), *ktisis* (creation), *ta panta* (universe)
2. Everyone   *pantes* (all), *ethnê* (nations)
3. Life   *bios, zoê, psychê* (all meaning life)
4. World order   *aion* (age), *genea* (generation)
5. This world   *sarx* (flesh), *phthora* (corruption), *kakia* (wickedness)

The five senses are not wholly unconnected, and both Paul and John find it possible to move freely from one to another. John can even use three of them in a single verse (1:10). But there are some contexts in which it is important to decide which is intended. What, for example, does Paul mean when he says: 'the form of this world is passing away' (1 Cor. 7:31)? In such cases the substitution test is indispensable. Does he mean that the physical universe is coming to an end (world^C), that this life is transitory (world^L), or that the old world order, rendered obsolete by the coming of Christ, is tottering to its fall (world^{TW})? The AV opted for world^L: 'the fashion of this world passeth away'. The modern tendency has been to assume, almost without argument, that world^C is what Paul had in mind, or that Paul did not distinguish between the end of world^C and the end of world^{TW}. Yet apart from passages which refer to the foundation or beginning of the world, Paul never uses *cosmos* of the physical universe, but rather *ktisis* or *ta panta*. There is no serious reason to suppose that in the passage under discussion he means more than 'the world as it now is'.

The first conclusion to be drawn from any word grid is that words and concepts only rarely coincide. Most words cover a variety of concepts, and all concepts are expressed by a complex assortment of synonyms and antonyms. The dangers of the word-concept fallacy are well illustrated by a study of the term 'heaven'. Many readers of the Bible have, I suspect, a unitary concept of heaven as the place where God lives (Ps. 11:4; Eccl. 5:2) and to which the righteous go when they die (Luke 6:35; Col. 1:5; Rev. 11:12). But this takes no account of the first sentence in the Bible, which tells us that heaven, as well as earth, was created by God; or of the penultimate scene, in which the old heaven and earth disappear, to make room for a new creation. Often heaven is no more than the sky (Gen. 27:28; Zech. 2:6); and the first mistake we can make is to imagine the people of biblical times naive enough to believe that God lived in the sky. There are always some naive people in any age, our own as well as theirs. But the writers of the Bible and its leading figures were not among them. They might, to be sure, look up to heaven in token of looking up to God (Mark 7:34). They might imagine the stars as angels, and the host of heaven as a privy council around the throne of God (1 Kings 22:19). But they knew that this was only a picture: 'heaven itself, the highest heaven, cannot contain you; how much less this house that I have built' (1 Kings 8:27).

But there is a worse trap to come in Matthew's phrase 'the kingdom of heaven'. Here the temptation is to assume that the kingdom of heaven is the same thing as heaven, and that to enter the kingdom is the same as going to heaven. Grammatically this is possible, since the genitive could be a genitive of apposition or definition, as in the City of Oxford. But in fact it is a subjective genitive, and the proof of this is that, where Matthew has 'kingdom of heaven', the other evangelists have 'kingdom of God'.[6] The kingdom of God exists wherever God reigns, and the kingdom of heaven exists wherever Heaven reigns. 'Heaven' is simply a title for God, as it is also in Luke 15:18 ('I have sinned against Heaven'). But because of the word-concept fallacy, and because Matthew's Gospel comes first and is the one from which lectionary readings are taken, the idea that the kingdom of heaven is an otherworldly sphere of existence is still prevalent, notwithstanding the central affirmation of the teaching of Jesus that the kingdom of God had arrived (Matt. 12:28) and was already being entered by the most unexpected people (Matt. 21:31).

For the biblical translator the counterpart of the word-concept fallacy is the notion that the same word in English (or French or German) ought to be used for every occurrence of any given word in Hebrew or Greek. A word in one language rarely covers exactly the same territory as its nearest equivalent in another. The French 'esprit' and the German 'Geist' overlap with the English 'spirit' for a large part of its range, but neither of them can be used of alcohol. None of these three can do all that is done with *ruaḥ* in Hebrew or *pneuma* in Greek, both of which can mean 'spirit', 'breath' and

---

[6] On the ambiguities of the genitive see below, pp. 97–100.

'wind'; and this poses insoluble problems for the translator of Ezek. 37:1-14, where all three senses occur, with 'point of the compass' thrown in for good measure.

In the AV the Hebrew *basar* and the Greek *sarx* were uniformly translated by the English 'flesh'. This might indeed be justified by the plea that the ambiguities of the English fairly reproduce the ambiguities of the original, and percipient and studious readers have no doubt always been able to cope with the resultant complexities. Cruden's Concordance, for example, remarks that 'flesh is understood in different ways', and proceeds to list eleven of them. But for the popular understanding of Christian ethics, and of the teaching of Paul in particular, this indiscriminate rendering has proved disastrous, since it has given the impression that Christians ought to adopt a negative and disapproving attitude to the body and its passions. When Paul uses *sarx* pejoratively, he is not talking about the body, but about the whole sinful nature of unredeemed mankind. His 'works of the flesh' include many that we should call sins of the spirit, such as envy and selfish ambition (Gal. 5:20). To be 'in the flesh' is the same thing as to be 'in Adam', in the old humanity, enslaved to sin and death. Christians are not, in this sense, 'in the flesh' (Rom. 8:9); and by this Paul does not mean that they are already disembodied spirits or that they have sloughed off their essential human nature.[7]

(b) *Etymology*

Etymology is the study of the derivation of words. The name enshrines one of the classical errors of linguistics, for it is derived from a Greek adjective which means 'true' or 'genuine', and its implication is that words have a 'proper meaning', which can be ascertained by tracing them to their source. In fact words continually change their meaning, in ways which we shall discuss in the next chapter, sometimes moving out of any recognisable contact with their origin. The English 'nice', which today means 'pleasant' and in the eighteenth century meant 'precise', is derived from the Latin *nescius* (ignorant). It is nowadays generally agreed that only current usage determines meaning; and one instance of

[7] I leave the biologists and psychologists to argue whether these remarks ought to be modified in the light of such works as *The Selfish Gene* by Richard Dawkins.

this is that we continue to use the word 'etymology', even though we no longer believe in what it etymologically stands for.

Etymology is an indispensable tool for deciphering unknown words, and also for tracing the historical development by which words have acquired the meanings they have at the time of use; though both these exercises are beset with pitfalls for the unwary. But in what sense may we claim that etymology is itself an ingredient of meaning? Only to this limited extent, that there are occasions when a speaker may make conscious use of a word's origin and rely on a corresponding awareness in his audience.

It is not difficult to find evidence in the Old and New Testaments that ancient writers had an interest in etymology, though much of it has to do with the (frequently spurious) derivations of proper names. Strictly speaking, a proper name is a word with denotation but no connotation, reference but no sense; and etymology is an attempt to provide it with connotation also. Thus Jacob's name is derived from the word for 'heel' and explained by the curious circumstance of his birth (Gen. 25:26); in modern terms, he was Heel by name and spent most of his life living up to it. In the midst of a sea of names in I Chronicles, we come across the pathetic little life story of Jabez, which appears to have been generated from the supposition that his name meant Sorrowful (4:9–10). The author of Hebrews makes some theological capital out of the name Melchizedek, which means king of righteousness (7:2). And Paul puns on the name of Onesimus, once Useless but now Useful (Phn. 11). There are also stories which offer etymological explanations of the names of places, such as Bethel and Peniel (Gen. 28:19; 32:30); and it is still a matter of debate among anthropologists whether the story is more likely to have given rise to the name or the name to the story.

Of all these many excursions into etymology by far the most important is the derivation of the divine name YHWH from the verb 'to be': 'I AM; that is who I am. Tell them that I AM has sent you to them' (Exod. 3:14). It is possible that the original narrator meant the verbs to be taken as futures, and that 'I will be as I will be' was a promise of the presence of God as and when he chose to be present; for the same verb occurs two verses earlier in the form 'I will be with you'. This line of thought leads us directly to the child whose name is Immanuel (Isa. 7:14), to the application of that name to Jesus (Matt. 1:23), and to the promise with which Matthew's Gospel ends, 'I am with you always, to the end of time' (28:20). But that is not the way in which the translators of the Septuagint understood the revelation of the divine name. They translated it by ὁ ὤν, 'he who exists', and so made it possible for later writers, beginning with the author of the Wisdom of Solomon (13:1), to make a synthesis between the theology of the Old Testament and the philosophy of the Greeks. Yet a third line of development is the elaboration of the name in the Revelation of John: 'Grace to you and peace from him who is and was and is coming' (1:4).

The Septuagint translators regularly resorted to etymology when they were defeated by the Hebrew text, and some of the results they produced proved to be influential. We have already seen that the significance of the Urim and Thummim had been lost by the time the Priestly Code was compiled. The translators derived the one from the word for 'light' and the other from the word for 'truth', so that in their version what the high priest carried in his breastpiece were the tokens of revelation and truth (Ecclus. 45:10). In the prophecies of Jeremiah (23:5; 33:15) and Zechariah (3:8; 6:12) we find the title 'the Branch' used of the king who is expected to restore the dynasty of David. This puzzled the translators, perhaps because it is not the same word as is used in Isa. 11:1, and they rendered it by the Greek *anatolē*, which normally means sunrise; and it is this oddity which lies behind the promise in the song of the other Zechariah that 'the morning sun from heaven will rise upon us' (Luke 1:78).

(c) *Sound*

The sound of words is clearly more important to their meaning when they are spoken than when they are written, but it has to be remembered that unvoiced reading is comparatively modern and that ancient authors wrote for reading aloud. The contribution of sound to sense is most obvious in onomatopoeic words like buzz and boom, and both Hebrew and Greek have their fair share of them. Most students of poetry would claim that there is a certain element of onomatopoeia in all consonants and vowel sounds, or at least in the reiteration of them, but it is doubtful whether this applies to prose. Repeated sibilants are supposed to produce 'a universal hiss', yet it can hardly be significant that there are six of them in the Greek form of 'your faith has saved you' (Mark 5:34). In any case such points as these can be studied only in the original language.

For our purpose it is more important that the sound of words frequently establishes associations of thought which the speaker will expect his hearers to be able to follow. Let us take as an example two versions of a familiar verse from John's Gospel (14:2): 'in my Father's house are many mansions' (AV); 'there are many dwelling-places in my Father's house' (NEB). Anyone who attempts to see this as visual imagery in either version will be in trouble, with a mental picture of heaven either as a garden suburb or as a block of luxury flats. John is not here dealing in pictures, but in an association of sound. The word for mansions or dwelling-places is *monai*, the cognate noun of the verb *meno*, for which the AV uses four English words (abide, dwell, continue, remain) and the NEB nine (stay, rest, find home, dwell, have permanent standing, belong, remain, continue, last). This is one of the many word-themes which John weaves like gold threads into his rich tapestry. It begins when two disciples ask Jesus, 'Where are you staying?' (1:38). Superficially this is a question about his address in Bethany, and the following verse picks it up at this level. But John is never content with the surface meaning of anything. At a deeper level he intends us to hear this as a question about Jesus' permanent home, a question which is not answered until the questioner understands that Jesus is the only Son, who dwells in the Father's house (8:35), in the Father (14:10), in the Father's love (15:10), and that in dying he is preparing a place for others, so that they may be where he is, where there is room for many to dwell. The AV with 'mansions' has abandoned all links of sound or sense between the noun and the verb (though it used 'abode' for the noun at 14:23). No translator can hope to do equal justice to all John's intentions, but the NEB has retained the link of sound with some of the other passages and a conceptual link with all of them.

One association of sound which appears on the face of it to have nothing to do with sense is the pun. Yet this form of assonance regularly provided the mental mechanism or stimulus for the oracles of the prophets. A basket of summer fruit (*qais*) becomes a portent of Israel's end (*qes*) (Amos 8:2). An almond tree (*shaqed*) is a reminder that God is keeping watch (*shoqed*) over his word (Jer. 1:11). 'He looked for justice (*mishpat*) and found oppression (*mishpah*), for righteousness (*ṣᵉdaqah*) and heard cries of distress (*ṣᵉʿaqah*)' (Isa. 5:7). 'God is able from these stones (*'ebnayya*) to make children (*bᵉnayya*) for Abraham' (Matt. 3:9). A pun can also be made on two senses of a single word. David, for example, is told by Nathan that he is not to build a house (temple) for God; rather, God is to build a house (dynasty) for him (2 Sam. 7).[8]

(d) *Feeling*

Besides their definition, all words (and not just the obviously expressive or evocative ones) have to a greater or lesser degree an aura of feeling about them, which can properly be regarded as part of their public meaning. It provides one of the most important criteria for discriminating between words which are otherwise synonymous.[9] The Greek words *laos* and *ethnos* both mean 'people' or 'nation', and in many contexts could be used interchangeably (e.g. Rev. 7:9). But in the New Testament they generally have a different feeling, inasmuch as the one is associated with Israel and the other with the Gentiles. Even a single word may evoke two different sorts of feeling in two different contexts. Ullmann has pointed out that the English word 'home' has one kind of feeling in 'Home, Sweet Home' and another in 'Home Office' (op. cit., p. 52). To call something 'new' may be to approve (Ps. 98:1; Heb. 8:13; Rev. 21:1) or to disapprove of it (Luke 5:39; Acts 17:21). A rock may give us a feeling of security (Isa. 32:2; Matt. 7:24), futility (Amos 6:12; Luke 8:6), or menace (Isa. 8:14; Rom. 9:33; 1 Pet. 2:8; Acts 27:29). A cloud impresses us differently according as it is a token of long-awaited rain (1 Kings 18:44), of misery and disaster (Ezek. 34:12), of mystery (Exod. 19:9), or of triumph (Rev. 1:7).

The feeling of a word is not always easy to reproduce in translation. When Paul and Silas were at Thessalonica, they were accused of 'acting against the decrees of Caesar, saying that there is another king, Jesus' (Acts 17:7 RSV). Now the Roman emperor was never called 'king' in Latin. Since the expulsion of the Tarquins in the sixth century B.C. the word *rex* had been loaded with unacceptable

---

[8] According to A. Guillaume, *Prophecy and Divination*, p. 121, the pun was a feature of prophecy among the Arabs also. For the more general use of puns see Sus. 54, 59.

[9] For this method of distinguishing synonyms see S. Ullmann, op. cit., pp. 142–3.

feeling, beyond the possibility of rehabilitation. In Italy the emperor was called *princeps*, first citizen. But in those parts of the empire where Greek was spoken he was known as *basileus*, which ought therefore to be translated 'emperor'. The accusation against the apostles was that they were setting up a rival emperor. But to translate the sentence in this way would be to miss the point that the charge was not a total fabrication, but had some basis of fact. Paul and Silas did believe that Jesus was in some sense king, the fulfilment of all the Old Testament promises of a messianic king to sit on the throne of David. It almost seems as if we have to choose between the Jewish associations and the Roman ones. But the NEB has found an ingenious way round the difficulty by putting the word 'emperor' back into the previous clause: 'they flout all the Emperor's laws, and assert that there is a rival king, Jesus.'

According to Paul the chief cause of moral depravity among the Gentiles was the futility of their thinking (Rom. 1:21; cf. Eph. 4:17). The general sense of the Greek word he uses is well enough represented by the English 'futility'. But we miss its overtones unless we recognise that this was a word used in the Septuagint in passages which inveigh against the unreality of pagan deities (Deut. 32:21; Jer. 14:22), and that for Paul therefore it carried all the revulsion against idolatry inherited from his Jewish past.

2. User's meaning

When we turn from language and what words are capable of meaning to what they actually do mean in any given item of speech, then, as we have already seen, the user is in control. Within the latitude of correctness marked out by public usage, or even slightly beyond it, he determines the sense of the words he uses, largely by the context in which he uses them, but partly also by his tone of voice, and to some extent by his choice of referent. These three clues ought to be enough to enable the listener to understand what the speaker has in mind, what he intends to convey; and in this sense intention is integral to meaning.

(a) Context

The first and weightiest rule of speech is that context determines meaning. But what do we mean by context? The words we use

have at least four types of setting, verbal, situational, traditional
and cultural, all of which have an influence on their sense. The
verbal context may be narrow or broad; the sentence in which a
word is used, the paragraph, the chapter or even the book. The
situational context includes such factors as the occasion of the
utterance and the occupation of the speaker. If we wish to understand the sentence 'There is something wrong with the table', we
need to know whether the speaker is a housewife in the dining-
room, a mason on a building site, a statistician in a computing
laboratory or an official of the Water Board. The words 'catholic',
'orthodox' and 'priest' may be used by two speakers in very much
the same situation, and yet with a difference of sense because the
speakers stand in different traditions. The context of culture is
important, for example, to a Frenchman attempting to translate
into his own language the sentence, 'I'm mad about my flat'; he
needs to know whether the speaker is an Englishman enthusiastic
about his living-quarters or an American furious about his puncture.

Proper attention to verbal context eliminates some of the apparent
inconsistencies of the Bible. There is a familiar contradiction, which
has caused a great deal of unnecessary trouble, between the
following two texts, here given in the literal translation of the AV.

To him that worketh not, but believeth on him that justifieth the
ungodly, his faith is counted for righteousness   (Rom. 4:5).

Ye see then how that by works a man is justified, and not by his faith
(Jas. 2:14).

The contexts show that the two writers are using 'faith' in different
senses and are not in any substantial disagreement. To Paul faith is
a confident commitment to the belief that God keeps his promises,
and indeed has kept all the promises of the Old Testament in the
sending of his Son (Rom. 4:20). The faith which James is attacking
is a mere intellectual assent to propositions about God, in which
even devils may share (2:19). A modern philosopher would query
whether such a faith can in fact ever exist, since even the sentence,
'I believe in the existence of one God', is a commissive statement
which entails creaturely dependence on the God in whom the
speaker professes to believe. James after his own fashion is making
exactly the same point: faith divorced from the commitment which

issues in conduct is a corpse (2:26). Similarly Paul, notwithstanding his vehement repudiation of 'works', i.e. deeds done in order to achieve a credit balance in the heavenly ledgers, thanks God 'that your faith has shown itself in action, your love in labour, and your hope of our Lord Jesus in fortitude' (1 Thess. 1:3).

The principle of contextual determination also delivers us from the worst excesses of the word-concept fallacy. The Greek *sôzô*, for example, regularly means 'save', but that is not to say that every time it or one of its cognates occurs in the New Testament we are dealing with the doctrine of salvation. In 1 Pet. 3:20 we are told, according to the AV, that in the ark 'eight souls were saved by water', which gives the misleading impression that the flood, the instrument of divine judgment, was the means of salvation for Noah and his family. What the Greek actually says is that they 'were brought to safety through the water' (NEB).

The story of the death of Ahab contains an interesting illustration of the importance of situation (1 Kings 22:10–17). Four hundred prophets have said, 'Attack Ramoth-Gilead and win the day; the Lord will deliver it into your hands.' Then comes a solitary prophet, Micaiah ben Imlah, who says exactly the same. Ahab, whatever his other faults, is no fool, and he recognises that, with the change of speaker, the words can no longer be taken at their face value. He therefore adjures Micaiah to drop the irony and to deliver his message in unambiguous terms.

A whole theology of the New Testament might well be written under this heading, since it is the contention of its contributors that with the coming of Jesus the whole situation of mankind has so altered as to change the semantic content of the word 'God'. God becomes 'the God and Father of our Lord Jesus Christ' (2 Cor. 1:3; Eph. 1:3; 1 Pet. 1:3). The Day of the Lord becomes 'the Day of our Lord Jesus' (2 Cor. 1:14). Against a schismatic group who have been claiming to share God's life, to know him and to love him after some esoteric fashion (1 John 1:6; 2:4; 4:20), the John of the First Epistle insists that we do not even know the meaning of the word 'love' and fill it with its true ethical content until we believe that the love of God took human form in Jesus and that God imparts that same love to others through his indwelling Spirit (1 John 4:7–16). The other John who wrote the Revelation is fond of a resonant title for God, 'the Omnipotent', which he uses nine times. But he repeatedly makes it clear that in using it he is recasting the concept of omnipotence, which he understands not as unlimited coercion but as unlimited persuasion. He hears a voice proclaim the victory of the Lion of Judah, but what he sees is 'a lamb with the marks of slaughter upon him' (Rev. 5:5–6); and it is by the blood of the sacrificed Lamb that the conquering martyrs win their victory, which is the only victory of God (12:11).

What appears to be a difference of meaning within two parallel traditions often turns out to be a difference only of reference, not of sense. The Jews and the Samaritans agreed about the sense of the words in Deut. 12:11, 'the place which the Lord your God shall choose as a dwelling for his name'; but the Jews took it to refer to Mount Zion and the Samaritans to Mount Gerizim (John 4:20). The Pharisees and the Sadducees would have defined 'Scripture' in identical terms; but the Pharisees regarded Law, Prophets and Writings as Scripture, and the Sadducees only the Law. But there are occasions when tradition can make a difference to the sense of words as well. The author of Hebrews begins his epistle: 'When in former times God spoke to our forefathers, he spoke in fragmentary and varied fashion through the prophets.' Yet in the argument which follows he quotes frequently from the Pentateuch and the Psalms and only rarely from the prophetical books. He does not restrict the term 'prophets' to Isaiah, Jeremiah, Ezekiel and the Twelve. For him the whole of the Old Testament is prophecy. Nor is this merely an extension of reference. The Old Testament is prophecy partly because through it God spoke to the forefathers and still speaks to the present generation, partly because it looks forward in all its parts to the better things which God has kept in store for 'these last days'.

The question of cultural context confronts us in an acute form when we try to translate the opening verse of the Fourth Gospel: 'In the beginning was the Logos.' The question 'What did John mean by Logos?' is a question about the cultural background to which he and his readers belonged. Was he writing to commend the gospel to educated Greeks, well schooled in the popular philosophy of the day, in which the Logos or Reason was at one and the same time the immanent rationality which gives order to the universe and also the rational quality in man which is capable of grasping the cosmic Logos and living in harmony with it? Was he a traditional

Christian with his roots in the Old Testament, looking back to the word of God which inspired the prophets and which was subsequently identified with the personified Wisdom? Or was he one of those who stood at the confluence of the Jewish and Greek worlds, trying to expound a teaching which was fundamentally Jewish in terms which would capture the imagination and respect of the educated Greek? The danger here is that we should think of culture in fixed and exclusive terms. It used to be held that Palestinian Judaism and the Hellenistic Judaism of the Dispersion were two homogeneous and contrasting systems. Now it is very generally held that neither was ever homogeneous, and that the contrasts existed as much within the two types as between them. Greek influence was felt not only in Alexandria but in Jerusalem, and strict Pharisees in Palestine had more in common with the strict Jews of Cyrene or Ephesus than any of them had with their more liberal neighbours.

This has important implications for the study of Hebrews. It was long held, almost without a dissentient voice, that the background to this epistle was the philosophical Judaism of Alexandria typified in the works of the learned Jew, Philo, who had expounded the Jewish scriptures in the light of the teachings of Plato and the Stoics. Did not the author believe that the earthly temple was a copy of the true temple in heaven and call the law a shadow of the things that were to come (8:5; 9:23; 10:1)? Since the author explicitly tells us that he derived the first of these ideas from the Old Testament (Exod. 25:40), this widely accepted theory was from the start precariously founded, and it has now undergone a total eclipse. The most that can be claimed is that the word 'shadow' may be a Platonic term picked up from popular vocabulary, much as a modern writer might make a reference to evolution without having read Darwin, or to relativity without being able to understand anything of Einstein.

(b) *Tone*

Anyone who attempts to read the Bible in public knows what a change of meaning can be effected by changing the inflexions of the voice, and how hard it is to be sure that the inflexions are correct. Let us consider by way of example Matthew's parable of the talents (25:14–30). We have no difficulty with the tone of the third servant's reply: 'I knew you to be a hard man: you reap where you have not sown, you gather where you have not scattered.' But what tone are we to use when the master picks up his words and repeats them? A flat, factual tone will suggest that the master accepts this description of his character and agrees with it. But it is possible, and surely correct, to read the words with a note of question rather than acceptance: 'I am not what you think me, but even if I had been all that, your conduct would still have been inexcusable!' Part of our difficulty is that the written word has no tone. Nowadays we attempt to supply this lack by punctuation, and so the NEB has added a question mark to the end of the sentence.

Paul, for all the eloquence of his pen, knew what a poor substitute a letter can be for the warmth and intimacy of the spoken word. 'I wish I could be with you now; then I could modify my tone; as it is, I am at my wits' end about you' (Gal. 4:20). He does not mean that he would alter what he has to say about their aberrations if he were face to face with them, but simply that it would all sound very different if they could hear the changing inflexions of his voice.

Some of the recorded sayings of Jesus need to be read with this point in mind. His words to the Syro-Phoenician woman, 'it is not fair to take the children's bread and throw it to the dogs' (Mark 7:27), which seem so austere in cold print, must have been spoken with a smile and in a tone of voice which invited the woman's witty reply. His answer to his mother at the wedding in Cana is in the AV version downright rude: 'Woman, what have I to do with thee?' (John 2:4). Among modern versions the most successful attempt to strike the right note is that of the Translator's New Testament: 'Mother, why are you interfering with me?'.

(c) *Referent*

The distinction between sense and referent is so indispensable to any discussion of meaning, and so self-evident once it has been pointed out, that it is a shock to find learned writers ignoring it. Among the arguments put forward to prove that Paul could not have written Ephesians there is one which states that *mysterion* has a meaning in Ephesians different from that which it has in Colossians. In fact the sense of the word is identical in both letters: it means 'a secret';

and it is only the referent, the nature or content of the secret, that is different. Yet there is no reason why one writer should not have detected in the person of Christ two different, though related, secrets.

Nevertheless, sense and referent are so intimately linked that failure to identify the referent is bound to diminish our understanding of the sense, which is then left hanging in the air. When someone speaks about a person or a thing we do not know, the words go over our heads. Some readers of the Bible are content to read it in this way, but the reader who wants to understand will ask, with the Ethiopian civil servant, 'Who is it that the prophet is speaking about here: himself or someone else?' (Acts 8:34).

The prophet John describes a war in heaven in which Michael and his angels were victorious over the Devil and his angels. Later Christian tradition, by the fallacy of misplaced concreteness, treated this as a precosmic event in its own right, quite failing to recognise that John's imagery had an earthly referent, as he makes inescapably plain in the sequel: 'This is the hour of victory for our God ... the accuser of our brothers is overthrown ... by the sacrifice of the Lamb they have conquered him' (Rev. 12:7-11). In other words, the victory in heaven is the symbolic counterpart of Christ's victory on the cross, which carries with it the guarantee of victory for his martyred followers.

There is another sort of problem in identifying the referent in John 6:53: 'unless you eat the flesh of the Son of man and drink his blood you can have no life in you.' Most commentators have held that here John is talking about the Eucharist; he does not record the act of institution in the upper room, but has transferred what he wanted to say about the sacrament to the sermon which expounds the significance of the feeding of the five thousand. Now there can be little doubt that his language here is eucharistic, since the main argument of the sermon is a contrast between the manna which Moses gave (i.e. the Torah) and the bread from heaven which is the incarnate Jesus, and the transition from eating bread to drinking blood must be occasioned by eucharistic memories. But the Eucharist is the source of John's language, not the theme or referent of the discourse. 'Flesh' in this Gospel is the symbol of incarnation (1:14), and what the hearers are being told is that they cannot come to full belief in the incarnation except through the ensuing death of Christ. 'You do not understand now what I am doing, but one day you will' (13:7). By the principle of ambiguity of predication (see pp. 9–10), the use of eucharistic language to talk about something more fundamental will reflect back on our understanding of the Eucharist, but only if we have first clearly understood where John is putting the central emphasis.

The last two chapters of this book will be devoted to the problem of identifying the referent where the language used is the cosmic language of myth and eschatology, and we shall find overwhelming reasons for being dissatisfied with the conventional notion that biblical writers took such language literally to refer to the beginning and end of the world.

(d) *Intention*

In the brief discussion of intention at the beginning of this chapter we noted that intention affects meaning in three ways, and we must now look more closely at each in turn. In the first place, words have the sense the speaker intends them to have. The most important corollary of this is that the speaker's intention determines whether his words are to be taken literally or figuratively. This enormous subject will occupy the whole of Part Two, and here a single illustration must suffice.

When Jeremiah reports his own answer to God, 'I see the stem of an almond tree' (1:11), how does he intend us to understand the word 'see'? Did he literally see an almond tree in the vicinity of Anathoth and think to himself that it was a good sermon illustration? Did the experience present itself to his mind's eye in a vision without any external stimulus? Or does the truth lie somewhere between the two: the sight of an actual almond tree induced the prophetic trance?

Secondly, the speaker's intention determines the type of language use. Readers of the Book of Jonah have commonly been too preoccupied with problems of marine biology to pay attention to the much more important theological difficulty that Jonah is ordered to prophecy something that does not happen: 'in forty days Nineveh shall be overthrown' (3:4). As McCurdy has put it, 'many things were foretold precisely that they might not come to pass'.[10] What

---

[10] Quoted by John Paterson, *The Goodly Fellowship of the Prophets*, p. 6.

we have to decide is whether the prophecy was intended as a prediction or as a warning. If it was a prediction, a plain statement of fact about the future, then it was absolute, and it was falsified by the event. If it was a warning, it carried an unexpressed conditional clause, 'unless they repent'. In a later chapter we shall see that it is characteristic of Semitic style to express ideas absolutely and to leave the listener to fill in for himself the implicit qualifications. In the story Jonah, being a bigotted nationalist, hoped that his prophecy was a prediction and was bitterly disappointed when it turned out to be only a warning, though all along he had suspected that God would act as he did (4:1–2).

Thirdly, a word has the referent a speaker intends it to have. Here at last we have reached a point at which we can revert to the question raised earlier, whether an utterance can have a meaning beyond what the original speaker intended. Provided that we restrict ourselves to meaning^R, we can give a clear affirmative answer. For a referent may be of five different kinds. (1) At one extreme there are statements about particular persons or things which are clearly not transferable: 'In the fifteenth year of the Emperor Tiberias . . . the word of God came to John son of Zechariah in the wilderness' (Luke 3:1–2). (2) At the other extreme there are general statements which can properly be applied to any member of a class: 'It is easier for a camel to pass through the eye of a needle than for a rich man to enter the kingdom of God' (Mark 10:25). But in between there are three other kinds of referent which merit closer attention. (3) Sometimes a speaker makes a statement about a particular referent which contains enough general truth to make it readily transferable to another. When, for example, Jesus says, 'How well did Isaiah prophesy about you hypocrites' (Mark 7:6), he is not suggesting that Isaiah was gazing into the future across eight centuries, but rather that in speaking of his own generation Isaiah might equally have been speaking about the contemporaries of Jesus: 'Isaiah might well have been prophesying about you.' (4) The fourth type is like a Situation Vacant advertisement: it describes in some detail a person whose identity is not yet known to the writer. In this category we must place the description of the servant of the Lord in Isaiah 53. The context makes it clear that the prophet believed Israel to be God's servant (e.g. 49:3), and that he was inviting Israel to see her national sufferings in the light of his

3

prophecy. But he was very unsure of any response. Was the servant to be the whole nation or only a remnant, to be many, few or one? The reason why modern scholars have endlessly debated these questions is that the prophet himself did not know the answers. It is as though he had published an advertisement, 'Wanted, a servant of the Lord', accompanied by a job description. He was undoubtedly aware that many famous men, such as Moses and Jeremiah, had sat for the composite portrait he was drawing. What he could not know was that in the end there would be only one applicant for the post.

(5) Closely allied to the Situation Vacant advertisement is the use of what Ogden and Richards (p. 131) called 'mendicants', words thrown out at a not fully grasped object. The Old Testament is full of such words, and a part of its inexhaustible usefulness to us lies in its 'majestic mendicancy'. Let us take as an illustration the word 'atonement', which occurs most frequently in the Priestly Code and gives a characteristic flavour to its sacrificial regulations. The priests who drew up the Code had no very clear idea of what they meant by atonement or how it worked. The nearest they ever came to a definition was: 'it is the blood, that is the life, that makes expiation' (Lev. 17:11). They were heirs to three centuries of criticism from prophets who had protested that sacrifice does not atone, and that it was not what God required;[11] yet they maintained and elaborated the ritual because they felt the need for atonement. Thus when the author of Hebrews says that the law, with its temple, priesthood and sacrifices, had 'a shadow of the good things to come', he is not sending us back to the Old Testament to find there light to throw on the mystery of the death of Christ, but is claiming that, once we see the fulness of sacrifice in the cross, we understand what the sacrificial worship of the Old Testament was groping after.

These last three types of reference together provide the linguistic justification for most of the instances in which the Old Testament is said to be fulfilled in the New. In all such cases it is legitimate to transfer an utterance to a fresh referent without violence to the principle that its sense is determined by the intention of the original speaker.

---

[11] Amos 5:21–25; Hos. 6:6; Isa. 1:10–17; Mic. 6:6–8; Jer. 7:21–23; cf. Ps. 40:6–8; 50:7–14; 51:16–17.

Some sayings, then, can properly acquire a new referent. But can they also properly be said to acquire a new sense? To a limited degree it would appear that we are already committed to assent to this as well. By the ambiguity of predication we have seen that every act of reference casts some reflexion back on the sense. Thus, when we apply Isaiah 53 to Jesus, this is bound to have some effect on the way in which we read the chapter; it has a new depth of meaning for the person who so applies it (beware meaning^V). But ought we to attribute such additional meaning to the original? I am inclined to think that it is wiser not to do so. This is admittedly not a question to which there is a right and a wrong answer, it is a matter of terminology; yet the terminology we choose influences the clarity of our thinking. My own choice, therefore, is to speak of the legitimate use of Scripture and not of finding new meanings in it. For this I have good scriptural precedent. When Paul tells us that there is a hidden meaning in Gen. 2:24, he is quick to add: 'I for my part take it to refer to Christ and the church' (Eph. 5:32). This is Pauline theology, not the theology of Genesis.

When we come in the next chapter to consider language historically, we shall see the full benefit of this distinction. Much of the material in the Bible has gone through a process of repeated editing, and the reason for the process is that each succeeding editor has wished to impose a meaning of his own on the tradition. The intentions of the Chronicler are very different from those of the sources on which he drew. So too in the Gospels we must always be ready to discriminate between what a saying meant on the lips of Jesus and what it came to mean to the evangelist who recorded it. The parable of the Lost Sheep is recorded by both Luke and Matthew. But in Luke (15:3–7) it has a setting in the life of Jesus as a defence against the accusation that he kept bad company, while in Matthew (18:12–14) it has a setting in the life of the church as an instruction to pastors on the treatment of the straying member of their flock. Matthew has made a legitimate use of the parable, but it would be confusing to say that this was part of its original sense.

There remains one final question. We have insisted that meaning is determined by the intention of the speaker. But who in the Bible is the speaker? This question requires an answer at no fewer than three levels: the characters in the narrative, the author and God. We rapidly learn to distinguish the first two levels, and not to assume that the authors of the Old Testament approve of all that is said or done by the characters in their story, or that the point of view of Jesus is that of the unjust judge (Luke 18:1–8). But is there such a thing as God's meaning to be distinguished from the intention of the human author? That this is an entirely proper question is demonstrated by the case of Jonah cited above, where the intention of God proved to be different from that of his spokesman. The Bible contains many instances in which the intention of God differs from that of his agent or messenger. 'You meant to do me harm, but God meant to bring good out of it' (Gen. 50:20). God uses the Assyrian as a punitive rod, though the Assyrian has other designs (Isa. 10:5–11), and he uses Cyrus as his anointed servant though Cyrus has not known him (Isa. 45:1–4). In the story of Job, what Satan intends as temptation God intends as test, and the same may be said of the temptations of Jesus.[12]

It is reasonable, then, to question whether the messengers of God have always correctly understood his intentions. We may doubt, either because we are squeamish or because we are Christian, whether God really ordered Saul to slaughter all the Amalekites (not that that would absolve Saul from a charge of disobedience to what he thought was a divine command). What we may not do is to invent something to put in the place of what we reject. There is an analogy here with those sceptics who find that they cannot believe the biblical account of the trial, death and resurrection of Jesus and undertake to tell us instead 'what actually happened': Caiaphas was *really* trying to save Jesus, it was all *really* part of a Zealot plot, Joseph of Arimathaea *actually* took Jesus down alive from the cross, etc. There is no harm in such conceits as long as they are recognised for what they are, sheer fiction. But anyone who takes them seriously is more credulous than the most naive believer in the biblical text. After all, there is evidence, some of it almost contemporary (1 Cor. 15:3–8), for the resurrection. We can respect the genuine agnostic who is content to live in doubt because he considers the evidence inadequate for belief, but not the spurious

---

[12] This helps to elucidate, though not to solve, the difficulty we have with the clause about temptation in the Lord's Prayer. God does not tempt us, and we ought not to ask him not to test us. 'Do not bring us to the time of trial' is an outrageous evasion of the problem. The prayer is a request that in the time of trial we may be tested without being tempted; but it is hard to light on an adequate way of putting this.

agnostic who prefers fantasy to evidence. Similarly in dealing with the words of the Bible we are bound by evidence. Literary critics have wisely warned us against the intentional fallacy, the error of supposing that a writer meant something other than he has actually written. We have no access to the mind of Jeremiah or Paul except through their recorded words. A fortiori, we have no access to the word of God in the Bible except through the words and the minds of those who claim to speak in his name. We may disbelieve them, that is our right; but if we try, without evidence, to penetrate to a meaning more ultimate than the one the writers intended, that is our meaning, not theirs or God's.

Chapter Three

Changes of Meaning

Current usage determines public meaning. But current usage changes, either by gradual development, or suddenly when a Humpty Dumpty pays a word extra to work overtime. The scientific study of semantic change is recent, but recognition of its existence is as old as the Books of Samuel. When Saul was looking for his father's lost donkeys, his servant proposed that they should consult the seer Samuel, and a later editor has added a parenthesis, informing us that 'what is nowadays called a prophet used to be called a seer' (1 Sam. 9:9). The editor is aware that in the early days there were two classes of holy man: the prophet (*nabi'*), who belonged to a group, and whose inspiration came in the form of mass ecstasy, often stimulated by music and rhythmical movement;[1] and the seer (*rô'eh*), the solitary whose inspiration came in the form of trance.[2] But in the course of time the prophetic guilds disappeared, and the name *nabi'* was transferred to the solitary prophet. To this we must add that the verb 'prophesy' (*hithnabbe'*) takes its meaning from the current sense of the noun and signifies 'to do whatever it is that prophets do'. When we are told that the four hundred prophets of Baal 'prophesied until the hour of sacrifice' (1 Kings 18:29), we are not to picture them delivering a choral sermon, but engaging in their frenzied dervish dance with ritual incantations. Yet at a later date the same verb connotes the delivery of such oracles as are found in the prophetic books. When we come to the prophets of the New Testament, we find a further

[1] In the expression 'sons of the prophets' the word 'son' (*ben*) is what grammarians call the *ben* of classification and does not necessarily imply parentage. When Amos says (7:14), 'I am no prophet, nor am I a prophet's son', he means that he is not a member of the trade union. But *ben* could be used in this way because, in a static society, sons tended to follow the trade of their fathers.

[2] Cf. the description of Balaam, 'who with staring eyes sees in a trance the vision from the Almighty' (Numb. 24:4).

semantic shift, since prophecy, at least as it is represented in the Revelation of John, includes the inspired reinterpretation of the Old Testament and of the sayings of Jesus.[3]

Two of the commonest forms of semantic change are the broadening and the narrowing of a word's scope, and these are well illustrated by the history of the two biblical names, David and Christ. When we first meet the word 'David', it is a proper noun, the personal name of the youngest son of Jesse. But David became King of Israel and received a promise that his descendants would sit upon his throne in perpetuity (2 Sam. 7:8-16; Ps. 89:3-4). So his personal name became a dynastic title. The Psalms of David were not so called because he wrote them (though he certainly was a poet and may have written one or two of them), but because they were a collection made for use in the chapel royal. When the dynasty came to an end in 587 B.C. with the destruction of Jerusalem, Ezekiel predicted its restoration: 'I, the Lord, will become their God, and my servant David shall be a prince among them' (34:24). Here 'David' is not of course the son of Jesse, but a new and ideal member of the Davidic line, 'great David's greater son'. There is a close parallel in the history of the name 'Caesar', which began as the personal name of Julius Caesar, became the dynastic name of all succeeding emperors, and survived into modern times in the German Kaiser and the Russian Czar.

The contrary process is seen in the word *christos*, which began as an adjective and ended as a proper name. Behind the Greek word lies the Hebrew adjective *mashiah* (anointed), from which our 'messiah' is derived. Anointing with oil was a practice common enough in secular contexts, e.g. as a courtesy to a guest (Ps. 23:5; Luke 7:46), or as a normal element in the toilet (Ruth 3:3; 2 Sam. 12:20; Matt. 6:17). In religious symbolism it was a rite of appointment to any high office, king, priest or prophet (1 Kings 19:15; Isa. 45:1; 61:1), or of the consecration of sacred objects (Gen. 31:13). But *mashiah* is used almost exclusively of two persons, the anointed king (1 Sam. 24:7) and the anointed priest (Lev. 4:3), the two 'sons of oil' (Zech. 4:14). In the Old Testament, however, it never connotes either of these without help from the context; i.e.

---

[3] See E. G. Selwyn, *The First Epistle of Peter*, pp. 259–68 and L. Hartman, *Prophecy Interpreted*.

in the one case the king is always 'the Lord's (my, your, his) anointed', and in the other case the word 'priest' is always added; and the same holds for *christos* in the Septuagint. Yet in the New Testament *Christos*, without such contextual support, has come to mean 'Messiah' (Acts 2:36; 9:22), and within twenty years of the crucifixion Paul is using the word as a proper name (1 Thess. 1:1).

In the previous chapter we defined the meaning[5] of a word as the contribution it makes to the sentence in which it stands, and we can now see the usefulness of this definition as a criterion for judging whether or not semantic change has taken place. In the Old Testament and Septuagint passages the ideas of 'king' and 'priest' are not supplied by *mashiah* or *christos*, but by other elements in the context. Only when these words connote 'promised king from the line of David', without support from the context, can we properly speak of semantic change and translate them as 'Messiah'. It is probably therefore a mistake to speak of a belief in 'two Messiahs' at Qumran, since 'the anointed ones of Aaron and Israel' in the Community Rule (ix) are simply the two familiar Old Testament figures, the anointed priest and the anointed king.

The causes of semantic change are many and complex, and some of them, the purely linguistic ones, cannot be adequately studied without a knowledge of the language in which they occur. Here we shall restrict ourselves to five causes which are within the competence of those who study the Bible in English.

1. Habitual denotation

We have seen that *mashiah* had the king as its referent or denotation for centuries before it absorbed kingship into its sense or connotation. It is a reasonable supposition that habitual denotation was the cause which brought about the change. This was certainly what caused the similar narrowing in the scope of the English 'furniture'. Up to the eighteenth century 'furniture' had a much wider meaning than it has today: 'that with which a person or thing is furnished or supplied'. When Marlowe says:

> With Nature's pride and richest furniture
> His looks do menace heaven and dare the Gods.

he is describing Tamburlane's natural endowment of gifts and graces, not his upholstery. When Bishop Berkeley says 'All the choir of heaven and furniture of earth—in a word, all those bodies which compose the mighty frame of the world—have not any subsistence without a mind', the parenthesis tells us what he was denoting by 'furniture'. The Bishop could have spoken in another context of 'my furniture' and meant 'my household effects'; but in that case 'household effects' would have been the word's denotation, not its connotation. But by repeated use in this sense the word has now come to connote 'household effects', and this sense has driven out the wider one.

Sometimes it is possible to trace the stages of habitual reference in considerably greater detail. Both in Hebrew and in Greek 'witness' is in origin a legal term, but the Greek noun (*martys*) is also the source of the English 'martyr'. The stages in the development of the cognate verb seem to have been as follows:

(a) to give evidence, in or out of court;
(b) to make a solemn affirmation, e.g. of one's faith;
(c) to witness to one's faith, even at the cost of death;
(d) to witness to one's faith by the acceptance of death;
(e) to be a martyr.

The development was complicated by the fact that at stage (c) witness to one's faith was frequently given in a court of law, so that the original sense persisted through all successive changes. There can be no doubt whatever that in the *Martyrdom of Polycarp* (1:1; 19:1) stage (e) has been reached (*c.* A.D. 156), since there the verb cannot be translated in any other way than 'died a martyr's death'. But according to Liddell and Scott that stage had already been reached in A.D. 95 when the Revelation was written: Antipas, so the lexicon tells us, was 'my faithful martyr' (2:13). It may freely be granted that John expected witnesses to die for their faith, but that is not to say that the word on his lips or pen already meant 'martyr'. For in the difficult chapter about the two witnesses (11:3 ff.) we read: 'when they have completed their testimony, the beast that comes up from the abyss will wage war upon them and will defeat and kill them.' Since their death occurs only after their

3*

witness is over, it would appear that John's usage is not yet at stage (d), let alone at stage (e).

Changes through habitual denotation occur most frequently among metaphors. A metaphor is the transference of a term from one referent with which it naturally belongs to a second referent, in order that the second may be illuminated by comparison with the first or by being 'seen as' the first. It continues to be a living metaphor just as long as speaker and hearer are aware of the double reference, and while this is still the case the connotation or sense of the word remains unchanged. But by repeated use it becomes a stock or faded metaphor, and at that point the dictionary will list the new reference as part of its sense, labelling it as figurative. The final stage is the dead metaphor, when users are no longer conscious of the word's origin, and the label (fig.) drops from the dictionary definition. A large proportion of the word-stock of any language will prove on scrutiny to have come into existence in this fashion. Consider for example the metaphorical use of parts of the body (see p. 16): we are not normally conscious of using a metaphor when we speak of the eye of a needle or the mouth of a river, or even of our hearts being where our treasure is (Matt. 6:21).

There has, however, been some considerable confusion over the application of this principle to the biblical words for the emotions. Hebrew uses not only 'heart' (as in English), but 'liver', 'kidneys' (AV 'reins') and 'bowels' to denote a variety of emotions, and in the Greek of the New Testament *splanchna* (innards) has a similar function. In this last instance there can be no doubt that we are dealing with a metaphor, and a dead metaphor at that, since Paul can refer to Onesimus as 'my own innards' (Phn. 12). There is therefore nothing to be said in favour of the ludicrous literalism of the AV, either in that passage or in 2 Cor. 6:11–13:

> O ye Corinthians, our mouth is open unto you, our heart is enlarged. Ye are not straitened in us, but ye are straitened in your own bowels. Now for a recompense in the same (I speak as unto my children) be ye also enlarged.

Even the most fervent admirer of the AV can scarcely here deny the superiority of the NEB:

Men of Corinth, we have spoken very frankly to you; we have opened our heart wide to you all. On our part there is no constraint; any constraint there may be is in yourselves. In fair exchange then (may a father speak so to his children?) open your hearts wide to us.

Many Hebraists have been slow to recognise the linguistic status of the words under consideration. G. R. Driver argued that this usage was symptomatic of a general lack of abstract nouns in Hebrew. 'The first point to be remarked is that almost all words can be traced back to roots denoting originally something that can be grasped by the senses: intellectual ideas, therefore, are expressed by roots of concrete significance and the passions by words indicating primarily the organs of the body.'[4] He appears to have overlooked the fact that exactly the same might be said of such English words as 'grasp', 'contemplate', 'nerve', 'spirit', 'mettle', and 'phlegmatic', and that other languages could produce a similar list. Most abstract terms in any language 'can be traced back to roots denoting originally something that can be grasped by the senses'; but that does not make them any the less abstract.

A much more radical approach was proposed by H. Wheeler Robinson, who argued that the ancient Israelite believed the consciousness to be diffused throughout the organs of the body. If then the Preacher asks whether the eye is not surfeited with seeing and the ear sated with hearing, he means us to understand that a sense of satiety is located in the organ. 'What the educated man frequently does not know, or, at any rate, forgets, is the fact that such a usage is *not* metaphor in the Bible, but represents the extent of current scientific knowledge. This non-metaphorical point of view underlies the use of every physiological term for physical activities, including the peripheral sense-organs (eye, ear, etc.).'[5] But the state of scientific knowledge has little, if anything, to do with whether words are used metaphorically or literally. Much of our own language is pre-scientific, as we shall see in the next section, and particularly our language of the emotions. When Mrs Bennet says 'nobody feels for my poor nerves',[6] she is admitting to an emotional instability which is an attribute of her

---

[4] *The People and the Book*, p. 118.
[5] *The Christian Doctrine of Man*, p. 21.
[6] Jane Austen, *Pride and Prejudice*, ch. 20.

character and not a defect in her sympathetic nervous system. Scientific knowledge may, to be sure, affect the sense of a metaphor. When 'head' is used metaphorically in the Bible, we must beware against supposing that what is meant is 'controlling intelligence', since the ancient world knew nothing of the function of the brain, but spoke of the heart as the seat of thought; but the usage is none the less metaphorical. Robinson's case for diffused consciousness, then, rests solely on his unsupported assertion that the language in question is being used literally, and must be tested by the normal criteria by which we judge the presence or absence of metaphor (see pp. 186–191). Let us then apply to the AV of Lam. 2:11 the test of Impossible Literality, which we have already used on the language of Paul. 'Mine eyes do fail with tears, my bowels are troubled, my liver is poured upon the earth.' Since the author is still alive, the last clause cannot be intended literally (cf. 2 Sam. 20:10). The NEB takes 'liver' by metonymy to mean 'bile', though there does not seem to be any evidence for such usage. Nausea is admittedly a well-known reaction to shock caused by sights of violence, but this is not what the poet is talking about. He is talking about the nervous exhaustion which supervenes upon the prolonged harrowing of the emotions (cf. Luke 22:45): he has no tears left to shed, his feelings are in chaos, his passion spent. Here at least we are dealing with faded or dead metaphors exactly on a par with the English use of 'heart', and the last thing we must do is to translate these Hebrew words by English anatomical terms which have no such metaphorical sense.[7]

2. *Evolution of the referent*

Language is more conservative than life. Words continue to be used even when their original referent has changed beyond recognition, whether through advances in technology and knowledge or through shifts in social structure or convention. The English still write with a 'pen' and the French with a 'plume', though it is no longer constructed out of a feather. We still speak of 'sun-rise', though we know that this is but an optical effect caused by the rotation of the earth. Unlike the mud bricks of Egypt (Exod. 5:7), modern bricks

---

[7] English terminology of this sort has recently been increased by 'gut-reaction'.

are made without straw, yet politicians still delight in reminding the opposite party of the impossibility of doing so. The Hebrew word for 'altar' (*mizbeaḥ*) is derived from the verb 'to slaughter', but it continued to be used in the Jerusalem temple, not only for the altar of burnt offering at a time when the slaughter was carried out elsewhere, but also for the altar of incense (Exod. 30:1–6).

There is an episode in the early history of David which splendidly illustrates this conservatism of language. David, an outlaw in exile from the court, shouts across a valley to Saul and asks who are the men that have set Saul against him and 'have ousted me today from my share in the Lord's inheritance and have banished me to serve other gods' (1 Sam. 26:19). Most commentators have taken this as evidence that David was not a monotheist but a henotheist, believing that Yahweh's writ extended only to the borders of Israel, and that in foreign countries one must worship the god to whom the land belonged.[8] But the narrator of the story cannot have intended the words to be taken in this literalistic fashion. For he portrays David as from start to finish a pious worshipper of Yahweh, whether he is in Israelite territory or Philistine: he consults Yahweh, through the ephod oracle (23:1), prays to Yahweh (23:10; 25:39), appeals to him (24:12; 30:6), attributes victory to him (30:23), and regards Saul as sacrosanct because he is 'the Lord's anointed' (24:6; 26:9,11). On the lips of David 'to serve other gods' could be intended only as a picturesque turn of phrase, a survival from earlier times when a literal interpretation was conceivable. We may compare the fondness of eighteenth- and nineteenth-century authors for the phrase 'household gods'. When Thomson wrote of 'the redbreast, sacred to the household gods',[9] or Longfellow of ships 'bearing a nation with all its household gods into exile',[10] the reader was not intended to imagine a recrudescence of the Roman worship of Lares and Penates either in rural England or among the Acadians of Nova Scotia.

The history of the Old Testament priesthood is a complex story in which many influences, social, ideological and technological

[8] It is interesting to note in passing that even Jezebel did not believe in such territorial limitations.

[9] J. Thomson, *The Seasons: Winter*, l. 246.

[10] H. W. Longfellow, *Evangeline* II.1.3.

combined to produce semantic change. It is not possible to document the whole process precisely, because many of the older sources were rewritten by later editors with a theological axe to grind. But the main stages are clear enough.

(1) In the earliest period accessible to us 'levite' was a professional designation, as yet unconnected with the name of Levi, since we read of a levite who not only came from Bethlehem in Judah but is explicitly said to be a member of the clan of Judah (Judg. 17:7).[11]

(2) Once the link with Levi had been established, priests were recognised as having a triple function (Deut. 33:8–11): custody of the ephod oracle with its Urim and Thummim; *torah*, i.e. the giving of authoritative rulings on matters of religion and conduct out of a traditional body of legal lore; and sacrifice, which was the least important duty of the three, since others besides priests could offer it (e.g. 1 Sam. 7:9; 1 Kings 18:30 ff.).

(3) After the early disappearance of the ephod oracle, *torah* became the distinctive activity of the priest until the end of the seventh century B.C. '*Torah* shall not perish from the priest, nor counsel from the sage, nor the word from the prophet' (Jer. 18:18).

(4) In the Code of Deuteronomy 'priest' and 'levite' were synonymous, and it was the intention of the authors of this code that, with the centralisation of the cultus, all levites should have equal rights of access to the central shrine (Deut. 12:11–14; 18:6–8).

(5) When Josiah reformed the temple worship in accordance with Deuteronomic law, the one point he was unable to implement was the equal status of all levites (2 Kings 23:9). No doubt the Jerusalem priests clung to their metropolitan privileges, and so inaugurated the distinction between priest and levite which is found in all later documents.

(6) During their exile in Babylon the Jerusalem priests, in defence of their superior status, hit on the idea that all priests must be descended from Aaron (Lev. 1:5; Numb. 18:1–7; 1 Chr. 6:49). They could trace their descent back to David's priest, Zadok, and Ezekiel had thought this an adequate distinction (Ezek. 44:15 f.).

---

[11] There is a similar problem about the origin of other names. *Qayin* is the personal name of Cain and the tribal name of the Kenites, and probably also means a blacksmith. Did Cain give his name to a tribe of smiths, or was he an eponym, i.e. a hero invented as an explanation of tribal origins?

Zadok, like his predecessor Melchizedek, had appeared on the Israelite scene without father, mother or genealogy. He was therefore conveniently provided with Aaronic pedigree at the expense of his discredited rival Abiathar. The Hebrew text of 2 Sam. 8:17 reads: 'Zadok the son of Ahitub and Ahimelech the son of Abiathar were priests.' But this is clearly in disarray, because we know that Abiathar was son of Ahimelech and grandson of Ahitub, and that he was the sole survivor when the whole priestly family was massacred by Doeg on Saul's order (1 Sam. 22:18–22). Someone has reversed the names in 2 Sam. 8:17 in order to supply Zadok with the correct parentage, and the Chronicler has adopted this revised version in his own geneaological table (1 Chr. 6:8).

(7) The theory of Aaronic succession tended to put the emphasis on the cultic aspect of the priesthood, and this tendency was accelerated by a shift from the spoken to the written word. Once the law was reduced to writing, the pious enquirer no longer needed to go to the priest for an authoritative answer; he could go to the scribe, the scholar who knew how to look up the answer in the book. Ezra was both priest and scribe, but it was his qualifications as scribe that mattered most when he came to read and interpret the written law (Ezr. 7:6; Neh. 8:1–8). The priest has become the offerer of sacrifice.

(8) While the priests were busy magnifying their office, two other factors were combining to erode it, the prophetic criticism of sacrifice and the Dispersion. Prophets from Amos to Jeremiah had declared that what God required was not sacrifice but the spiritual realities which sacrifice purported to symbolise, loyalty, obedience and humility (see above Chapter Two, note 11), and their protest had won a permanent place in Israel's worship through the Psalter. Josiah's reform and the centralisation of the sacrificial cultus in Jerusalem in 621 B.C., which attempted to meet these criticisms, proved in some ways counter-productive, since fewer worshippers could now be regularly present at the offering of sacrifice. In the centuries that followed, when Jews were scattered throughout almost all the countries of the known world, their religious needs were met by the spiritualisation of sacrifice.

> Keeping the law is worth many offerings;
> to heed the commandments is to sacrifice a thank-offering.

A kindness repaid is an offering of flour,
and to give alms is a praise offering.
The way to please the Lord is to renounce evil;
and to renounce wrongdoing is to make atonement.
Yet do not appear before the Lord empty-handed;
perform these sacrifices because they are commanded.

(Ecclus. 35:1–5)

For purposes of personal piety and synagogue worship the levitical code is to be spiritualised (taken metaphorically). On visits to Jerusalem it must be taken literally, but only because it is part of the written law which every Jew must obey. This major shift of religious focus was assisted by a verbal ambiguity. 'A sacrifice of thanksgiving' (Amos 4:5; Ps. 107:22; 116:17) originally denoted a thank-offering, an animal sacrifice in token of thanks (Lev. 7:12; 22:29). But the same phrase could also be used of an act of worship in which thanksgiving was offered to God, that and nothing more (Ps. 50:14). It is important also to note that the spiritualisation of sacrifice is also the laicisation of it. It does not take a priest to offer to God the sacrifice of a contrite heart.

3. Taboo

The emotive forces of attraction and repulsion operate unevenly on language. Attraction and dominant interest have their effect mainly on style. Paul, for example, betrays his urban origins by his metaphors. But repulsion, acting through taboos of delicacy, fear or reverence, alters the permissible currency of the word-stock.

Taboos of delicacy produce euphemisms, of which there are a few in the Old Testament, mostly involving some use of the word 'feet' (Deut. 28:57; Judg. 3:24; 1 Sam. 24:3; Isa. 7:20; Ezek. 16:25). In abuse and mockery euphemism has an advantage over direct speech in that it lends itself to innuendo, as Elijah demonstrates when ridiculing the domestic habits of Baal: 'it may be he is . . . engaged' (1 Kings 18:27 NEB).

The nearest equivalent to taboo in Hebrew is the *ḥerem* or ban placed upon all that has been consecrated to an alien deity. Whatever is banned is declared unholy and prohibited from both sacred and common use.[12] Some of the effect of this on language we have already observed in the finding of offensive substitutes for the name of Baal (p. 31). A later instance of the same procedure is found in the Book of Daniel. In 167 B.C. Antiochus Epiphanes ordered the erection of an altar to Zeus Olympios in the Jerusalem temple, and this is the 'abomination of desolation' or 'desecrating horror' of Dan. 11:31 and 12:11. It has been plausibly conjectured that the author arrived at this designation by the familiar method of verbal corruption. The Hebrew for Olympios would be *ba'al shamayim* (lord of the heavens). Daniel had only to substitute a 'horror'-word for Baal and retain the consonants of the second word (vowels were not yet written in the Hebrew text) to produce *shiqquṣ shomem*. We cannot indeed be sure that this is an accurate account of his mental processes, but there can be no doubt that a new term was added to the vocabulary of theology, since his phrase was taken up in the New Testament and made a title for Antichrist (Mark 13:14).

Far more important for the student of the Bible than the taboos of delicacy and fear is the taboo of reverence, which manifests itself in a variety of ways. The personal name Yahweh was early withdrawn from common speech, to be used only by the high priest in pronouncing the blessing (Ecclus. 50:20). In its place the name Adonai (my Lord) was used, and this in turn gave rise to the Greek *Kyrios*, the Latin *Dominus* and the English 'Lord'. When the vowels were eventually written in the Hebrew text, the vowels of Adonai were added to the consonants of the tetragrammaton YHWH to produce the hybrid form Jehovah.[13] One of the earliest pieces of evidence for the reverential evasion of the divine name is in a group of psalms from which an editor has systematically eliminated the name Yahweh and put *Elohim* (God) in its place (esp. cf. Ps. 14 with Ps. 53). In the rules of the Qumran community a member was to be expelled for uttering the divine name (1 QS 6:27—7:2).

The first of the Elohim psalms contains another type of reverential

[12] We know from the Mesha Inscription that the *ḥerem* could operate in reverse. The Moabite king declares unholy to Ashtar–Chemosh the city of Nebo which had belonged to Yahweh. As N. Snaith has put it: 'What was *qodesh* to Jehovah was *cherem* to Chemosh. Contrariwise, what was *qodesh* to Chemosh was *cherem* to Jehovah. One god's *qodesh* was another god's *cherem*' (*Distinctive Ideas of the Old Testament*, p. 33).

[13] This was in accordance with the general practice in any place where emendation was required. The sacred text could not be altered, but the vowels supplied were those of the *Qere* (what is read) and not of the *Kethib* (what is written).

alteration (Ps. 42:2). Originally the psalmist's question ran: 'When shall I come to see the face of God?' To 'see the face of' a person was a regular Hebrew idiom for being received in audience by someone of consequence (e.g. Gen. 43:3,5; 2 Sam. 14:24). It was therefore a natural term to use of access to the presence of God, and the psalmist who so used it was apparently undeterred by the knowledge that, in quite another sense of the word 'see', it was held that nobody could see God and live (Exod. 33:20). As we shall see in another chapter, pedantic anxieties of this kind are always the work of a later semi-sophistication. In the end, however, pious pedantry prevailed and editors changed the verb to the passive form: 'when shall I come to appear before God?'[14]

A growing sense of the divine transcendence led also to the introduction of what we may call verbal insulators placed between the holiness of God and the world. When Israel is promised the protective company of an angel, the word 'angel' is so obviously a way of talking about God's own presence that we feel no incongruity when the promise continues in the first person rather than the third: 'my angel will go before you and bring you to the Amorites . . . and I will make an end of them' (Exod. 23:23). The Deuteronomist cannot bring himself to speak of God dwelling on earth, so he refers to the temple as 'the place which the Lord your God will choose as a dwelling for his name' (Deut. 12:11). Ezekiel cannot do with fewer than three insulators: 'this was the likeness of the appearance of the glory of the Lord' (1:28). Later writers, copying Ezekiel, spoke of the temple as 'the place where your glory dwells' (Ps. 26:8; cf. Exod. 29:43). The terms 'angel', 'name' and 'glory' are purely linguistic devices and have no referent other than God himself, just as in English courtly diction 'the Queen's Most Excellent Majesty' is a way of talking about the sovereign. We have already seen that Matthew uses 'Heaven' as a surrogate for God (p. 43),[15] and it is not difficult to add a list of other New Testament examples: 'the right hand of Power' (Mark

---

[14] The same was done in other passages (Exod. 23:15; 34:20, 23, 24; Deut. 16:16; 31:11; 1 Sam. 1:22; Isa. 1:12). In each case the NEB has 'enter the presence of'.

[15] Cf. also the English use of Providence:

> The world was all before them, where to choose
> Their place of rest, and Providence their guide.
> Milton, *Paradise Lost* x. 646–7.

14:62), 'the Majesty on high' (Heb. 1:3), 'the sublime Presence'
(2 Pet. 1:17). But there are two other instances which might not be
so readily detected. The italics in the AV translation of Col. 1:19
show that the translators have inserted a subject for the verb which
is not present in the Greek: 'it pleased *the Father* that in him should
all fulness dwell.' This gratuitous addition is not only grammatically
improbable, since a sudden change of subject needs to be explicitly
indicated, but also unnecessary. The subject is 'all fulness', here
used to mean 'the complete being of God' (NEB; cf. Col. 2:9): 'in
him God in all his fulness chose to come and dwell.'

The other case requires a brief excursus on Rabbinic usage. At
the climax of the Revelation a voice from heaven declares that 'the
tabernacle of God is with men' (Rev. 21:3). The Greek word *skênê*
was used in the LXX for the tabernacle in the wilderness, but this
fact is far from being in the foreground of John's thought. He is
using *skênê* on grounds of sound as well as sense, as the equivalent
of the Hebrew *shekinah*, a word derived from the verb 'to dwell'
and used in Rabbinic writings to mean 'the Presence'. In the
Targums[16] we find three reverential insulators, *memra* (word),
shekinta (presence) and *yeqara* (glory), regularly used without regard
for syntax to avoid any suggestion of direct contact between God
and man. Where the Hebrew says that God spoke, dwelt among
Israel, or was seen by men, the Targum has 'the *memra* spoke', the
shekinta dwelt', 'they saw the *yeqara* of God'. Sometimes these
words even occur in combination: 'my eyes have seen the *yeqara* of
the *shekinta* of the Lord of the ages' (Targum of Jonathan on Isa.
6:5). Some commentators have thought it significant that all three
are juxtaposed in a single verse of John's Gospel: 'The Word
became flesh and tabernacled among us . . . and we saw his
glory.'

4. *Arbitrary causes*

It occasionally happens that a particular user or group of users will
seize on a word and give it a twist which diverts it to a new meaning.
Whereas other forms of semantic change are gradual, and are

---

[16] Aramaic versions of the Old Testament books, dating from the middle of the
second century A.D. or later, but containing much traditional interpretation.

perceptible only in retrospect, arbitrary change is datable. In 1940 such a change overtook the German 'Blitz', which till then had meant 'lightning'. When Hitler spoke of a *Blitzkrieg*, he meant a war which would be over in a flash. But Londoners took up this foreign word and used it to refer to the German air raids; and when they said that a house had been blitzed, they did not mean it had been struck by lightning.

In the year 598 B.C., the year of the first deportation of Jews to Babylon, something of the same sort happened to the Hebrew word *kabod* (glory).[17] The root *k-b-d* signifies weight, but there is no recorded instance of the literal use of *kabod*; it is always used metaphorically to connote a person's importance, authority or rank (cf. the Latin *gravis*, the English 'weight', the German *Gewicht*), and in a derivative sense the honour or esteem accorded to greatness. Joseph, for example, tells his brothers to carry word back to their father of all his glory, i.e. what a grand person he has become (Gen. 45:3). In the very few early passages in which it is used of God *kabod* means his majesty, all those qualities which call forth worship and praise. The answer to Moses' request, 'Show me your glory' is 'I will make all my goodness pass before you' (Exod. 33:18). In Deut. 5:24 'glory' and 'greatness' are intended as a pair of synonyms. The parallelism in Ps. 19:1 shows that 'the glory of God' declared by the heavens is the stamp of divine artistry which the Creator impresses on all his handiwork, and this is exactly what the word signifies in the song of the seraphim heard by Isaiah (Isa. 6:3). But in 598 B.C. Ezekiel had his vision of the chariot of the cherubim with its multi-directional wheels, surmounted by a firmament on which was enthroned a figure of celestial radiance. This he called 'the glory of the Lord', and from that moment on, so influential was his vision on all who succeeded him, 'radiance' became part of the connotation of *kabod*. 'Arise, Jerusalem, rise clothed in light; your light has come and the glory of the Lord shines over you' (Isa. 60:1). Wherever in the story of Moses we read of the glory of the Lord appearing in the cloud (e.g. Exod. 16:10), we can be sure that the passage is part of the Priestly Document, written in Babylon under the influence of Ezekiel.

[17] Did Lewis Carroll know how well the biblical history of this word exemplified Humpty Dumpty's theme of mastery?

5. *Translation*

'You are asked then to read with sympathetic attention, and make allowances if, in spite of all the devoted work I have put into the translation, some of the expressions appear inadequate. For it is impossible for a translator to find precise equivalents for the original Hebrew in another language. Not only with this book, but with the law, the prophets, and the rest of the writings, it makes no small difference to read them in the original' (Ecclus., Prologue). In thus venting the frustration he experienced in translating his grandfather's work into Greek, the grandson of Jesus ben Sira speaks for all translators. Translation is an impossible task because, as he reminds us, words in one language rarely coincide in sense and scope with words in another. When we translate from language A into language B, one of two things is bound to happen: either the words of language B will be dominant and will distort the text by imposing their own shades of meaning on it; or the words and context of language A will be strong enough to impose their meaning on language B and so bring about semantic change in its vocabulary. Both these results can be exemplified from the Greek translation of the Hebrew scriptures; but, just because the original was a sacred text, the balance was firmly tipped in favour of the second. For the same reason, among the forces which have combined to mould the English language, none has been more potent than the Authorised Version of the Bible.

For an illustration of the effect of the LXX translation on the Greek language we cannot do better than return to the study of 'glory'. The Greek *doxa* is derived from a verb which means 'to seem' and in classical Greek the noun had two senses: 'opinion' (what seems to me) and 'reputation' (what I seem to others). In the second of these senses it shows a partial overlap with the Hebrew *kabod*, and is a reasonable rendering of it in passages where *kabod* means 'the honour in which a person is held'. To cover the full range of *kabod* Greek had no exact equivalent. The translators might have chosen *timê* (honour). But *timê* also means 'price' and, since this is the sense it commonly has in the Greek Bible, this may have been the reason why they avoided it. Whatever their reasons, they chose *doxa* to represent *kabod* in almost all its occurrences, and used *timê* for 'honour' only in passages where the presence of two synonyms in the Hebrew demanded the use of two different words in the translation (e.g. Exod. 28:2; cf. Ps. 8:5). Thus, through the principle of contextual determination, *doxa* acquired all the senses of *kabod*, without any apparent interference from its pre-biblical background; and this was true not only in the written text of Scripture, but for the daily speech of Hellenistic Jews and subsequently also of Greek-speaking Christians, as is obvious from the use of the word in the New Testament. But there is some evidence that the change was even more far-reaching and affected even the vernacular Greek of the pagan environment. In some of the collections of magical texts found in Egypt the word *doxa* has the sense of 'radiance' or 'splendour'; and the presence in these same texts of names such as Abraham, Isaac and Jacob strongly suggests that the magicians had been influenced by the language of the Greek Old Testament.[18]

There has long been controversy over the Greek translation of Isa. 7:14, and it will be useful to state the facts afresh, particularly because they are frequently misrepresented.

(1) The Hebrew text runs: 'A young woman (*'almah*) is with child, and she will bear a son, and will call him Immanuel.' There is a Hebrew word which means 'virgin' (*bᵉtulah*), but Isaiah does not use it. The sign he offers to Ahaz is in the child's name (cf. 7:3; 8:1,16), not in anything remarkable about his birth.

(2) The Greek translation uses *parthenos*, and this has often been unjustly called a mistranslation. The translator of Isaiah was admittedly more erratic than the translators of most of the other books, but at this point there is no cause for complaint. *Parthenos* can mean 'virgin', but need not; its basic meaning is 'girl', 'young woman', and there is not the slightest reason to suppose that the translator intended by it anything other than the sense he found in the original Hebrew.

(3) It was however open to any reader of the Greek version to understand the word in its restricted sense and take the prophecy to refer to a virgin birth; and this is the way Matthew appears to have read the text (1:23).

(4) Such a use of the Old Testament could occur only in a wholly

---

[18] See *Papyri Graecae Magicae*, ed K. Preisendanz, and esp. papyrus XIII, ll. 64, 189, 298 ff., 514. For further examples of Septuagintal influence on Hellenistic Greek, see C. H. Dodd, *The Bible and the Greeks*.

Greek-speaking community. If Isa. 7:14 was ever used of Jesus in the Palestinian, Aramaic-speaking church, it must have been used for the name Immanuel and not as a proof-text for a miraculous birth.

(5) Luke, as well as Matthew, believed in a miraculous birth, but he made no use of the Isaiah prophecy, and his belief is not expressed in his use of the word *parthenos* (1:27), which is correctly translated 'girl'.

(6) It is linguistically quite feasible that the belief in a virgin birth grew out of a misunderstanding of the Isaiah prophecy in its Greek guise, particularly if the text was already popular in the Aramaic-speaking church because of the name Immanuel; but the linguist, qua linguist, cannot prove that this is what actually happened.

If we are to interpret accurately biblical texts written over a period of many centuries, it is obviously important to be able to tell when semantic change has occurred, but it may sometimes be equally important to establish that it has not. As a salutary example let us cite the definitions of the Greek *sophia* given in the ninth edition of Liddell and Scott:

σοφία—prop. *cleverness* or *skill* in handicraft or art . . . 2. *skill* . . . in matters of common life, sound judgment, intelligence, practical wisdom . . . also *cunning, shrewdness, craft* . . . 3. *learning, wisdom* . . . 4. among the Jews, ἀρχὴ σοφίας φόβος Κυρίου LXX *Pr.* 1.7 . . . Σοφία, recognised first as an attribute of God, was later identified with the Spirit of God cf. LXX *Pr.* 8 with *Sir.* 24 sq.

This one entry contains a bewildering variety of error. We may pass over the little word 'prop.', with its implication, which no modern linguist would accept, that an early attested sense of a word is somehow more proper than a later one, and concentrate on the section beginning 'among the Jews', which claims that by its use in the LXX as a translation of the Hebrew *hokmah*, by becoming a technical term of Hellenistic Jewish religion, and above all through the personification of wisdom in Pr. 8 and Ecclus. 24, *sophia* underwent semantic change. In fact *hokmah* in Hebrew covers almost exactly the same range of meaning as that given for *sophia* in non-biblical Greek. The quotation from Pr. 1:7 ('The beginning of wisdom is the fear of the Lord') is a statement about wisdom, not a definition of the word: it tells the reader how to set about becoming wise, not what the word 'wise' signifies. Personification is a literary device whereby we treat as a person that which is recognised to be not a person, and there is no a priori reason why the use of this figure of speech should be an occasion for semantic change. In the case of *sophia* there is one simple test which shows that no such change has occurred. In every context in which *sophia* is used to denote the personified wisdom of God it is used also of the practical understanding of life which men ought to have and which God out of his own wisdom is prepared to bestow on them, and in such a way that the two forms of wisdom are unmistakably identified. From first to last wisdom for the Jew, whether personified or not, meant know-how, and particularly knowing how to live.

Up to this point we have been looking at semantic changes which took place during the thousand years in which the books of the Bible were being written. But for the student of the Bible it is equally necessary to be alert to the changes which biblical words have undergone in the ensuing centuries of Christian history. In what follows I shall not be attempting either to solve or to dissolve with a wave of the linguist's wand all the outstanding differences of Catholic, Protestant and Orthodox theology and churchmanship, but simply to illustrate the linguistic hazards of which Christians of differing traditions must be aware before ever they can converse with one another at all. It is precisely when theologians have claimed biblical authority for their own beliefs and practices that they have been peculiarly exposed to the universal temptation against which Ogden and Richards have warned us (see above, p. 10), namely of jumping to the conclusion that the biblical writer is referring to what they would be referring to were they speaking the words themselves. 'As new shopkeepers who have "bought the goodwill" of their predecessor's business keep his name for a while over their door, so ... innovators want to retain the prestige, almost the "selling-power", of the consecrated word.'[19] Consider, for example, the long and still continuing debate about baptism, whether it is right to baptize infants or only consenting adults. Both sides have claimed scriptural authority, and both have fallen into the trap of

[19] C. S. Lewis, *Studies in Words*, p. 104.

assuming that biblical writers are referring to what we refer to when we speak of baptism, i.e. a rite administered to all who themselves seek, or whose parents seek for them, membership of the church. But in New Testament times baptism was administered only to converts, who were baptized with their whole household. Children born to parents already Christian were not baptized either in infancy or later in adulthood, because they had been born into the household of faith.

For a more extended, and perhaps even more contentious, example let us take the following sentence from the Book of Common Prayer: 'It is evident unto all men diligently reading Holy Scripture and ancient Authors, that from the Apostles' time there have been these orders of Ministers in Christ's church: Bishops, Priests, and Deacons.' That kind of diligence is fortunately less common today than it used to be. To the modern linguist the only thing that is evident is that these three English words, together with the Latin and Greek words from which they are derived, have been in continuous use from a time considerably earlier than that of the apostles. What is very far from evident is that their connotation has remained constant or that they have been used at all times to denote the same ministerial offices. All three words present interesting linguistic problems, which in the case of 'priest' are of great complexity. The simplest way of keeping the old name over the door is by using modern words to translate the Greek words from which they are derived, no matter how much semantic change has happened in the mean time.

The English 'bishop' is derived, via the Latin, from the Greek *episkopos* (overseer). In the Septuagint this word is used to denote a variety of persons in positions of authority: army officers (Numb. 31:14; Jugd. 9:28; 4 Kgms. 11:15, 18), foremen in charge of building operations (2 Paral. 34:12, 17), business managers (Neh. 11:9, 14, 22), city officials (Isa. 60:17), and the superintendents appointed by Antiochus Epiphanes to enforce his decree against the Jewish religion (1 Macc. 1:51). The only priest so designated is Eleazar in his capacity of custodian of the tabernacle (Numb. 4:16). The earliest use of *episkopos* in the New Testament is in Philippians, which is addressed to 'God's people who live at Philippi, including *episkopoi* and *diakonoi*.' It is still a matter of conjecture what Paul can have understood by these words in this context.

Since there was a plurality of each type of leader in the one small church of Philippi, it would manifestly be an anachronism to translate them as 'bishops and deacons'. Paul mentions no such offices in any other church to which he writes. It is safest simply to call them 'overseers and assistants' and admit that we have no idea what their functions were. In the letter to Titus instructions are given for the appointment of elders in every city, who are to be men of unimpeachable character; 'for the *episkopos* must be a man of unimpeachable character.' Here there is no doubt that elder and *episkopos* are one and the same, and the probability is that 'elder' is the title of the office and *episkopos* a functional term, 'the man who exercises oversight'. But a little later, in 1 Timothy, the *episkopos* seems to be emerging as the holder of a distinct office. We appear to be moving rapidly towards the state of affairs recommended by Ignatius (*c.* A.D. 115), who declared that every local church ought to have *episkopos*, elders and deacons, and that without these no body of Christians could properly be called a church (Trall. iii.1). But even with Ignatius we are still a long way from the diocesan bishop.

The English 'priest' has a dual source: etymologically it is derived from the Greek *presbyteros* (elder) via the Latin *presbyter*; but it is also the standard English translation of the Greek *hiereus* and the Latin *sacerdos*. That in the course of time *presbyteros* and *presbyter* underwent semantic change so as to become synonyms for *hiereus* and *sacerdos* is not disputed; but this development certainly did not belong to the age of the apostles.

In the Old Testament elders are the heads of families who are responsible for local government (e.g. 1 Sam. 16:4), though there is always some doubt whether the word denotes an office or an age-group, since they are frequently contrasted with the young (e.g. Lam. 5:14), and the same ambiguity still attaches to the use of the word in the New Testament (1 Pet. 5:1, 5). When the author of 2 and 3 John calls himself 'the Elder', this is a claim to belong to the older generation which is the church's link with the apostolic past, not the title of an office to which he has been appointed; and it is probably for a similar reason that Peter is called 'your fellow-elder. There is however ample evidence to show that in the second half of the first century many local churches were governed by elders, some of whom were qualified to teach.

On the other hand, no member of the church is ever in the New Testament entitled 'priest'. We have seen that 'priest' had long since come to mean 'one qualified to offer sacrifice', and Christ's self-offering had made the sacrifices of the temple obsolete. In much later times the office of priest was to be particularly associated with the offering of the Eucharist, conceived as a representational sacrifice, but in New Testament times there was a compelling reason why this connexion of thought could not be made. The Eucharist had its origin in the last celebration of the Passover by Jesus and his disciples. But at Passover the function of the priest was restricted to the slaughter of the Paschal lamb in the temple precincts; the commemorative meal was presided over by the head of each household. To a Jewish Christian therefore it would be self-evident that the only priest of his liturgy was Christ, who had offered himself once for all as the Paschal lamb, leaving the laity thereafter to celebrate the commemoration of his death.

'Deacon' is derived from the Greek *diakonos* (servant), which is the most general ministerial term in the New Testament, freely used of all types of ministry, but especially of the ministry of Jesus himself (Mark 10:45; Rom. 15:8). It is the word used in the warnings Jesus gave to his disciples not to aspire to other rank or greatness than to be 'last of all and servant of all' (Mark 9:35; cf. 10:43; Matt. 23:11; Luke 22:26). Paul is *diakonos*, and so are Apollos, Epaphras, Tychicus and Timothy. Apart from Phil. 1:1, there is only one passage in the New Testament where the word has a more specialised reference (1 Tim. 3:8–12), and in that same epistle it is still being used in the wider sense (4:6; cf. 1:12). On this evidence we may say that the semantic change which transformed *diakonos* (minister) into *diakonos* (deacon) has just begun by the time 1 Timothy was written, though the new sense had not yet begun to oust the old. But what are we to say of Phoebe from Cenchreae, who belongs to an earlier generation (Rom. 16:1)? Was she the church's servant, or its minister, or its deacon?

There is of course no reason why words should not be allowed to change their meaning by the evolution of the referent. Humpty Dumpty has his rightful place among the theologians; Canute does not. What is indefensible is the notion that the conservatism of language is a guarantee of eternal and unchanging truth. On this point perhaps the Red Queen would be a more reliable guide:

because we live in a linguistically mobile world, we need to keep running if we are to remain in the same place. We also need to remember that words have evocative power as well as sense and reference. Some words are naturally emotive or are deliberately used to evoke emotion; others, including those we are here discussing, acquire emotive associations, good or bad, through partisan use. Few words succeed in living down their history, least of all their emotive associations. When a word has been on the battle-front for generations, it does not readily settle down to the dispassionate commerce of armchair theology.

Chapter Four

Opacity, Vagueness and Ambiguity

The time has come when we must examine more closely and distinguish more exactly those linguistic obstacles to communication which we have so far encountered only in a haphazard fashion. All such obstacles may be classified under three heads. The first of these, opacity, is integral to the very nature of language, and all we can do is come to terms with it. The second, vagueness, is in one sense an inescapable quality of language, in another sense a disease of language, and in a third sense a particular style of speech. The third, ambiguity, though frequently confused with polysemy, the multiple senses covered by the dictionary definition of words, is more usefully regarded as a characteristic of speech, being sometimes a defect in the use of language and sometimes a deliberate exploitation of multiple meaning.

1. Transparency and opacity

A language is transparent insofar as its meaning lies open to any intelligent but uninstructed observer, and opaque insofar as it has to be learnt; and anyone who has grappled with a hitherto unfamiliar language will be only too ready to believe that in all languages the opaque vastly exceeds the transparent. Transparency is of three kinds,[1] and it is important to note that languages vary both in the degree and in the incidence of their transparency.

(i) *Phonetic transparency* (*onomatopoeia*). Total transparency occurs only where words reproduce the sounds they signify, as in the English 'bang' or 'fizzy'. But onomatopoeia accounts for only a tiny proportion of the word-stock of any language and does not

---

[1] In a sign language, such as that of international road signs, there is also visual transparency.

substantially qualify the general rule that the relation between words and what they signify is arbitrary or conventional. Even with the most obvious instances of onomatopoeia a certain element of convention enters in: the cock says 'cockadoodledoo' in England, 'cocorico' in France, and 'kikeriki' in Germany and Greece. Classical Hebrew appears to offer comparatively few instances of this deviation from arbitrariness.[2] This may be because the ear of the western lexicographer is not attuned to pick up assonances which would have been obvious to the native Hebrew-speaker. But a more probable reason is that onomatopoeia depends to a large extent on vowel sounds, and Hebrew is a language in which in most words only the consonants remain unchanged while the vowels are modified by inflexion. Examples do, however, occur, and some are readily recognisable by English readers: e.g. *has* (hush) and *yalal* (yell).

(ii) *Morphological transparency.* Much more important is the relative transparency effected by the two processes of inflexion and word-building. If we know the meaning of a root and the rules of inflexion and morphology, it is usually possible to work out for ourselves the meaning of cognate forms. In this respect English is more transparent than French and less transparent than agglutinative languages such as Greek or German. But all languages have their own areas both of transparency and of opacity.[3]

This is one of the many linguistic facts which have been overlooked by those who have tried to find in the Hebrew language evidence for some special quality of the Hebrew mind. J. Pedersen, for example, is one of those who have claimed that Hebrew is a primitive language because it is deficient in abstract terms, and that the Hebrew thinker did not think abstractly because he grasped each object or action in its undivided totality. 'When we speak of going, going in, going out, going up or down, then it is for us the same action, only performed in a different manner and leading to different results, because we have the abstract idea, i.e. to "go", which may be supplemented now in one, now in another direction. To the Israelite these are perfectly different actions, seeing that he

[2] Brown, Driver and Briggs in their Hebrew lexicon use the sign 'onomat.' only rarely in their explanations of the origins of words.

[3] There is also a secondary transparency between languages of a single family, e.g. the Romance languages. Some elements of English are transparent to those who know Greek and Latin.

considers the totality-character of the action with its special stamp.'[4]
Barr has pointed out that Pedersen here confused general terms
with abstract ones, and that French also uses a variety of terms for
going in various directions (*monter*, *partir*, *sortir*, *entrer* etc.),
instead of qualifying the general term *aller* with directional
markers.[5] The possession of general terms which can be the basis
for word-building distinguishes transparent languages from opaque
ones, not the developed from the primitive. The other point which
Pedersen overlooked is that Hebrew has its own areas of transparency. The Hebrew word for 'teach' (*limmad*) is a causative stem
of the verb 'learn' (*lamad*). The verb 'to see' has a passive stem
meaning 'appear' and a causative stem meaning 'show'. Yet the
absence of such verbal conveniences in English does not imply
that we regard teaching and learning, or seeing and appearing, as
totally unrelated processes.

The lack of congruence between any two languages in their areas
of transparency can cause serious problems for the translator.
What, for example, is the English translator to make of *dikaiosynē*
(righteousness) in Romans. Greek, like Hebrew, possesses here a
full range of cognate forms (verb, adjective, adverb and noun), but
English does not. The judge in a law court, faced with two litigants,
justifies one of them, i.e. declares right to be on his side, gives the
verdict in his favour. In the opening chapters of Romans Paul
discusses on what grounds God justifies men and women,
declares them to be in the right. English has the noun 'justification'
to connote the judicial act, but no cognate word to signify the
character of the judge whose verdict is sound or the status of the
person justified, and has to make do with 'righteous' and 'righteousness' instead. 'Just' and 'justice' will not do, because they are
already pre-empted by long usage for quite a different meaning.
But the traditional rendering is almost as unsatisfactory, since
'righteous' has come to have a moral connotation, usually nowadays

[4] *Israel*, p. 111. Cf. also G. A. Smith, 'The Hebrew genius' in *The Legacy of Israel*:
'Hebrew may be called primarily a language of the senses' (p. 10); 'Few abstract terms
exist in ancient Hebrew and no compound words. Abstraction and constructive power
are almost as absent from the grammar and the syntax as from the vocabulary' (p. 11).

[5] Op. cit., pp. 30 f. For the distinction between general and abstract, see J. S. Mill's
attack on Locke (*A System of Logic*, bk. 1. ch. ii 4). Cf. S. Ullmann, op. cit., p. 119; and
on 'primitive languages' see ibid., p. 120. Also O. Barfield, *Poetic Diction*, p. 74: 'that
luckless dustbin of pseudo-scientific fantasies, the mind of primitive man.'

with a slightly disparaging tone, and certainly does not convey to the modern reader the notion of 'being in the right' or 'winning a lawsuit'. R. Knox went further than this, dismissing 'righteousness' as 'a meaningless token word: 'to use such a token word is to abrogate your duty as a translator.'[6] The duty of the translator is to tell the reader what the original means, and this he cannot do by using token words which, like algebraical symbols, are devoid of semantic content. Yet if in Rom. 1:17 we translate *dikaiosynê* in such a way as to explain what it means, shall we not be short-circuiting Paul's argument, since he takes four chapters to do precisely that?

A language, then, is transparent to the extent that the significance of its words may be deduced from a knowledge of their simpler elements. But there are two ways in which the importance of morphology can be overestimated. There is first a common human tendency to resent opacity and to try and enlarge the area of transparency. We have already seen that the writers of the Old Testament were not immune from it (pp. 45–6). God took Adam from the ground—(*ᵃdamah* (Gen. 2:7). Naphtali was so called because Rachel wrestled (*naphal*) with Leah and won (Gen. 30:8). Even the more sophisticated writers take delight in exploring morphological links in ways that come near to punning. Isaiah's dictum to Ahaz, 'Have firm faith, or you will not stand firm', plays upon the common etymology of two verbal forms which are not commonly related in sense (Isa. 7:9). Paul makes even more elaborate play out of simple and compound forms of the one verb *krinô* (1 Cor. 11:29–32). But such conceits have more to do with style than with meaning. It is well for the student of the Bible to recognise this stylistic tendency where it is in evidence, but he must not treat it as a warrant for indulging his own etymological fancies. Even where a genuine etymological link exists, a word may grow away from its origins in the direction of opacity. The Greek *charis* (grace), for example, like *chara* (joy), is derived from the verbal root *chairein*, but none of its varied uses in the New Testament could be deduced from its etymology, and no New Testament writer ever attempts to establish a sibling link of sense between these two words of common ancestry.[7]

---

[6] *On Englishing the Bible*, p. 11.

[7] Very occasionally they were confused by copyists (e.g. 2 Cor. 1:15; 3 John 4), but these are errors of sight or sound rather than of sense.

The second danger arising from morphology is less obvious, but no less important. The grammar of a language, at least as it is set out in elementary manuals of instruction, has traditionally been dictated by morphology. Nouns and adjectives are set out in declensions, verbs in conjugations. Inflected languages of the Indo-European family (e.g. Greek, Latin, French and German) roughly conform to a single pattern. English, a relatively un-inflected language of the same family, fits the pattern less comfortably. But Hebrew is a Semitic language with a totally different grammatical structure. It is very easy therefore to draw the conclusion that Hebrew must be just as different from the European languages as a means of expressing thought, and this fallacy has had a good deal of support from those who ought to have known better.

(1) Hebrew has been supposed deficient in adjectives. By the standard of Greek or Latin morphology this may be true, but the reason is that in Hebrew the function of the adjective is frequently discharged by two other grammatical forms: the stative verb (to be small, old, heavy etc.) and the construct state of the noun ('my holy hill' is literally 'the hill of my holiness'), both of which might properly be described as adjectival. Incidentally, the Hebrew noun does not morphologically have a genitive case, but the construct state shares most of the functions and, as we shall see later in this chapter, the ambiguities of the Greek and Latin genitive.

(2) The Hebrew verb does not have tenses like those of Greek and Latin verbs. It has accordingly been argued that the Hebrew people had a different concept of time from ours.[8] But the users of Hebrew were quite capable of expressing the difference between past, present and future by the use of other elements in their syntax.

(3) With the majority of Hebrew roots the simplest form is that of the verb, from which noun and adjective are therefore said to be derived. In a Hebrew dictionary words are arranged wherever possible under the verbal form. So Hebrew grammarians have found it necessary to invent a technical term for verbs derived from nouns—denominative (see p. 62). But the denominative verb is familiar enough in other languages, whose grammarians have not felt the need of a special name for it, e.g. in Greek *basileuein* (to be or act as king) or the English 'to salt', 'to chair', 'to paper'.

---

[8] See J. Barr, *The Biblical Words for Time.*

4

(4) The Hebrew verb has a stem, the *niphal*, which can be either passive or reflexive, but has also a wide range of subsidiary uses, including the *niphal tolerativum*, which signifies allowing someone to do to you the action connoted by the verb. Thus *darash* means 'to seek' and one of the senses of *nidrash* is 'to allow oneself to be sought' (Isa. 65:1). But once this usage has been pointed out to us in Hebrew, we soon become aware that it exists without a name in other languages. Joseph went to Bethlehem 'to get himself enrolled' (Luke 2:5). 'Why,' says Paul to the Colossians, 'do you let yourselves be dictated to?' (Col. 2:21). It occurs in fact whenever a passive verb is used in the imperative. 'Do not be bullied' is shorthand for 'do not let anyone bully you.'

Illustrations of this sort go far to substantiate the main point which is being made by linguists of the structuralist school, who maintain that beneath the surface structure dictated by the morphology of languages there is a deep structure which is common to all.[9]

(iii) *Analogical transparency (metaphor)*. Most of the words in common use in any language have a wide range of metaphorical meaning which depends for intelligibility on an obvious similarity between the literal and the metaphorical referents. All we need to do is to identify the point of comparison. Much of this transparency can survive translation, provided that the objects or practices denoted by the literal sense exist in both cultures. We have no great difficulty with the following Hebrew metaphors:

The head of Syria is Damascus and the head of Damascus is Rezin ... the head of Ephraim is Samaria and the head of Samaria is Remaliah's son   (Isa. 7:8–9).

Harvest is past, summer is over, and we are not saved. I am wounded at the sight of my people's wound ... Is there no balm in Gilead, no physician there? Why has no new skin grown over their wound?
                                                                              (Jer. 8:20–22).

Ephraim is a half-baked scone   (Hos. 7:8).

[9] Cf. O. Barfield, op. cit., p. 82: 'The service rendered by these latter [*sc.* grammarians and philologists] both to speech and to thought is of the utmost importance; their error merely lay in supposing that life actually created language after the manner in which their logic reconstructed it.'

Even when we discover that the ancient Israelite killed his enemies 'with the mouth of the sword', the comparison of the sword with a ravenous beast overcomes any sense of unfamiliarity (e.g. Gen. 34:26).

One of the pitfalls for the biblical translator is that, in his eagerness to tell the reader exactly what the text before him means, he may ignore analogical transparency and quite unnecessarily unpack the metaphors, leaving the language flat and sterile. When, for example, Paul calls Christ 'the firstfruits of the harvest of the dead' (1 Cor. 15:20 NEB), it can be assumed that the harvesting of crops is such a universal phenomenon that even the Translator's New Testament, produced as an aid for translators into a thousand tongues, hardly needed to resort to the paraphrase: 'this is the guarantee that those who have died will be raised also.'

2. *Vagueness*

Vagueness covers three quite distinct aspects of linguistic usage, generalisation, indeterminacy and economy; and it is important not to confuse them.

(i) *Generalisation*. General terms are obviously less precise than particular ones: tree is less precise than cedar, weapon than sword, craftsman than potter, sin than covetousness. Yet general terms are, as we have seen, the indispensable means by which we organise and understand our experience. There is no truth in the claim that the Hebrew language is deficient in general terms, as anyone may demonstrate by running off a list of those which occur in the Old Testament.

It is, however, true that for a variety of reasons the biblical style avoids this type of vagueness. Much of the Bible is narrative, in which generalisations are inevitably sparse. The proverbial literature contains a fair number of vague moral commonplaces, but frequently prefers to teach by instance and illustration (e.g. Prov. 6:16–19). The poetical passages share with all other poetry a love of the particular (e.g. Isa. 11:6–8; 55:13). And the legal codes have at their core a body of case law (Exod. 21:1—23:19). In the interpretation of the law there was always a tendency to eliminate vagueness by exact definition. The commandment to love your neighbour as yourself invited the lawyer's question, 'Who is my neighbour?' (Lev. 19:18; Luke 10:29). If the law forbad work on the sabbath, the rabbis would naturally ask what the law intended by 'work' and answer their own question with a list of thirty-nine categories (*Mishna*, Shab. 7.2).

Yet there can be dangers in too great precision. Jesus' reply to the lawyer denied him the right to limit his liabilities by definition. At other times Jesus attacked the Pharisees because, in their determination to know exactly what the Torah meant so that they might live in total obedience to it, they concentrated on the minor and practicable pieties, to the neglect of the broad and inexhaustible principles, 'justice, mercy and good faith' (Matt. 23:23). A sound ethical system cannot dispense with the vague generality of the unattainable ideal.

(ii) *Indeterminacy*. In the examples cited above it will be obvious that the distinction between particular and general applies equally to concrete and to abstract terms. But some abstract terms are of such a high degree of generality that on close scrutiny they are found to have no clearly defined referent. One of the reasons why Socrates annoyed his contemporaries was that he pointed out to them how they used words without knowing what it was they were talking about. 'Socrates found that his fellow-Athenians attached the greatest importance to *aretê* [virtue, excellence], and each wanted his sons to be taught it; but, in questioning them closely, he again and again discovered that not one of them knew what this prize was which they valued so highly. Neither did Socrates; but, as he would genially point out to his interlocutors, there was this difference between him and them—they thought that they knew, but he knew that he did not.'[10]

The causes of indeterminacy are various. Occasionally the weakness is congenital: 'There is no ultimately correct and single meaning to words like "romanticism".'[11] More often it happens that words, which at other times and in other contexts can convey a clear meaning, fall victim to careless or polemical use or to fashion, as did 'wit' in the eighteenth century. 'It also suffered the worst fate any word has to fear; it became the fashionable term of

---

[10] J. D. P. Bolton, *Glory, Jest and Riddle*, p. 43.
[11] S. I. Hayakawa, *Symbol, Status and Personality*, p. 20.

approval among critics. This made it a prey to tactical definitions of a more than usually unscrupulous type, and in the heat of controversy there was some danger of its becoming a mere rallying-cry, semantically null.'[12] For a similar cause Jeremiah rebukes people for claiming to possess the law of the Lord without considering what it is they are talking about, and complains that prophets and priests say 'Peace, peace', when there is nothing in the contemporary situation to which the word can rightly apply (Jer. 8:8, 11).

In the Graeco-oriental background of early Christianity *gnôsis* (knowledge) had become a fashionable term, annexed by the champions of many incompatible cults, in which it was subjected to tactical definition (1 Tim. 6:20). The New Testament writers combat its spurious popularity in a variety of ways. With the 'strong party' at Corinth Paul sympathises, but insists that knowledge shall be subordinate to love (1 Cor. 8:1-11; 13:2, 8). To the Colossians he argues that the only knowledge worth having is the knowledge of God revealed in Christ (Col. 2:2). The author of 1 John denies that knowledge is the monopoly of any esoteric sect (2:20); it is the common possession of all who have inherited the apostolic tradition (1:1-4), and the test of its possession is obedience (2:3). In all three communities there had been a group using the fashionable word as a means of bullying their less assertive fellow members. But the evidence of the three epistles does not indicate that these groups had much else in common with each other, let alone with the developed Gnostic sects of the middle of the second century. It is therefore tendentious and confusing to use the word 'Gnosticism' of the beliefs of these somewhat shadowy groups, as though they were the beginnings of a homogeneous and clearly defined movement, sharing all the marks of Gnosticism properly so-called.

(iii) *Economy*. Erich Auerbach has drawn attention to a striking difference between the epic styles of Homer and Genesis in his contrast between the stories of Odysseus' scar and the binding of Isaac. The old nurse Euryclea recognises the returning Odysseus by a scar on his thigh, whereupon Homer spends more than seventy lines explaining how he came by the wound in a boar hunt.

---

[12] C. S. Lewis, op. cit., p. 86. A tactical definition is one in which a term is so defined as to guarantee the conclusion required.

In this, as in other Homeric narratives, every detail of time, place, circumstance, feeling and motive is explicit; all is foreground and every contour is sharply defined. In the biblical story we are not told why God gave Abraham the command to sacrifice Isaac, where Abraham was or what thoughts went through his mind. The story is told in starkest outline and all else is left to the imagination. 'It would be difficult, then, to imagine styles more contrasted than those of those two equally ancient and equally epic texts. On the one hand, externalised, uniformly illuminated phenomena, at a definite time and in a definite place, connected together without lacunae in a perpetual foreground; thoughts and feelings completely expressed; events taking place in a leisurely fashion and with very little suspense. On the other hand, the externalisation of only so much of the phenomena as is necessary for the purpose of the narrative, all else left in obscurity; the decisive points of the narrative alone are emphasised, what lies behind is non-existent; time and place are unidentified and call for interpretation; thoughts and feelings remain unexpressed, are only suggested by the silence and the fragmentary speeches; the whole, permeated with the most unrelieved suspense and directed toward a single goal (and to that extent far more of a unity), remains mysterious and "fraught with background".'[13]

I do not for a moment suggest that the vagueness of economy, which Auerbach finds so impressive and so redolent of mystery in this story, is peculiar to the Bible, or that it arises out of any unique properties of the Hebrew language. It is, as he himself says, a matter of style; and no doubt a similar economy of style may be found in the literature of other cultures. It is, however, characteristic of many other biblical narratives, and particularly of the stories in the Synoptic Gospels. In the parable of the Good Samaritan we are not told who the man was, what was the object of his journey or whether he ever in the end achieved it, what business brought the Samaritan to those parts, or the site of the inn. We do not need to know all this. Almost, it might be argued, we need not to know.[14]

Since the advent of Form Criticism it has been fashionable to

[13] *Mimesis*, p. 9.
[14] For a structural analysis of this story, which tabulates all the missing features, see D. Patte, *What is Structural Exegesis?*

attribute the absence of personal and circumstantial detail in the Gospels to the attritional effect of oral transmission, acting on each unit like the tide smoothing pebbles on a beach. No doubt the stories of Genesis too were orally transmitted before ever they were written down (see the reference to bards in Num. 21:27). But tradition is supposed also to have had something to do with the formation of the Homeric poems and their very different style. One cannot help wondering therefore whether too much has been ascribed to its influence.

3. Ambiguity

Ambiguity is not a characteristic of language but of speech. It occurs when an utterance may bear more than one meaning and we are left in doubt which of the possible meanings is intended. Language is not ambiguous in itself, though it supplies the raw material for ambiguity; it becomes ambiguous in use, when neither context nor tone provide adequate clues to the speaker's intention. The types of ambiguity may thus be classified in two ways: (a) according to the linguistic area in which the doubt arises; and (b) according to the reason why that doubt is left unresolved.[15]

(a) *Areas of ambiguity*
(i) *Phonetic.* There are words of different sense which sound identical (homophons) and can therefore be mistaken for one another. Ambiguity of this kind occurs only in the spoken word, and it impinges on the study of the Bible only through variants in the text and through the constraints which it imposes on translation.

Manuscripts were frequently copied by dictation, and in this way homophony could cause errors of transcription. The chance of this happening in the text of the New Testament was considerably increased by the modification of vowels in Hellenistic Greek: the classical distinction between the long and the short O (omega and omicron) had been eroded, and three vowels (η, ι, υ) and three diphthongs (ει, οι, υι), which were phonetically distinct in classical times, were already, as in Modern Greek, pronounced

---

[15] W. Empson in his *Seven Types of Ambiguity* includes some types from each class, along with that type of vagueness here called indeterminacy.

alike (ēē as in the English 'meet'). Thus in Romans 5:1, half the manuscripts read the indicative ('we have peace') and half the subjunctive ('let us have peace'), and the only difference between the two readings is the length of a vowel, which would not have been aurally discernible. In 1 Pet. 2:3 the majority reading is 'if you have tasted that the Lord is good (chrestos)', but one manuscript has 'if you have tasted that the Lord is Christ (christos)'. In this case there is no real doubt, since the clause is a quotation from Ps. 34:8, but the error is worth mentioning because of a probable parallel elsewhere. Aquila and Priscilla were expelled from Rome along with other Jews by an edict of Claudius (Acts 18:2), which Suetonius (*Claud.* 16) records in these terms: 'he banned from Rome the Jews who were in a constant state of riot at the instigation of Chrestus.'[16] There may have been a Jewish agitator named Chrestus, but it is much more likely that some Roman official got hold of the wrong end of the stick, and that the root of the trouble was anti-Christian rioting.

Because the Bible is regularly read and quoted in public, the translator has constantly to take note of phonetic ambiguity and avoid such words as 'succour' for fear that they will be wrongly heard. A Roman Catholic priest told me that, when his church adopted a liturgy in the vernacular, in which the Lord's Prayer was introduced as 'the prayer he taught us', some children asked to see the prairie tortoise.

(ii) *Lexical.* The commonest occasion for ambiguity is polysemy, which may leave us guessing which sense of a word is intended. Since in text book descriptions of polysemy (see above, pp. 41–2) the examples given tend to be nouns, it is important to note that multiple meaning may be found in any part of speech: pronoun, preposition, conjunction and interjection, as well as noun, verb, adjective and adverb. Hebrew, for instance, has a multipurpose preposition *b-*, which can mean in, during, at, against, down upon, with, by means of, through, for (at the cost of), on account of, in spite of etc. In Hellenistic Greek the preposition ἐν was almost as versatile, and its range was even further enlarged in biblical Greek by its frequent use as the equivalent of *b-*.

With all this wealth of possibility it is remarkable how rarely

---

[16] *Iudaeos impulsore Chresto assidue tumultuantes Roma expulit.*

lexical ambiguity in fact occurs, and how often the context enables us to settle upon a precise sense. Yet there remain enough instances which leave us in unresolved doubt. Does the prophet (Isa. 13:5) foresee the devastation of the whole land (AV, NEB) or of the whole earth (JB)? and are the meek to inherit the land (Ps. 37:11) or the earth (Matt. 5:4)? Is the steward in Jesus' parable called a bad steward because he was dishonest, or because he was incompetent, or because he had broken the law against usury by charging interest on his master's loans (Luke 16:8)? Does the 'now' of Eph. 3:5 denote the present of the Christian era, separated from former generations by the coming of Christ, or is the dividing line between past and present some more specific and more recent experience of revelation? When Paul says 'we', is he referring to himself alone, to himself and his colleagues, to Jewish Christians contrasted with 'you Gentiles', or to all Christians without discrimination? Does Paul date the Last Supper on the night when Jesus was 'betrayed' (AV), 'arrested' (NEB) or 'delivered up' (TNT)? When Paul says that God 'chose to reveal his Son in me' (Gal. 1:16), does he mean 'to me', 'in my heart', 'through me', or simply 'in my case'? Does the conjunction 'for' in Phil. 3:3 introduce the reason why the Philippians are to be on their guard or the reason why Paul has elected to use the opprobrious word 'mutilation' to describe those who prided themselves on being 'the Circumcision'? Is the interjection *ouai* (Luke 6:24–26; 11:42–52; Matt. 23:13–31) a term of imprecation ('woe to') or of lament ('alas for')?

(iii) *Grammatical.* Up to this point we have treated polysemy as though it were a property of words alone, but it is found not only in the eight parts of speech, but also in almost all of the much more numerous grammatical forms and syntactical constructions. The only grammatical form which appears to be wholly unequivocal is the vocative case. We may of course be left in doubt about the referent of a word in the vocative (are the people addressed in Gal. 3:1 north Galatians living in Ancyra and Pessinus, or south Galatians living in Antioch, Iconium, Lystra and Derbe?), or about the degree of emotional intensity involved (John 2:4); but in neither instance does the doubt arise from the use of the vocative.

Some of the most important ambiguities arise in the uses of the

4*

Greek genitive. With the majority of these uses, particularly those in which the genitive is governed by a preposition or a verb, we need not be concerned.[17] But there are seven uses, enumerated below, which together constitute an area of ambiguity, and these are the more interesting for us in that most of them have their parallels in the Hebrew and English equivalents to the genitive, the Hebrew construct state and the English 'of' or s with an apostrophe:

(1) The possessive genitive: 'the mountain of the Lord' (Ps. 24:3); 'the house of Simon and Andrew' (Mark 1:29).

(2) The genitive of relation: 'Abner son of Ner' (2 Sam. 2:8); 'Mary wife of Clopas' (John 19:25); 'Mark cousin of Barnabas' (Col. 4:10).

(3) The subjective genitive: 'the works of your father', i.e. such as your father would do (John 8:41); 'your labour of love', i.e. the labour which love undertakes (1 Thess. 1:3).

(4) The objective genitive: 'the fear of the Lord' (Job 28:28); 'the zeal of your house' (Ps. 69:9; John 2:17).

(5) The partitive genitive: 'the half of my goods' (Luke 19:8); 'the firstfruits of them that sleep' (1 Cor. 15:20).

(6) The genitive of apposition or definition: 'the cities of Sodom and Gomorrah' (2 Pet. 2:6); 'the shield of faith' (Eph. 6:16).

(7) The genitive of quality: 'this body of death', i.e. this body beset by death as a physical and spiritual reality (Rom. 7:24). The genitive of quality is particularly common in the Old Testament because of the adjectival use of the construct state ('paths of righteousness' = right paths in Ps. 23:3), and because of the frequent use of *ben* (son) in the ben of classification ('sons of the prophets' = members of the prophetic guild; 'sons of Belial' = riffraff). Hebraisms of both sorts are found in the New Testament: e.g. 'the mammon of unrighteousness' (Luke 16:9) = worldly wealth (NEB), and 'children of wrath' (Eph. 2:3) = those whose lives expose them to retribution.

---

[17] See Blass-Debrunner-Funk, *A Grammar of New Testament Greek*, §§ 169–86.

Even within these categories there can be ambiguity. In English 'Jane's Thomas' might, to anyone who did not know Jane, mean her husband, her son or her gardener. Was then 'James's Judas' (Luke 6:16) his son (NEB) or his brother (AV)? More often ambiguity arises because the genitive might belong to either of two categories. 'The love of God' is certainly subjective in the benediction of 2 Cor. 13:14 and certainly objective in Luke 11:42. But is the love of God which the Spirit pours into Christian hearts God's love or love for God (Rom. 5:5; cf. 5:8, 8:28)? The same question must be asked about the love which Jesus finds lacking in his critics (John 5:42). Here the NEB decides for the objective: 'you have no love for God in you.' This may well be correct, though some slight doubt is raised when later we find Jesus praying to God for his friends 'that the love you had for me may be in them' (John 17:26). Five times in his letters Paul uses the phrase 'faith of (Jesus) Christ' (Rom. 3:22; Gal. 2:16 *bis*; 3:22; Phil. 3:9; cf. Eph. 3:12). In a literal English translation this sounds like a subjective genitive, referring to the faith which Jesus exemplified; and it has been argued that this is what Paul means, since elsewhere faith in Christ is expressed in prepositional phrases. But in Greek there is no difficulty at all in taking the genitive as objective, and the overwhelming majority of translators and commentators have held that this is in each case the sense required by the context.

Sometimes the choice is between the partitive and the appositive. When Paul describes Epaenetus as 'the firstfruits of Asia' (Rom. 16:5), the household of Stephanas as firstfruits of Achaea (1 Cor. 16:15), and Christ as 'the firstfruits of them that sleep' (1 Cor. 15:20), these are all beyond question examples of the partitive. But when he speaks of 'the firstfruits of the Spirit' (Rom. 8:23), this may be either partitive (a first instalment of the Spirit) or appositive (the Spirit as the first instalment of a harvest to come). In another letter Paul twice uses the phrase 'the down-payment of the Spirit', using the term *arrhabon* which we know from secular papyri to have been in common commercial use (2 Cor. 1:22; 5:5). Here the same doubt arises. But in Eph. 1:14, where we are told that the Spirit is the *arrhabon* of our inheritance, the doubt is resolved in favour of apposition. We are faced with a similar choice in Eph. 4:9, where 'the lower regions of earth' can be either partitive (those regions of earth which are below, i.e. Hades) or appositive (the earth below). Over the centuries opinion has swung now this way, now that, always with a strong assertion that the one sense was correct and the other inadmissible. E. J. Goodspeed even used this verse as an argument against the Pauline authorship of Ephesians on the ground that Christ's descent into Hades is not mentioned in the other Pauline letters. It did not seem to occur to him that this might be an argument for adopting the alternative interpretation.[18]

From the possible ambiguities which may arise within the vast territory of syntax let us take as an example the simplest of all structures, predication (see also above, pp. 9–10), and in particular the uses of the verb 'to be'. In English, as in Greek and Latin, the verb 'to be' may be used either in statements of existence or as a copula linking two ideas in statements which may be of four kinds: identity, attribute, sequence or cause, resemblance or equivalence. It is sometimes inaccurately stated that the Hebrew language has no verb 'to be'. It is more accurate to say that it has a verb (*yesh*) for use in statements of existence, but does not commonly employ any verb as copula, except in the future tense where the sense approximates to 'become' (e.g. 2 Sam. 7:14: 'I will be father to him and he shall be son to me'). The confusion between statements of existence and statements involving the use of a copula, which so bedevilled Greek philosophy that even Plato and Aristotle barely fought their way free of it, could not readily have occurred in Hebrew. The only places in the Bible where we meet anything like it are those which refer to pagan gods. Sometimes it is far from clear whether the prophet or apostle intends to deny their existence or merely that they have the attributes of deity. Deutero-Isaiah appears explicit enough. 'I am the Lord, there is no other; there is no god beside me' (45:5). Apart from the one Creator, the word 'god' has no referent other than the man-made images to which other nations look in vain for help (45:20). But does this hold also for Jeremiah when he calls pagan deities no-gods (2:11; 5:7)? Paul can on occasion be as absolute as Deutero-Isaiah: 'a false god has no existence in the real world' (1 Cor. 8:4; cf. Eph. 2:12). Yet in

---

[18] For the evidence in favour of the appositive, see G. B. Caird, *Paul's Letters from Prison*, ad loc. Rabbinic exegesis understood Ps. 68 to be about Moses' ascent of Sinai to receive the law and his descent to give it to Israel. The author of Ephesians (be he Paul or another) claims that the psalm is about Christ's ascent to heaven and his return 'to earth below' at Pentecost to bestow spiritual gifts on the church.

another context he can speak of pagan religion as slavery 'to beings which in their nature are no gods', and appears to identify these with 'the weak and beggarly elementals', the powers of the old world order (Gal. 4:8–9).

We turn then to look more closely at copular predication, noting that Hebrew is not alone in being able to achieve this without the actual use of the copula. Here is an example of each of the main types with the copula suppressed in Greek:

(1) Identity. 'Is the law sin?' (Rom. 7:7).

(2) Attribute. 'No one is good except God alone' (Mark 10:18).

(3) Cause. 'To be carnally minded is death' (Rom. 8:6).

(4) Resemblance. 'The tongue is a fire' (Jas. 3:6).

Ambiguity sets in when we are unable to determine which of these types of predication was intended.

If we may judge by the acrimonious debates and mutual recriminations it has engendered, the sentence 'this is my body' (Matt. 26:26; Mark 14:22; Luke 22:19; 1 Cor. 11:24) must be one of the most ambiguous in the New Testament. There are those who print the words THIS IS in large capitals in their prayer books, as though to assert that this particular instance of predication is unique, not to be compared with any other use of the verb 'to be'. Yet they are only marginally more naive than those (of whom I myself have been one) who accuse them of absurdity on the ground that Hebrew and Aaramaic possess no copula, as though that debarred speakers in those languages from predication altogether. The statement cannot be one of identity, since Jesus cannot be supposed to have identified the bread in his hands with the living body of which those hands were part; and if it be claimed that the word 'body' in this instance has a different referent, then it is being used metaphorically, and all metaphorical statements belong to class (4). But if we conclude that 'is' here stands for 'represents' or 'symbolises', the traditional riposte is that the eucharistic elements are not to be regarded as 'mere symbols'. The fallacy in this objection lies in the assumption that symbols are invariably substitutes for the reality they signify, bearing the same relation to it as a still-life painting to real fruit and fish, whetting but not satisfying the appetite. But many symbols, such as a kiss, a handshake and the presentation of a latchkey, are a means, or even the means, of conveying what they represent. The most natural way of taking the copula in the eucharistic saying, therefore, is 'represents', with the understanding that Jesus intended the gift of bread to convey the reality it symbolised.

Another verse of notorious difficulty is the opening sentence of the Fourth Gospel: 'In the beginning the Logos already existed, and the Logos was in God's presence, and the Logos was God.' The third clause looks like a statement of identity, yet the second denies the possibility of taking it so. The NEB has attempted to take it as attributive ('what God was the Word was'); but, since God is a class of one, whoever has all the attributes of God is God, so that the attributive converts into a statement of identity. Is it possible, then, that we have manufactured our own difficulty by leaving Logos untranslated, as though it were a proper noun, and that bold translation would resolve the problem. 'In the beginning was a purpose, a purpose in the mind of God, a purpose which was God's own being.' It is surely a conceivable thought that God is wholly identified with his purpose of love, and that this purpose took human form in Jesus of Nazareth. Yet by this resort we have only postponed our difficulty to the prayer in which Jesus speaks of the glory he had and the love with which the Father loved him before the world began (17:5, 24). Perhaps in the end it is best to conclude that John intended to write an opening sentence which would 'tease us out of thought as doth eternity'.

(iv) *Functional.* Further ambiguities may arise out of the use to which words are put, and of these it is unnecessary at this point to give illustrations. We have already seen in the first two chapters examples of the possible confusion between the referential, commissive and social uses of language. The need to discriminate between the literal and the non-literal will be dealt with at length in Parts II and III.

(b) *Causes of ambiguity*

The reasons why ambiguity may be unresolved are of three kinds, accidental, historical and deliberate. That is to say, a speaker may have intended to be unambiguous and yet have failed to notice that what he said could be taken in a way he did not intend; his utterance may have been unambiguous to his original audience and have become ambiguous to us because, with the passage of time, we lack the contextual knowledge available to them; or he may have intended the ambiguity, and that in a variety of ways which we may classify as oracular, ironic, parabolic, exploratory and associative.

Accidental and historical ambiguities are straightforward and need not delay us. Paul in 1 Corinthians has to correct a false impression given by a previous letter, in which he had warned his converts not to associate with immoral persons, not intending to refer to pagans, since 'to avoid them you would have to get out of the world altogether' (5:10). Both his letters to the Thessalonians contain passages written because they (in common with some modern scholars) had wrongly taken his preaching about the coming of Christ from heaven to mean that he expected the world to end shortly. Much of 1 Corinthians can be taken in more than one way because it was an answer to a letter from Corinth of which we know neither the exact content nor the tenor (1 Cor. 7:1). In two of his letters Paul refers to 'the elements of the world' (Gal. 4:3, 9; Col. 2:8, 20), which can mean either 'the elemental powers controlling the present world order' or 'the elementary teaching characteristic of this world'; and the original readers were probably familiar enough with the term to be in no doubt which sense was intended, whereas we have to make our choice on a calculation of probabilities. But the deliberate exploitation of ambiguity requires closer attention.

(i) Oracular ambiguity is commonly associated with Delphi and the Sibyl. When Croesus consulted the Delphic oracle, he was told, 'if Croesus crosses the Halys, he will destroy a great empire'; and with this equivocal encouragement he destroyed his own (Aristotle, *Rhet.* iii.5). Maxentius, on the eve of his death in battle against Constantine, consulted the Sibylline books and was told that the enemy of Rome would die (Lactantius, *M.P.* 44). The Old Testament prophets did not as a rule indulge in this hedging of bets, though we might perhaps assign to this category Jeremiah's prediction of destruction at the hands of an enemy from the north (Jer. 1:13; 4:6). Brewer's *Dictionary of Phrase and Fable* cites as a parallel Micaiah's prophecy to Ahab (1 Kings 22:15), but there it is not the sense or the referent of the oracle that is ambiguous, but the intention: Ahab is meant to think that God intends him to conquer, whereas in fact God means him to die. A better instance would be Joseph's interpretation of the dreams of the head butler and head baker, both of whom are told that 'within three days Pharaoh will lift up your head', though in the one case this means restoration to favour and in the other hanging (Gen. 40:12, 19). The evasive responses of the Pythian priestess and the Sibyl were of course designed to protect the oracle against recrimination, and it is possible that John thought Pilate to be covering himself in a similar fashion in causing the title 'King of the Jews' to be nailed to the cross. This could be taken either as a statement of the charge of which he had been found guilty or as a simple designation, and Pilate refused to remove the ambiguity (John 19:19–22).

(ii) The prophecy of Caiaphas, on the other hand, is not oracular but ironical. Dramatic irony is a form of speech which assumes a double audience, the first understanding nothing beyond the face value of the words, the second seeing both the deeper meaning and the incomprehension of the first. It is well exemplified in the conversation between Joseph and his brothers, where the reader knows the identity of Joseph and the brothers do not (Gen. 42). Similarly when Caiaphas declares that it is expedient that one man should die for the people and not the whole nation perish (John 11:50), his is the voice of *Realpolitik*, but John attributes a deeper, theological meaning to his words and credits him with the unwitting faculty of prophecy on the strength of his priestly office. Dramatic irony is one of the most prominent stylistic features of the Fourth Gospel, based on the evangelist's belief that all earthly things are capable of being symbols of things heavenly, and that this is preeminently so in the words and works of Jesus (3:12). In one incident after another the interlocutor takes the words of Jesus at the earthly level, and his sights, or those of the reader at least, have to be raised to the heavenly. The bystanders who hear Jesus say 'Destroy this temple, and in three days I will raise it again' remonstrate that it has already been forty-six years under construction; and John's comment is that 'the temple he was speaking of was his body' (John 2:19–21). Nicodemus has to be taught that rebirth is not reentry into the womb but spiritual renewal (3:3–8), the Samaritan woman that living water is an inner spring which cannot be piped into her house (4:10–15), Martha that resurrection is not an event at the end of time but a recreative power already present in Jesus (11:23–26).

(iii) Parabolic ambiguity is well illustrated by Nathan's parable (2 Sam. 12:1–10). Nathan tells David the story of the rich man who took the poor man's ewe lamb, and asks him as head of the judiciary to give his official ruling on the case, with the intention that his own verdict on the hypothetical situation may be seen to apply to the real offence of his treatment of Uriah. Many of the parables of Jesus contain, explicitly or implicitly, a similar invitation to the hearer to judge, and incidentally to judge himself. 'What will the owner of the vineyard do?' (Mark 12:9). 'Which of the two did as his father wished?' (Matt. 21:31). 'Which of the three do you think was neighbour to the man who fell into the hands of the robbers?' (Luke 10:36).

(iv) Some deliberate uses of ambiguity must be called exploratory, because the speaker has not made up his mind between two senses, but is discovering a new truth by investigating the interconnexion between them. In our study of the genitive case above we have seen that the phrase 'the love of God' can be either subjective or objective, and that both uses are found in the New Testament. In 1 John this ambiguity is exploited to the full. The letter was written to encourage the faithful survivors of a schismatic split, caused by the departure of an influential group who had been making startling claims for themselves (2:19): they knew God with an esoteric knowledge not vouchsafed to other members, and they loved him with an intensity which put them beyond sin and gave them a share in his divine life (1:6, 8; 2:4; 4:20). Since, then, the author writes to controvert the schismatics' claim that they love God, we may assume that the objective sense of 'the love of God' is the starting point of his argument, and in one passage this is un-ambiguously expressed. 'When we love God and obey his commands we love his children too. For this is the love of God, that we keep his commands' (5:2–3). In three other passages it is doubtful whether the objective or the subjective is meant. 'If anyone keeps his word, in him the love of God comes to its perfection' (2:5). 'If anyone loves the world, the love of the Father is not in him' (2:15). 'If anyone has enough to live on and yet when he sees his brother in need shuts up his heart against him, how can it be said that the love of God dwells in him?' (3:17). In a fifth passage the sense intended is clearly the subjective. 'God himself dwells in us if we love one another; his love is brought to perfection within us' (4:12). In the light of the two unambiguous passages it appears probable that in the three ambiguous ones both senses are being intended at once. For John's argument is that love for God entails love for our fellows, so that the one cannot exist without the other; and that when we love our fellows, it is not merely we who love, but God who loves through us; so that all human love which is genuine is the indwelling of God. God is love, and only by the experience of loving can one have experience of God (4:7–9).

The teaching attributed to Jesus in the Gospels strongly suggests that he used this device of deliberate ambiguity to provoke his hearers into thought about ultimate questions. Consider the following passage, which is quoted in the first instance from the RV.

> If any man would come after me, let him deny himself and take up his cross and follow me. For whosoever would save his life shall lose it; and whosoever shall lose his life for my sake and the gospel's shall save it. For what doth it profit a man, to gain the whole world and forfeit his life? For what should a man give in exchange for his life?
>
> (Mark 8:34–37).

Here the Greek word *psychê* is used four times in quick succession, and the revisers decided to render it uniformly by 'life'. But *psychê* can mean life is a wide variety of senses, ranging from 'being alive' through 'life that is worth living' to 'true self' or 'soul'. Ought not the translation then to be more explicit? The opening reference to the cross, the Roman method of execution, indicates that the starting point of the discussion is the risk of physical death entailed in discipleship. Yet it simply is not true that to lose one's life in this sense is to save it. And is there not a curious clash between the warning against saving one's life and the warning against forfeiting it? It was considerations such as these that had prompted the AV to render *psychê* in verse 35 by 'life' and in verses 36–37 by 'soul': 'what shall it profit a man, if he gain the whole world and lose his own soul? Or what shall a man give in exchange for his soul?' But this has the double disadvantage of breaking the verbal link without solving the problem. Accordingly the NEB made a bolder attempt at giving the sense of the passage.

> Anyone who wishes to be a follower of mine must leave self behind: he must take up his cross, and come with me. Whoever cares for his own safety is lost; but if a man will let himself be lost for my sake and for the gospel, that man is safe. What does a man gain by winning the whole world at the cost of his true self? What can he give to buy that self back?

The intention was excellent; but it did not produce such an increase in clarity as to compensate for the loss of directness and force. The commentator may of course cut the knot with the scissors of Form Criticism, by arguing that the four sayings in this passage came to Mark as independent units of tradition which he threaded together by the catchword *psychê*, much as the three sayings of 9:50 are threaded together by the catchword 'salt'; but that extreme and improbable view is no help to the translator, who has to try and make sense of the passage as it stands. I would suggest, rather, that Jesus was deliberately exploiting the ambiguity of 'life', and this view finds some support in other parts of the gospel tradition. 'I bid you put away anxious thoughts about food and drink to keep you alive, and clothes to cover your body. Surely life is more than food, the body more than clothes' (Matt. 6:25). But if that is so, this is one of those rare passages where a word of many meanings must be rendered by a single English word throughout.

(v) Closely akin to the exploratory is that use of ambiguity known as associative thinking. This device is more popular with creative thinkers than with logicians, who tend to look askance at it, since in it the argument does not proceed by logical and compelling steps, but by the exploitation of polysemy. Nathan's prophecy, for example, which was the ground of later belief in the eternity of David's dynasty, and therefore also, once that dynasty had been interrupted, of the confidence that God would one day restore it by the sending of a Messiah, was constructed out of a word-play on two meanings of the word 'house'. David is not to build a house (temple) for God; God will build a house (dynasty) for David

(2 Sam. 7:5–11). An even more elaborate play on the same word is found in Eph. 2:19–22. The church is God's house (household), in which Gentile Christians have now joined Jewish Christians as members of the one family. They are therefore built as living stones into a house (building) of which Christ is the cornerstone, and which grows into a temple or house (dwellingplace) for God.

This kind of associative link was particularly important in the exegesis of Scripture. Jewish exegetes had a name for it, *g^ezerah sh^ewa*, which signified the explication of one text by cross-reference to another which had some verbal link with it; and Christian exegetes followed their example. The author of 1 Peter has brought together three Old Testament texts which have in common only the word 'stone' (Isa. 8:14; 28:16; Ps. 118:22), and out of them has fashioned the sonorous and impressive declaration that Christ is the precious stone set by God in Zion, a foundation stone to those who believe and are built as living stones into the same temple, but to unbelievers the stone which the builders rejected and which is therefore left lying around for them and others to trip over.[19]

---

[19] Since two of these Old Testament passages are cited together in Rom. 9:32–33, it is a plausible suggestion that both writers were using a common source, perhaps an early Christian hymn in which the quotations were already associated. See E. G. Selwyn, *The First Epistle of Peter*, pp. 268–81.

Chapter Five

Hebrew Idiom and Hebrew Thought

Within the latitude of correctness, the bounds of intelligibility marked off by the word-stock and grammar of a language, it is usually possible to express any given idea in a variety of ways. If this were not so, it would be impossible to compile a dictionary. Yet it often happens that among the possible forms of expression one is regarded as normal usage and characteristic of native speakers of the language, and such normal usage we call idiom.

In Chapter Four we saw that Hebrew commonly prefers to use a noun in the construct or a verb where English uses an adjective. It is not that adjectives do not exist. There is an adjective *ṣaddiq* which means 'just' or 'right', and it can be used attributively, as in 'just laws' (Deut. 4:8); but the preferred idiom is 'laws of justice' (Deut. 16:18), using the noun *ṣedeq* with the word for laws in the construct. When the narrator tells us that 'Abraham and Sarah had grown old' (Gen. 18:11), he uses an adjective, but when two verses later he has Sarah say, 'Shall I indeed bear a child when I am old?', she uses the idiomatic stative verb.

I have begun with these examples in order to make it clear that most idioms are purely stylistic in character and imply nothing in particular about the mental processes of the user. It is necessary to emphasise this point, because the amount of material which survives in classical Hebrew is so small that facts of style have all too often been treated as though they were facts of language. Nevertheless there are some idioms which are more closely related to thought, and this chapter will be devoted to the study of two such usages which are characteristic of Biblical Hebrew and also, through Semitic influence, of biblical Greek. Neither of these usages is peculiar to the biblical languages, and no claim is being made that they point to anything distinctive in the forms of biblical thought. What is important is that the reader should be able to recognise them when he meets them and to make allowances for them in his interpretation.

1. Hyperbole and absoluteness

Hyperbole or overstatement is a figure of speech common to all languages. But among the Semitic peoples its frequent use arises out of a habitual cast of mind, which I have called absoluteness—a tendency to think in extremes without qualification, in black and white without intervening shades of grey. When T. E. Lawrence was living among the Arabs during the First World War, this was the quality of their speech and thought which most vividly impressed him.

> In the very outset, at the first meeting with them, was found a universal clearness or hardness of belief, almost mathematical in its limitation, and repellant in its unsympathetic form. Semites had no half-tones in their register of vision. They were a people of primary colours, or rather of black and white, who saw the world always in contour. They were a dogmatic people, despising doubt, our modern crown of thorns. They did not understand our metaphysical difficulties, our introspective questionings. They knew only truth and untruth, belief and unbelief, without our hesitating retinue of finer shades.
>
> This people was black and white, not only in vision, but by inmost furnishing: black and white not merely in clarity, but in apposition. Their thoughts were at ease only in extremes. They inhabited superlatives by choice. Sometimes inconsistents seemed to possess them at once in joint sway; but they never compromised: they pursued the logic of several incompatible opinions to absurd ends, without perceiving the incongruity. With cool head and tranquil judgment, imperturbably unconscious of the flight, they oscillated from asymptote to asymptote.[1]

This description of the modern Arab could equally well have been written about the ancient Hebrew. One does not have to go to Gnosticism to find the origin of the contrast between love and hate, light and darkness, good and evil, truth and falsehood, which is so

---

[1] *The Seven Pillars of Wisdom*, ch. 3. In a footnote Lawrence explains that he was under the erroneous impression that an asymptote was one of the branches of a hyperbola.

prominent in the documents of Qumran and in the Johannine writings, since in each case it is derived from their common background in the Old Testament. Consider the use of the words 'love' and 'hate'. When the Hebrew uses these words, he may mean by them what we should mean, i.e. affection and detestation; but he may merely be using an absolute turn of phrase to express a preference. Where we should say 'I prefer A to B', he says 'I love A and hate B'. 'Jacob loved Rachel more than Leah . . . the Lord saw that Leah was hated' (Gen. 29:30–31). These two forms of expression are clearly interchangeable, and the use of both in successive verses is sure proof that the narrator could distinguish between hate (detest) and hate (love less); he was not a prisoner within his own hyperbole. The same idiom is found three times in the teaching of Jesus, and it is interesting to note that in one instance Luke has recorded a saying in the Semitic idiom which Matthew gives in a form better attuned to Gentile ears and sensibilities.[2]

If anyone comes to me and does not hate his father and mother, wife and children, brothers and sisters, even his own life, he cannot be my disciple (Luke 14:26).

He who loves father or mother more than me is not worthy of me; he who loves son or daughter more than me is not worthy of me (Matt. 10:37).

The two versions are, allowing for minor differences, synonymous. Jesus is not advocating the abandonment of family ties, let alone misanthropy, but is demanding that, where there is a clash of loyalty between the claims of family and the claims of the kingdom of God, the service of the kingdom shall come first. In a different context he could declare with equal emphasis that duty to one's family takes precedence over the minor pieties of religious observance (Mark 7:9–13).

The second saying in which Jesus uses the idiomatic 'hate' contains an additional example of Semitic absoluteness. 'No man

---

[2] In recording sayings of Jesus Luke frequently employs a Semitic idiom which Matthew avoids, and this is one of the many facts fatal to any theory that Luke copied from Matthew the material which they have in common but did not derive from Mark (Q material).

can serve two masters; either he will hate the one and love the other, or he will be loyal to the one and take liberties with the other' (Matt. 6:24). The word *douleuein*, here translated 'serve', can mean 'be the slave of'; and it has been argued that, since it is, and was in the time of Jesus, possible for a free labourer to work for two employers, the first clause ought to run 'no man can be the slave of two masters'. But this is a platitude, hardly worth saying; and Jesus was not in the habit of warning his hearers against the inconceivable. The point is that, whereas we with our Western style of qualified speech would say, 'No man can take service under two masters without giving one of them preferential treatment', Jesus makes the first statement absolute and leaves the hearer to supply the connexion with what follows. The translator is left with the difficult choice between retaining the starkness of the original and supplying the logical link. If he is wise he will choose the first course and rely on the percipience of the reader; for the third passage defies any paraphrase: 'Anyone who loves his life loses it, and anyone who hates his life in this world will keep it for life eternal' (John 12:25).

Prophecy deals more often than not in absolutes. The prophets do not make carefully qualified predictions that the Israelites will be destroyed unless they repent. They make unqualified warnings of doom, accompanied by unqualified calls to repentance. Amos can say:

> As a shepherd rescues out of the jaws of a lion
> two shin bones or the tip of an ear,
> So shall the Israelites who live in Samaria be rescued
> like a corner of a couch or a chip from the leg of a bed,

but also:

> Seek good and not evil, that you may live,
> that the Lord of hosts may be firmly on your side,
> as you say he is   (3:12; 5:14).

What appears to be an unconditional verdict turns out to contain an unexpressed conditional clause. When Hezekiah is dangerously ill, Isaiah says to him, 'This is the word of the Lord: Give your last instructions to your household, for you are a dying man and will not recover' (Isa. 38:1). But once the king has offered a penitential prayer, the prognosis is reversed. The message Jonah is given to deliver to Nineveh runs, 'Within forty days Nineveh will be destroyed', but he admits afterwards that the reason why he ran away to Tarshish was that he knew God would relent if the Ninevites repented, and he was a narrow enough bigot not to want that to happen (Jon. 3:4; 4:1–3).

There is one episode in the life of Jeremiah which shows that the absoluteness of prophecy was well understood by at least some of the people. Jeremiah has foretold the destruction of city and temple, and there are those who wish to put him to death, presumably because they regard the prophetic oracle as a curse which has magical power to bring about the event it predicts. But some of the elders take Jeremiah's side. 'In the time of Hezekiah king of Judah, Micah of Moresheth was prophesying and said to all the people of Judah: "These are the words of the Lord of hosts: Zion shall become a ploughed field, Jerusalem a heap of ruins, and the temple-hill rough heath." Did King Hezekiah and all Judah put him to death? Did not the king show reverence for the Lord and seek to placate him? Then the Lord relented and revoked the disaster with which he had threatened them' (Jer. 26:18–19). According to Deut. 18:21–22, the prophet who uttered an unfulfilled prophecy was a false prophet, not speaking in the name of the Lord or by divine commission, and ought to be sentenced to death for having spoken presumptuously. Yet Micah, whose prophecy was unfulfilled, was not regarded as a false prophet: his was not truly an unfulfilled prophecy but a cancelled one, revoked once it had done its work in eliciting repentance.

Prophetic hyperbole is seen at its most vivid in passages where the judgment of God on a particular nation is depicted in terms of cosmic collapse.

> I saw the earth, and it was without form and void;
>   the heavens and their light was gone.
> I saw the mountains, and they reeled;
>   all the hills rocked to and fro.
> I saw, and there was no man,
>   and the very birds had taken flight.

I saw, and the farm-land was wilderness,
and the towns all razed to the ground,
before the Lord and his anger   (Jer. 4:23–26).

Jeremiah's vision is of the whole creation returning to its primaeval chaos; in the first line he uses the phrase *tohu wabohu*, which is used elsewhere only of the empty turbulence out of which God created heaven and earth (Gen. 1:2; cf. Isa. 34:11). But the referent of the vision, what it is intended to predict, is the coming devastation of Israel. A later prophet of the school of Isaiah announces the imminent arrival of the Day of the Lord.

The Day of the Lord is coming indeed,
that cruel day of wrath and fury,
to make the earth a desolation
and exterminate its wicked people.
The stars of heaven in their constellations shall give no light,
the sun shall be darkened at its rising,
and the moon refuse to shine.
I will bring disaster upon the world
and their due punishment upon the wicked   (Isa. 13:9–11).

On a superficial reading the referent of these verses might appear to be the end of the world, and it is in fact one of the passages out of which mediaeval theology constructed its gruesome picture of the Dies Irae. Yet when we read on it becomes apparent that what the prophet intended to describe, under the symbols of world judgment, was the end of Babylon's world, the coming destruction of the Babylonian empire by the invading armies of Cyrus the Mede.[3] Later in the same book we find a prophecy from yet another prophet, who may well have been familiar with the passage quoted above.

Approach, you nations, to listen,
and attend, you peoples;

[3] Scholars of a pedantic literalism have attempted to evade this conclusion by attributing the two parts of the poem to different hands. But even if their analysis were correct, we should still have to reckon with the editor who saw nothing incongruous in bringing them together. The application of surgery to a biblical text is more often than not an admission on the part of the surgeon that he has failed to comprehend it as it stands.

let the earth listen and everything in it,
　the world and all that it yields;
for the Lord's anger is turned against all the nations
　and his wrath against all the host of them. . . .
All the host of heaven shall crumble into nothing,
　the heavens shall be rolled up like a scroll,
and the starry host fade away,
　as the leaf withers from the vine
　and the ripening fruit from the fig-tree;
for the sword of the Lord appears in heaven,
　see how it descends in judgment on Edom
　　　　　　　　　　　　　　　(Isa. 34:1–5).

The stars are to fall from their courses and the heavens to collapse
on the head of Edom, because they took advantage of Israel's hour
of weakness to seek revenge for ancestral grievances.

The prophet is sometimes as absolute in his optimism as in his
forecasts of ruin. The Isaianic prophecy of the scion from the stock
of Jesse and his coming reign (Isa. 11:1–9) has commonly been
taken as a description of a Golden Age, and so in a sense it is. But
the brave new world of the prophet's vision is no unearthly paradise,
discontinuous with the present. It is rather an idealisation of the
existing monarchy: for the king must still reign over a realm which
calls for the administration of justice if the rights of the poor are
to be protected and the humble defended against aggression, a
realm in which the wolf has not ceased to be lupine or the lion
leonine. The passage has been rightly compared with Vergil's
Fourth Eclogue, the Pollio, which, for all its air of enchantment
('summers of the snakeless meadow, unlaborious earth and oarless
sea'), is an elegant piece of court flattery, depicting the benefits
expected to accrue from the inauguration of imperial rule under
Augustus.

Once we have acquired some familiarity with this prophetic
idiom through instances in which the referent is incontrovertibly
defined by the context, we may perhaps be ready to cope with
advanced hyperbole in which no such direct clue is provided. The
Book of Isaiah ends with a prediction of the final victory of God,
described in terms which the modern reader is apt to find as
repellant as anything Lawrence heard among his Arab friends.

For, as the new heavens and the new earth
which I am making shall endure in my sight,
    says the Lord,
so shall your race and your name endure;
and month by month at the new moon,
    week by week on the sabbath,
all mankind shall come to bow before me,
    says the Lord:
and they shall come out and see
the dead bodies of those who have rebelled against me;
their worm shall not die nor their fire be quenched,
and they shall be abhorred by all mankind
                                        (Isa. 66:22–24).

On this J. Muilenberg has written: 'Vss. 22–23 are a magnificent
climax not only to chs. 56–66 but to chs. 40–55 as well. Vs. 24,
however, has a different spirit . . . it is possible that there is another
hand here.'[4] Yet such dismemberment is necessary only if we
persist in taking the imagery literally, and even without the offend-
ing last verse it is quite out of the question that the prophet intended
that. Even if we restrict ourselves to the geographical limits of the
prophet's world and to the level of population in his day, the
prospect of all mankind travelling on weekly and monthly sight-
seeing tours to Jerusalem is too ludicrous to take literally; under
ancient conditions of travel, time alone would be enough to make
the idea impossibly absurd. We are dealing with a poet who has
chosen this hyperbolic symbol to express his confidence in the
coming of a new age in which the whole world will accept the
worship of the one true God. But the final verse also is a picture of
impossible literality: a dead body may be demolished by worms or
by fire, but the two together cancel each other out. The prophet
knows that in the world as it is war appears to breed war for ever,
and that the forces of resistance to the sovereignty of God have
great resilience, recovering and growing to even greater strength
every time they seem to be defeated, and constantly winning
sympathy and support from the gullible. The victories of God are
visible only to the eyes of faith and always in danger of being con-
troverted by brute fact. The picture of a new world therefore would

---

[4] *The Interpreter's Bible*, ad loc.

be incomplete and unconvincing unless that new world is established by a divine victory so final as to leave no room for the recrudescence of hostility, and attested by such empirical verification as to convince the credulous dupes of the opposition.

2. Parataxis

Parataxis is 'the placing of propositions or clauses one after another, without indicating by connecting words the relation between them' (OED). Its opposite is hypotaxis, the construction of a sentence with one main clause to which subsidiary ideas are linked in subordinate clauses introduced by conjunctions or prepositions which make the logical connections clear (relative, temporal, circumstantial, final, consecutive, causal, concessive, conditional, etc.). Classical Greek and Latin are severely hypotactical languages. Biblical Hebrew is paratactical. Even beginners cannot fail to be struck by this contrast. Yet there are eminent philologists who have drawn strangely faulty inferences from it. 'The Semitic sentence is a succession of short sentences linked together by simple co-ordinate conjunctions. The principal mark, therefore, of Hebrew and especially of classical Hebrew style is that it is what the Greeks called *lexis eiromenê* "speech strung together" like a row of beads . . . It will, therefore, be readily understood that philosophical reasoning and sustained argument were beyond the grasp of the Hebrew intellect or, at any rate, beyond its power of expression.'[5]

Driver is on sounder ground when he describes this as a feature of Hebrew style than when he attempts to deduce from it the limitations of Hebrew thought. Hebrew possesses words for 'if', 'because' and 'therefore'; and any language which has such words is capable of being used for logical thought.

If you return in safety, the Lord has not spoken by me (1 Kings 22:28).

Because you have done this . . . I will bless you abundantly
(Gen. 22:16).

For you alone have I cared among all the nations of the world; therefore will I punish you for all your iniquities   (Amos 3:2).

[5] G. R. Driver, in *The People of the Book*, p. 119.

Just because parataxis happens to be a mark of colloquial speech in many languages, it does not follow that it is a proof of naiveté when we find it in literary Hebrew. It is simply not true that the Hebrew speaker was unable to express logical connections. What is true is that Hebrew idiom prefers the paratactical style in which such connections are implicit and taken for granted.

The Hebrew word for 'and' is the single letter ו (waw) added to the beginning of a word, phrase or sentence. Here is a set of waw-sentences literally translated, from which it may be seen that the logical connections (supplied in parenthesis) are not very hard to detect:

Explicative:	Abel brought an offering from the firstborn of his flock, and (i.e.) their fat portions (Gen. 4:4).
Concessive:	You have said, 'You shall have peace, and (although) the sword is at your throats' (Jer. 4:10).
Circumstantial:	I saw Adonai enthroned and (with) his train filling the temple (Isa. 6:1).
Causal:	Do not detain me and (since) the Lord has made my journey successful (Gen. 24:56).
Comparative:	(As) a door turns on its hinges and (so) a sluggard turns on his bed (Pr. 26:14).
Final:	Bring it to me and (so that) I may eat it (Gen. 27:4).
Conditional:	(If you) cherish her and (then) she will lift you high (Pr. 4:8).

Parataxis occurs also in vernacular Greek, but its relative frequency in the New Testament is almost certainly due to Semitic influence.[6] 'But (if you) say the word and (then) my servant will be cured' (Luke 7:7). 'It was nine o'clock and (when) they crucified him' (Mark 15:25).

Anyone who habitually employs parataxis in expression will be sure to think paratactically as well. He will set two ideas side by side and allow the one to qualify the other without bothering to spell out in detail the relation between them. An excellent example is provided by the psalmist in his hymn on the eloquence of the celestial bodies.

---

[6] See Blass-Debrunner-Funk, op. cit., § 471.

They have no speech or language,
   their voice is not heard;
Their music[7] goes out through all the earth,
   their words reach to the end of the world
                    (Ps. 19:3-4).

In the Age of Reason it took Joseph Addison eight lines to say what the psalmist had said more succinctly in four.

What though in solemn silence all
Move round the dark terrestrial ball?
What though no real voice nor sound
Amid their radiant orbs be found?
In reason's ear they all rejoice,
And utter forth a glorious voice,
For ever singing, as they shine,
'The hand that made us is divine.'

Not all readers of the psalm have taken the point as well as Addison. The Septuagint translator who put the psalm into Greek in the third or second century B.C. seems to have thought it incredible that anyone should have said anything so manifestly self-contradictory. So he rendered the first couplet:

There is no speech or language
Where their voice is not heard.

This corrupted version passed, via the Vulgate, into the English AV. In his ICC commentary Briggs goes further than this and excises v. 3 as a pedantic gloss, though the pedantry is wholly his own.

Paratactical thinking enabled the ancient Hebrew to set in close proximity two different, and even apparently contradictory, senses of a word, without the discomfort felt by the modern reader. How many readers have been puzzled, for example, by the uses of 'repent' in the story of Saul's quarrel with Samuel in 1 Sam. 15?

[7] The Hebrew has *qawam* (their line), which the NEB, following Brown, Driver and Briggs, translated as 'their music'. But the music of the spheres was a Greek conceit not elsewhere mentioned in the Bible. So it may be that a letter has dropped out, and that we should read *qolam* (their voice), which would make the juxtaposition even more stark.

Then the word of the Lord came to Samuel: 'I repent (regret) that I have made Saul king' (v. 10).

'The Glory of Israel does not deceive or repent (change his mind): he is not a man that he should repent' (v. 29).

The Lord repented (regretted) that he had made Saul king over Israel (v. 35).

The logic by which these two divergent uses of the one verb are held together is all present in the context: God's regret for having made Saul king and his consequent withdrawal of legitimacy from his reign are not due to caprice or vacillation. God does not make mistakes and then have to change his plans, as men do. The appointment of Saul was from the start conditional on Saul's loyalty. 'You have rejected the word of the Lord and therefore the Lord has rejected you' (v. 26).

There is a yet greater wealth of concealed logic in the prayer attributed to Solomon at the dedication of the temple (1 Kings 8:12–53).

O Lord who set the sun in the heaven but chose to dwell in thick darkness, here have I built you a lofty house, a habitation for you to occupy for ever (vv. 12–13).

But can God indeed dwell on earth? Heaven itself, the highest heaven cannot contain you (v. 27).

Hear in heaven your dwelling, and when you hear forgive (v. 30).

The historian who compiled this prayer at least seven centuries before Christ did not tell his readers that he was using both 'dwell' and 'heaven' in different senses; he simply allowed the senses to stand side by side. We cannot suppose him to have been unaware of the problems which his paratactical style poses. Still less may we ascribe to him that primitive simplicity implied in Bultmann's demand that we demythologise the Bible, on the ground that biblical man had a mental picture of a three-storey universe which he naively took to be literally true, to be a kind of primitive science. Biblical man may indeed have pictured the world to himself with heaven above it and Sheol below; but, as A. M. Farrer has pointed out, he was not silly enough to imagine that aviation could reach the one or excavation the other.[8] Anybody who has ever accepted the three-storey picture as a description of the world he lived in has done so because it was also a permanent and universal symbol without which certain aspects of religious truth could neither be apprehended nor expressed.

Once this characteristic of thought and speech has been pointed out, examples of it spring to our notice. In his cavalcade of those who in the past have lived by faith, the author of Hebrews can say in a single paragraph that they 'saw God's promises fulfilled' and yet 'did not obtain the promise' (11:33, 39), leaving the reader to draw the proper distinction.

Hyperbole and parataxis go readily in double harness. Like Lawrence's Arab the ancient Hebrew 'inherited superlatives by choice' and was 'black and white not merely in clarity, but in apposition'. The absoluteness of the Sermon on the Mount has long been recognised, whether with admiration or with dismay. What is less frequently noticed is that many of the absolute (and daunting) commands are qualified by the juxtaposition of others. 'Pass no judgment, and you will not be judged' is immediately balanced by 'Do not give dogs what is holy; do not throw your pearls to the pigs' (Matt. 7:1–6). Perhaps it is in this direction that we should look for a resolution of some of the curious inconsistencies of eschatology. Mark has a whole chapter (13) in which he enumerates the premonitory signs that lead up to the day of the Son of Man, and concludes with the warning: 'begin watching now, for you do not know when the time will come.' Source critics detect here composite origin and clumsy editing; but Mark apparently is not uneasy about this juxtaposition of incompatibles. Nor does Paul betray any embarrassment when in one letter to Thessalonica he says, 'Watch, for it may happen at any moment', and in the next, written probably a few weeks later, 'Do not get excited, because it cannot happen yet'. The easy course is to deny that Paul wrote 2 Thessalonians, but it is not through that wide gate that we shall find the narrow path which leads to understanding.

---

[8] For Bultmann's essay see *Kerygma and Myth*, ed. H. W. Bartsch, Eng. tr. R. H. Fuller, pp. 1–16; and for Farrer's critique, pp. 212–23.

Chapter Six

The Septuagint

The lightning conquest of the Persian empire by Alexander the Great, begun at Granicus in 334 B.C. and completed at Gaugamela three years later, was one of the most remarkable events in the history of language. It made Greek for almost a millennium the lingua franca of the eastern Mediterranean. Jews living outside of Palestine were brought up with Greek as their first or only language, and even in Palestine there were Greek-speaking enclaves, so that most Jews must have had some familiarity with the universal tongue. The Christian church was from the start bilingual, numbering among its earliest Jewish converts Hellenists as well as Hebrews, i.e. Greek-speaking Jews as well as Aramaic-speaking ones (see Acts 6:1).

Thus for the student of the New Testament translation is not merely a task he has to perform on the original Greek text. It is also part of the stuff with which he has to work. The sayings of Jesus and some of the traditions of the early Palestinian church, which are preserved in Greek, are translations out of Aramaic, as may be plainly seen by the residual presence of Aramaic words: *talitha qum* (Mark 5:41), *ephphatha* Mark 7:34), *abba* (Mark 14:36; Rom. 8:15), *maranatha* (1 Cor. 16:22). Old Testament citations in the New Testament may be the author's own Greek rendering of the Hebrew, or they may be quoted from some collection of texts, first made in Hebrew and then translated by some unknown hand; but in the vast majority of cases they are quoted from the standard Greek translation, the Septuagint, which rapidly became the Bible of the early church.

Within forty years of the death of Alexander in 323 B.C. the Jews in Alexandria had embarked on the lengthy process of making a Greek version of their Scriptures. The name 'Septuagint', which by long usage has come to denote the whole Greek Old Testament, referred in the first instance only to the translation of the Torah, the five books of Moses. The name (Seventy) is derived from a legend, preserved in its earliest form in *The Letter of Aristeas*: Ptolemy II Philadelphus wished to add a copy of the Jewish Law to his new library at Alexandria and asked the high priest in Jerusalem to send translators; and seventy (or seventy-two) were sent, who 'completed the task, arriving at agreement by comparing each other's work'. In later forms of the legend the translators worked independently and, when their versions were compared, they proved to be identical, thus indicating that the translation shared the plenary inspiration of the original. The probable basis of truth in the legend is that the work was done in Alexandria and in the reign of Ptolemy II (285–246 B.C.). But the reason for it is more likely to have been the needs of the Jewish community itself than a collector's whim; and, to judge by the high quality of the translation, the size of the translation panel must have been considerably smaller than seventy.

The translation of the other books of the Old Testament followed at intervals over the next four centuries and was the work of many hands.[1] Their combined work was the first translation of a lengthy text ever made from one language to another, and, considering that it was undertaken without the aid of grammars, dictionaries or concordances, it was an amazing achievement. Unfortunately we cannot with any confidence reconstruct all the details of the story. Apart from the *Letter of Aristeas*, no ancient records survive, and all we can do is piece together such fragments of information as can be derived from the Septuagint itself. There is much still to be done in this field, because for the last hundred years ninety per cent of the work done on the Septuagint has concentrated on the problems of its text.[2]

In 1914 H. B. Swete could do no more than point to the wide differences of style, competence and date. 'The Pentateuch is on the whole a close and serviceable translation; the Psalms and more especially the Book of Isaiah show obvious signs of incompetence. The translator of Job was perhaps more familiar with Greek

---

[1] For evidence of this compare Ps. 18 with 2 Sam. 22, 2 Kings 18:13–20:19 with Isaiah 36:1–39:8, and Micah 4:1–5 with Isaiah 2:2–4, where the Hebrew is identical and the Greek radically different.

[2] See S. Jellicoe, *The Septuagint and Modern Study*.

124   *The Language and Imagery of the Bible*

pagan literature than with Semitic poetry; the translator of
Daniel indulges at times in a Midrashic paraphrase. The version
of Judges which appears in our oldest Greek uncial MS has
been suspected by a recent critic of being a work of the fourth
century A.D.; the Greek Ecclesiastes savours of the school of
Aquila.'[3]
The pioneer work was done by H. St. J. Thackeray in his
Schweich Lectures for 1921.[4] He showed by analysis of vocabulary
and style that the books of Jeremiah and Ezekiel were divided
between two translators, so that Jeremiah α was responsible for
chapters 1–28 and Jeremiah β for chapters 29–52, Ezekiel α for
chapters 1–27 and 40–48 and Ezekiel β for chapters 28–39; and the
Minor Prophets were also the work of Ezekiel α. In the four books
of Kingdoms (1 and 2 Samuel, 1 and 2 Kings) Thackeray detected
four hands (α 1 Kgms; β 2 Kgms 1:1—11:1; γ 3 Kgms 2:12—
21:29; δ 2 Kgms 11:2—24:25 and 3 Kgms 22—4 Kgms 25), but
in this case the translators were not contemporary collaborators, but
belonged to widely different periods, the latest being probably post-
Christian. He believed that Isaiah was the earliest of the prophetic
books to be translated, and that the translator 'was less competent
on the whole than the translator or translators of the Jeremiah
group, though he tries to hide his ignorance by paraphrase or
abbreviation, occasionally giving the general sense of a passage,
while omitting to render the difficult words'. Subsequent writers
have refined and modified Thackeray's conclusions without
substantially altering them.[5]
Thackeray's methods have been applied to other books as well.
G. Gerleman, for example, has shown that 1 and 2 Chronicles were
translated independently of the books of Kingdoms, and also of
Ezra and Nehemiah. He has raised the question whether Job and
Proverbs may not have been the work of one translator, since the
two versions show a similar style and a similar freedom in the
treatment of the Hebrew text. The Greek Job introduces allusions
to Greek mythology: in 41:22, where the Hebrew has a most
obscure description of the crocodile, the Greek calls it a dragon
'with all the gold of the sea beneath it'. The Greek Proverbs makes

[3] *An Introduction to the Old Testament in Greek*, pp. 315–16.
[4] *The Septuagint and the Jewish Worship*, pp. 9–37.
[5] For a full bibliography up to 1968, see Jellicoe.

allusions to Greek poetry and sometimes substitutes Greek maxims for those of the original.[6]

In the dating of these various translations we have one piece of solid evidence. The translator of Ecclesiasticus tells us in his prologue that he arrived in Egypt in 132 B.C. and at once set about translating his grandfather's book into Greek. The grandfather, Jesus ben Sira, had written a compendium of Old Testament instruction, ending with a catalogue of the heroes of Israel's national history (chs. 44–50), in compiling which he regularly quoted from the Hebrew of the Old Testament. The grandson recognised these quotations and, wherever possible, used the Septuagint version in his own translation. From this we can deduce that he was familiar with the Greek versions of the Pentateuch, 1 Samuel, Isaiah, Ezekiel and Psalms, but not with Joshua and Judges.

All the translations, whatever their date, are what we should call literal; that is, they take the text word by word rather than sentence by sentence, or, as S. P. Brock has put it, they aim to bring the reader to the original, not the original to the reader.[7] Even the best of them could never fail to be recognised as translations, even by readers unacquainted with the Hebrew. But there are degrees of literality. On the whole it is a safe generalisation that the early translations read smoothly, without any undue sense of strain or strangeness, whereas the later ones are stilted, crabbed and pedantic, adhering far too closely to Hebrew idiom, often resorting to transliteration of the Hebrew where its meaning appeared obscure. If this change was due at all to incompetence, it was the type of incompetence which tends to consort with a bigoted conviction that the sense matters less than the sanctity of the letter.

Swete and Thackeray agreed about the incompetence of the translator of Isaiah, and it will be worth our while to pause for a moment to see whether the evidence justifies the verdict. Erratic he certainly was. In comparison with the richness of the Hebrew, his

---

[6] *Studies in the Septuagint*; cf. H. S. Gehman, 'A theological approach to the Greek translator of Job', *JBL* LXVIII (1949); D. H. Gard, *The Exegetical Method of the Greek Translator of the Book of Job*.

[7] 'The Phenomenon of the LXX', *Oudtestamentische Studien* XVII, pp. 11 ff. He also points out that literalism would be less objectionable before the age of printing, since the text could always be expounded.

vocabulary often seems oddly thin, since he has a few favourite words which he uses over and over again to render a great variety of Hebrew words. On the other hand, he will sometimes surprise us with a rare word which occurs nowhere else in Greek literature except Homer (9:5) or Herodotus (1:22). It is as though he had learnt his Greek from a manual containing selections from great authors. On occasion he will take Isaiah's vigorous metaphors with flat-footed literalness. He turns 'Your silver has become dross, your wine mixed with water' into 'Your money is counterfeit, and the merchants are diluting the wine with water' (1:22). Yet even this takes on a fresh guise when we find that he has a proletarian grudge against the middle class and loses no chance of an attack on the merchants. He believes that Isaiah speaks to the social conditions of contemporary Egypt and makes his point by his style of translation. He appears also to have been critical of Jewish refugees who fled to Egypt to escape persecution. Where Isaiah tells eighth-century Jerusalem not to be 'afraid of the Assyrians when they smite with the rod and lift up their staff against you as the Egyptians did', he alters the last clause to make it read: 'for I am bringing upon you the plague of seeing the road that leads to Egypt' (10:24).

The Septuagint enriched the Greek language in three ways. First, as we have seen in Chapter Three, Greek words tended to undergo semantic change by taking on new meaning from the Hebrew words they were used to translate. Secondly, some Hebrew words which were either transliterated into Greek letters or otherwise given a Greek form (sabbath, manna, amen, alleluia, etc.) became naturalised in Greek and subsequently in other languages also. Thirdly, the translators coined new words, either deliberately or more probably by accident, because by analogy with similar words they assumed that such words must already exist. An English-speaking foreigner might, for example, assume by analogy that 'gruntled' and 'feckful' were current English.[8] In the same way the Septuagint translators coined such words as *hekousiazesthai* (to volunteer) and *trietizein* (to be three years old).

There is one other characteristic of the Septuagint to which we

---

[8] I have come across a thesis written in English by a German, containing frequent uses of 'resp.', when the word required by the sense was 'or'; because in German *beziehungsweise*, abbreviated to *bzw.*, can mean both 'alternatively' and 'respectively'.

shall return later. This is its occasional avoidance of anthropo-
morphisms or other language about God which seemed to the
translator irreverent.

Hebrew	LXX
Exod. 15:3 Yahweh is a man of war.	The Lord stamps out war.[9]
Exod. 15:8 With the blast of your nostrils.	With the spirit of your anger.
Exod. 24:10 They saw the God of Israel.	They saw the place where the God of Israel stood.
Exod. 24:11 Upon the nobles of the children of Israel he did not lay a hand.	Of the Elect of Israel not one was missing.
Ps. 17:15 I shall behold your face in righteousness, I shall be satisfied when I awake with your likeness.	I shall appear in your presence in righteousness, I shall be satisfied when your glory appears.[10]

For the development of New Testament theology it can be of
great importance that the Septuagint does not exactly coincide with
the Hebrew. The author of Hebrews, for instance, quotes Ps. 8 in
its Greek form:

> What is man that you remember him,
> Or the son of man that you visit him?
> You have made him *for a little while* lower than the angels;
> You have crowned him with glory and honour;
> You have put all things in subjection beneath his feet
>
> (Heb. 2:6–8).

He takes this to mean that God from the beginning planned man's
destiny in two stages, corresponding to the two ages of Jewish
eschatology. In the present age (for a little while) man was to live
under the authority of angels, i.e. those who accompanied God at
Sinai and were therefore the mediators and guardians of the law of
Moses.[11] In the age to come man was to be crowned with glory and

---

[9] Cf. Ps. 46(45):9; Judith 9:7; 16:3.
[10] See also above, pp. 73–5.
[11] See esp. 2:2, and cf. Acts 7:53; Gal. 3:19.

supreme over the universe, and that age the author declares to have been inaugurated by the representative death of Jesus, who as pioneer has entered into the glory to which God intends to lead his many sons. Without the Septuagint the author might conceivably have arrived at the same conviction, but he could not have found scriptural warrant for it in the Hebrew version of Ps. 8.

There is one further way in which our study of the Septuagint may throw some light on the New Testament. In Luke 19:41–44 and 21:20–24 the evangelist has placed on the lips of Jesus two prophecies of the destruction of Jerusalem, which are couched in such picturesque detail that they used to be thought *vaticinia ex eventu*, i.e. prophecies compiled after and with knowledge of the event. But C. H. Dodd demonstrated that the siege as it is described in these passages does not follow the course of the actual siege in the war of A.D. 66–70, as it is described in the writings of Josephus, and that the prophecies are built up out of a cento of phrases drawn from the Septuagint version of Old Testament prophecies of the fall of Jerusalem in 587 B.C.[12] The implication of this appears to be that the Lucan prophecies were earlier than A.D. 70 in origin, but could not be attributed to Jesus, since he would not have used the Septuagint. But with the example of Ecclesiasticus before us we may envisage another possibility. Jesus could have compiled his prophecies in Hebrew or Aramaic, making deliberate use of echoes from the Old Testament, and the translator who put his words into Greek could, like ben Sira's grandson, have recognised the Old Testament allusions and turned to the corresponding passages of the Septuagint in order to make them clear to his Greek readers.

---

[12] 'The fall of Jerusalem and the "abomination of desolation" ', *Journal of Roman Studies* xxxvii (1947), pp. 47–54, reprinted in *More New Testament Studies*.

Part Two

METAPHOR

Chapter Seven

Literal and Non-Literal

'Our rector is literally the father of every boy and girl in the village.' It is easy enough to see what the examination candidate who wrote this sentence wanted to say: the rector was one of those clergymen whose parishioners address them as 'Father', and for every child in the village this expressed something real. Unfortunately, like many adults who ought to know better, she confused the real with the literal. Any statement, literal or metaphorical, may be true or false, and its referent may be real or unreal. 'The name body is the name of the class of real entities'[1] is a metaphorical statement. 'He was really the sinister son of Queen Victoria'[2] and 'There are fairies at the bottom of our garden' are literal. When Mark tells us that the Pharisees and Herodians tried to trap Jesus with a question (12:13), his diagnosis of their motive may be true or false, but the truth or falsity is not determined by the fact that he expressed it in a metaphor. When Isaiah predicts that 'on one day the Lord will cut off from Israel head and tail' (9:14), he would not have enhanced the likelihood of fulfilment by saying 'noble and baseborn'. Literal as well as metaphorical language may be used in performative or expressive utterances where the question of truth does not arise. In short, literal and metaphorical are terms which describe types of language, and the type of language we use has very little to do with the truth or falsity of what we say and with the existence or non-existence of the things we refer to.

It is necessary to start with this warning, because there are eminent scholars who make exactly the same mistake as the schoolgirl essay-writer. Here are two examples with a common theme. 'One must be chary of speaking of "the metaphor" of the Body of

---

[1] J. Bentham, *The Theory of Fictions.*

[2] Daisy Ashford, *The Young Visiters.* Admittedly the malapropism 'sinister' conceals a metaphor from heraldry, but without it the sentence is a literal, false statement.

Christ. Paul uses the analogy of the human body to elucidate his teaching that Christians form Christ's body. But the analogy holds because they are in literal fact the risen organism of Christ's person in all its concrete reality.'[3] 'While it contains of course a certain element of metaphor, the description of the Church as the Body of Christ is to be taken ontologically and realistically . . . It is not a mere metaphor, but the literal truth, that the Church is the Body of Christ.'[4] Both writers seem to be beset with the fear that, if once they admitted a word to be metaphor, they would forfeit the right to believe in the reality of that which it signified. This fear would be justified only on one of two assumptions: either that metaphor is an optional embroidery which adds nothing substantial to the meaning of a sentence; or that metaphor can be used only in emotive and evocative utterances which have no truth value. Both these assumptions we shall find to be ungrounded.

It may be well, however, to recognise in passing that fear of the figurative may arise from either of two very different causes. The first is the artificial cultivation of it in rhetoric, in which the primary motive is either entertainment or victory in debate. The second is what A. M. Farrer has called the problem of transcendence. 'The problem of transcendence . . . arises wherever we find ourselves asking to what reality symbolic descriptions refer. The only case which allows of a perfectly simple answer is one in which a non-symbolical description can be alternatively supplied. On the dramatic occasion on which Sherlock Holmes allowed himself the expression "the Napoleon of crime", he was not, indeed, referring to anyone named Napoleon, but he was referring to a person of whom the eminent detective would have been prepared to give an uncannily particular and literal description, down to the microscopic structure of his hair and the size of his boots. But when nothing at all of this kind can be done, philosophical difficulties arise, and they reach their maximum in the case of religious expressions.'[5] A book on language is not the place in which to wrestle with those difficulties. For us it is enough to note that if we call an expression 'literal' or 'metaphorical' we are talking about the nature of the

[3] J. A. T. Robinson, *The Body*, p. 51.
[4] E. L. Mascall, *Christ, the Christian and the Church*, pp. 112, 161.
[5] 'An English appreciation', in *Kerygma and Myth*, ed. H. W. Bartsch, tr. R. H. Fuller, pp. 216–17.

language employed, whereas if we call it 'ontological' we are talking about the reality of its referent. Linguistic statements must not be confused with metaphysical ones.[6]

Literality is easier to illustrate than to define, but provisionally we may say that words are used literally when they are meant to be understood in their primary, matter-of-fact sense. To this most dictionaries would add, 'not figurative or metaphorical', and both these contrasts may be misleading. For figurative language covers all uses of the classical figures of speech, and in several of these (simile, chiasmus, oxymoron, tmesis[7]) every term may be intended literally. The contrast between literal and metaphorical is unsatisfactory for the opposite reason, that there are several other forms of speech which are non-literal besides metaphor, as the following list will show.

1. Hyperbole

Overstatement is, as we have already seen, characteristic of the Hebrew style, and the Old Testament abounds in examples of it. It can be used in flattery, as in the song of the dancing women: 'Saul has killed his thousands and David his tens of thousands' (1 Sam. 18:7). But it can also be used in noble lament: 'They were swifter than eagles, stronger than lions' (2 Sam. 1:23). In the New Testament we find Jesus using it to startle his hearers into recognition of unfamiliar truth. 'First take the plank out of your own eye, and then you will see clearly to take the speck out of your brother's' (Matt. 7:5). 'Blind guides! You strain off a midge, yet gulp down a camel' (Matt. 23:24). 'It is easier for a camel to pass through the eye of a needle than for a rich man to enter the kingdom of God' (Mark 10:25). In this last instance plodding literalists have suggested that the needle's eye was the name for a low gate, like the door into the Church of the Nativity at Bethlehem, or that a camel was a kind of rope. But the Semitic bravura of Jesus' speech resists all such pathetic attempts to tame it.

---

[6] See also below, ch. 11 pp. 193–4.

[7] This figure, the splitting of two parts of a word, is vigorously illustrated by Ennius's *'cere comminuit brum'* (he split his head open). There are examples, less striking in the AV, e.g. 'to usward' (Eph. 1:9), but none that I know of in the Hebrew or Greek of the Bible.

2. *Litotes*

By contrast, the Hebrew people never discovered the emphatic use of understatement. Except for such phrases as 'a drop of water' (Gen. 18:4), no instances of it occur in the Old Testament. Greek influence presumably accounts for the handful of examples found in the New: 'a citizen of no mean city' (Acts 21:39); 'I must mention a practice I cannot commend' (1 Cor. 11:17); 'not all have responded to the gospel' (Rom. 10:16).[8]

3. *Irony*

In its simplest form irony consists in saying one thing and intending the opposite, usually with sarcasm both in tone and in the intent to hurt or ridicule. When Michal said to David, 'What a splendid display the king of Israel made today!' (2 Sam. 6:20), he had no difficulty in gathering that she was critical of his style of dancing. Jesus sometimes used irony to pierce the protective armour of his opponents. 'You have a fine way of setting aside the commandment of God in order to maintain your tradition' (Mark 7:9). Paul too can use it to shatter complacency. 'All of you, no doubt, have everything you could desire. You have come into your fortune already. You have come into your kingdom—and left us out' (1 Cor. 4:8). 'I never sponged on you; forgive me that wrong' (2 Cor. 12:13).

Dramatic irony differs from simple irony in that the contrast between what is said and what is meant is intended by the writer of the story, but there is always some character within the story, whether the speaker or another, who does not understand. The question addressed by King Xerxes to Haman is ironical, since its purpose is to make Haman think that it applies to himself, whereas in fact it applies to Mordecai (Esth. 6:6). Pilate is unaware that with the words 'Behold the man' he has hit upon the true identity of his prisoner as 'the Proper Man whom God himself hath bidden' (John 19:5).[9]

[8] Luke, the one Gentile contributor to the New Testament, is particularly fond of the use of the negative with expressions of quantity or quality: Acts 12:18; 15:2; 19:11, 23, 24; 20:12; 26:19,26; 27:20; 28:2.

[9] The quotation is from T. Carlyle's translation of Luther's hyman, *Ein Feste Burg*. For further examples of dramatic irony, see above, pp. 104–5.

4. Synecdoche

This is usually defined as the use of part for whole or whole for part, as when in English we say 'hands' when we mean factory workers, sailors or copyists, and when Hebrew uses 'wheels' to mean wheeled vehicles (e.g. Isa. 5:28; Ezek. 23:24; 26:10). But it also covers any use of a less inclusive term instead of a more inclusive one and vice versa. Luke, for example, tells us that the Samaritan put the injured man on his own beast, instead of calling it a donkey (Luke 10:34). When Paul is accused of taking a Gentile, Trophimus, into the temple, the accusers must be referring to those courts of the temple from which Gentiles were excluded, and not to the outer court, though it too could be called the temple (Acts 21:28; cf. Mark 11:15). In Heb. 13:24 'Italy' almost certainly denotes 'Rome'.

Frequently this figure is no more than a stylistic conceit, but it may be used to express a significant relationship. If, for instance, we say that Oxford beat Cambridge, this is something more than a short way of saying that eleven (or nine or fifteen) men from the one university beat a like number from the other; for a team is regarded as in some sense the representative of the whole. When we read that Israel was routed by the Philistines (1 Sam. 4:2), we naturally and correctly assume that the Israelite army is meant; in time of war there is much to be said for a mode of speech which identifies the fortunes of a nation with those of its army.

One specialised form of synecdoche is eponymy, whether this consists in the use of a genuine ancestor's name to denote also the tribe or nation claiming descent from him, or of the invention of an ancestor or hero to account for the name of a people. In the Old Testament Jacob is the name both of the individual man, son of Isaac and grandson of Abraham, and also of the nation which traced its lineage back to his twelve sons. The ancestor embodies, symbolises, represents the whole group of his descendants. The author of Hebrews can even argue for the superiority of Melchizedek to Levi on the grounds that Levi was in the loins of his ancestor Abraham when he paid tithes to Melchizedek and received his blessing (7:4-10). It is surprising that so little use was made in the Old Testament of the eponym Adam. In Hebrew *'adam* is the

ordinary word for 'man' or 'mankind',[10] and in the Old Testament
it is used only five times as a proper name (Gen. 4:25; 5:3, 4, 5;
I Chr. 1:1). In the story of man's creation and fall, the progenitor of
the human race is consistently referred to as 'the man'.[11] The
eponymous possibilities of the word are not exploited for theological purposes until we come to Paul's contrast between life 'in
Adam' and life 'in Christ' (1 Cor. 15:22; Rom. 5:12–21). Adam,
the first man, is a truly representative figure, since he is also the
typical man, Everyman, whose story is re-enacted by each human
being, and he is mankind, the corporate entity to which all individual men and women inescapably belong. Paul's argument is
that, because the natural solidarity of mankind in Adam is a fact of
experience, and because each individual is related to the threefold
Adam by inheritance, imitation and involvement, this establishes
the possibility of a new solidarity of grace 'in Christ'. Finally, there
are two examples of synecdoche in which Paul uses the word
'Christ' when we should have expected him to say 'the church'.
'Is Christ divided?' 'As the body is one, though it has many limbs
and organs . . . so it is with Christ' (1 Cor. 1:13; 12:12).

5. Metonymy

Metonymy is calling a thing by the name of something typically
associated with it: e.g. the Bench, the stage, the turf, the bottle may
stand for magistrates, the theatrical profession, horse-racing and
alcoholic liquor. In the Old Testament we find sceptre (Gen.
49:10) and key (Isa. 22:22; cf. Rev. 3:7) standing for authority,
sword for war (Lev. 26:6); and in the New Testament tongues for
languages (1 Cor. 12:30; 14:1–19), thrones for superhuman
powers (Col. 1:16), and the Circumcision for the Jews (Gal.
2:7–9, 12; Eph. 2:11; Col. 4:11). Mention has already been made of
euphemism, which is certainly a non-literal form of language, and
may reasonably be classed as metonymy (e.g. sleep for death, 1 Cor.
15:20; John 11:11 f.).

Closely allied to metonymy is personification, which is particularly common in proverbial literature. 'Wine is an insolent fellow'

---

[10] As in Greek and Latin, man = human being (*'adam, anthrôpos, homo*) is distinguished from man = male (*'ish, anêr, vir*).

[11] The definite article should be read at 2:20; 3:17, 21 as elsewhere.

personifies wine and makes it stand for all addicts (Prov. 20:1; cf. 27:4; 30:15–16; Ecclus. 10:10). Death is personified in Ecclus. 41:1–4 (cf. Job 28:22; Hos. 13:14), the Lady Stupidity in Prov. 9:13–18, and the word of God in Wisd. 18:14–16. The case of the personified wisdom is more complex, because of the frequency and variety of the imagery. She is represented as a mother, a bride, a taskmaster, and even, by a kaleidoscopic change, as a banquet (Ecclus. 4:11; 15:2; 6:18–31; 24:19–21). More often she is a hostess who presides over a salon of instruction and culture (Prov. 1:20 ff.; 8:1 ff.; 9:1 ff.), and in this guise she is contrasted with the Lady Simplicity, who keeps a house of low repute and hidden danger. But the hostess Wisdom who invites young men to study under her tuition is doing exactly what Jesus ben Sira does at the end of his book (Ecclus. 51:23); and she is thus a metonym standing for all wise teachers. On the other hand, when Wisdom is represented as a master-builder working in the service of God the Creator, this is a metonymic and picturesque way of talking about what God in his wisdom does (Prov. 8:22 ff.; Ecclus. 24:1 ff.). Because of the illegitimate use which biblical theologians have often made of the personified Wisdom, it cannot be too strongly emphasised that to personify is to treat as a person that which is not a person. In Proverbs and Ecclesiasticus the uses of wisdom as an attribute of God or of wise men, as a way of life, as a gift of God to men and as personification follow one another in rapid proximity; and anyone who takes the trouble to read through these books will need no further proof that their compilers were fully aware of the rhetorical nature of the language they were using.

Some linguists classify synecdoche and metonymy as metaphor, on the ground that all three consist in the transfer of a name from one referent to another. This usage, however, blurs one important distinction: in synecdoche and metonymy the link between the two referents is one of contiguity and in metaphor it is one of comparison. Metaphor is best understood when it is studied along with other forms of comparative language.

6. *Periphrasis or circumlocution*

This is more often than not a disease of speech, a preference of the convoluted or speciously elegant to the direct and the simple, a product of incompetence, affectation or self-importance; and Dickens in *Little Dorrit* had some justification for calling a government department 'the Circumlocution Office'. But as a figure of speech circumlocution has its legitimate use, particularly in expressions of reverence or respect. God can be called 'the Eminence of Israel' (1 Sam. 15:29) or 'the Majesty on high' (Heb. 1:4), and Abigail throughout her long speech to David can refer to herself as 'your handmaid' (1 Sam. 25:24 ff.; cf. 1:16).[12] Each of these phrases is a substitute for direct, literal reference; but it is something more than an exact equivalent, since it has an added connotative value. Wherever Abigail says 'your handmaid', she could equally well have said 'I' or 'me'; but by using the periphrasis she establishes her relationship to David as that of suppliant to patron.

This simple illustration, which could also be classified as synecdoche (the use of the general for the particular), throws some light on the meaning of the phrase 'son of man' on the lips of Jesus. G. Vermes has recently argued,[13] with an impressive array of evidence, that in the Palestinian Aramaic of the time of Jesus *bar nash(a)*[14] was never used as a title for the Messiah, but was either a generic term for man or a periphrastic self-reference. He recognises that in the examples he cites circumlocution is never an exact equivalent to a personal pronoun, but is always used out of modesty, distaste or embarrassment, or in some cases to create a deliberate double entendre, so that the hearer is left in doubt whether the speaker intends a reference to man in general or to himself in particular. He concludes that at least half of the Son of man sayings are genuinely attributed to Jesus, who used the circumlocution 'out of awe, reserve or humility'. All sayings which link the self-designation with Dan. 7:13 he regards as later products of church theology. He concedes that, since it is beyond question that the disciples noticed this verbal link, it is conceivable that Jesus may have done so before them, though he thinks this unlikely. 'The final dilemma which the historian is asked to solve is whether direct reference to Daniel 7:13 results from an attempt to render explicit the underlying significance of innuendos genuinely uttered by Jesus, or whether indirect references are secondary develop-

---

[12] For other examples see above, pp. 73–5.
[13] *Jesus the Jew*, pp. 160–91.
[14] *Bar nash* is the indefinite form, *bar nasha* the definite.

ments from the formal quotations just investigated.' The one flaw in this argument is that Dr Vermes has not carried far enough his analysis of the possible reasons why Jesus adopted the circumlocution at all. It is possible that Jesus said 'the Son of man has the right on earth to forgive sins' because it would have been immodest to say 'I' (though he immediately follows the circumlocution with an unambiguous first person singular). It is possible, though very unlikely, that distaste or fear of death prompted him to speak of his death as the death of the Son of man (though there are sayings such as Mark 10:38 and Luke 12:49–50 in which he appears to be under no such constraint). But awe, reserve and humility cannot explain the whole range of Son of man sayings which Vermes accepts as genuine: e.g. 'the Son of man has nowhere to lay his head' (Matt. 8:20; Luke 9:58); 'the Son of man came eating and drinking, and they say, "Look at him! a glutton and a drinker" ' (Matt. 11:19; Luke 7:34). Nor do they explain the fact that 'Son of man' was a habitual and characteristic self-designation. In view of what Vermes himself has said about the use of double entendre in the Aramaic sources he has examined, is it not much more probable that Jesus too was deliberately exploiting the ambiguities of the phrase, that he had pondered what Psalm 8 had to say about the destiny of man and what Daniel 7 had to say about the destiny of Israel, and was inviting his hearers to consider how his ministry was related to both these themes and what implications it held for themselves? What was linguistically possible for the early Aramaic-speaking church cannot have been linguistically impossible for the Aramaic-speaking Jesus.

7. *Legal fiction*

In addition to the classical figures already considered there is a widespread usage which has some title to be classified as non-literal speech. In Roman law foreigners were admitted to some of the rights of citizenship by a fictitious allegation of citizenship. In English law before 1852 a writ of *Quominus* gave jurisdiction to the Court of Exchequer over cases which would otherwise have been outside its competence, and for the same reason places overseas could be deemed to be in England. Bentham denounced all legal fictions as plain falsehood, declaring that fiction is of use to justice exactly as swindling is to trade. 'Everything is sham that finds its way into that receptacle, as everything is foul that finds its way out of Fleet-ditch into the Thames.'[15] But what he overlooked is that this practice was not prompted by any intention to deceive and that nobody was deceived by it. It was subsequently defended by both Maine and Salmond.

Maine's contention was that there are three ways in which law may be adapted to the changing needs of society, legal fiction, equity and legislation; and that in the ancient world, where law was regarded as immutable, whether because of religious sanction or definitive codification, legal fictions offered the simplest, if not the only, road of advance. 'At a particular stage of social progress they are invaluable expedients for overcoming the rigidity of law, and, indeed, without one of them, the Fiction of Adoption which permits the family tie to be artificially created, it is difficult to understand how society would ever have escaped from its swaddling-clothes and taken its first step towards civilisation.'[16] Salmond carried the argument a stage further. 'In early law the purpose of most legal fictions was to alter indirectly and covertly a legal system so rigid that it could not be effectively altered in this respect by the direct and open process of legislation. The practical effect of any rule of law depends on the nature of the rule and on the nature of the facts to which it is applied. If the rule cannot itself be altered, its effect may be altered by establishing a legal fiction as to the nature of the facts.'[17]

The case for regarding legal fiction as a form of non-literal language is well supported by Maine's instance of adoption: adoptive parents, who are known not to be the literal parents of a child, are in law regarded as having the duties and rights of parents. The Old Testament legal codes contain no law of adoption, therein differing from the Code of Hammurabi and the Nuzi laws; and the only two certain instances of adoption in the Old Testament are those of Moses and Esther, both occurring in a foreign country (Exod. 2:10; Esth. 2:7).[18] It is the more remarkable that as a

---

[15] J. Bentham, op. cit., Appendix A.
[16] H. J. S. Maine, *Ancient Law*, ch. 2.
[17] J. Salmond, *Jurisprudence*, 12th ed. p. 74 note (p).
[18] There may be a third reference in Gen. 15:2-3, but the text is too corrupt for certainty.

metaphor adoption is common enough, either as a description of God's election of Israel (Deut. 14:1–2; Hos. 11:1), or in passages relating to the enthronement of the king (2 Sam. 7:14; Ps. 2:7; 89:27).

The nearest counterpart to adoption in the Old Testament is levirate marriage (Deut. 25:5–10; cf. Gen. 38:6–26; Ruth 4:1–17). If a man married and then died childless, the law required his brother to marry his widow; and the first child of the second marriage was deemed to be the legitimate issue of the first. Anthropologists have speculated that the origins of this custom are to be found in fraternal polyandry or group marriage, i.e. marriage between a group of brothers and a group of sisters. But even if this theory could be proved, it would throw little light on the significance of the custom in the more highly developed society of biblical times. For in polyandrous or group marriage it is only the family that matters, and individual paternity is of no interest, whereas in each of the three biblical texts the main point of levirate marriage is that the natural paternity is known, but is disregarded in order to supply a particular member of the family with an heir. According to the Deuteronomist, the object was to perpetuate the dead husband's name, i.e. both his reputation and his memory: his reputation must be protected from the shame of childlessness, which would either be removed by the birth of a putative heir or be transferred by the shoe-loosing ceremony to the next-of-kin who refused his levirate obligation; and his memory must be kept alive as the only form of immortality available in a culture without a belief in an afterlife (cf. Ecclus. 44:12–14). The story of Tamar, from which the shame sanction is absent, shows that the custom long antedates the shame culture of Deuteronomy, and this is confirmed by the story of Ruth, in which marriage to the widow is inseparable from redemption of the family property, the duty of the next-of-kin is 'to restore the name of the dead to his inheritance' (4:5), and the ceremony of shoe-loosing is a purely legal transaction without any ignominy attached to it. Naomi has been forced by poverty to sell her property, and the next-of-kin is keen to redeem it until he is reminded that he must also marry the widow. To the modern reader his refusal to do this may appear to be a lack of gallantry, but his true reason is that, since the first son would inherit the property, he would be paying the cost of redemption without retaining a title to the property. When Ruth bears her first son to Boaz, the neighbours announce that Naomi has a son, i.e. grandson, since the child is reckoned to be the issue of Ruth's first marriage. There is thus a strong probability that behind the legal fiction of the levirate lies some strict law or custom about the inalienability of family property.

All the Old Testament codes contain stringent prohibitions of usury (Exod. 22:25; Lev. 25:35; Deut. 23:19-20), designed to protect the destitute against the exploitation of their necessity by the rich. The law was much broken (Ezek. 18:8, 13, 17; Neh. 5:6 ff.; Prov. 28:8); and even when it was observed, it tended to defeat its own purpose, since borrowers were lax about repayment and lenders reluctant to risk their money for no return (Ecclus. 29:3-7; cf. 8:12). When a commercial middle-class began to spring up, they found the law an impediment to investment for mutual benefit. Those who wanted to evade the letter of the law and yet maintain a reputation for pious observance had a convenient legal fiction ready to hand. A borrower could write a receipt, not for the actual sum borrowed, but for capital plus interest, thus leaving no evidence on which a charge of evasion could lie. In the parable of Jesus (Luke 16:1-8), the steward is not dismissed for dishonesty, but for incompetence. He is called 'unjust' because, as his master's agent, he had been breaking the Mosaic law by charging interest. One debtor had borrowed fifty measures of oil (or more probably the monetary equivalent) and had given a receipt for a hundred. Another had borrowed eighty measures of wheat, and had given a receipt for a hundred. On dismissal the steward gained the friendship of the debtors by allowing them to make out a fresh receipt for the capital only, as they should have done in the first place under a strict adherence to the law. The master recognised that he could not complain without making a public admission that he charged interest, and chose instead, by praising the steward's action, to gain a reputation for meticulous legal observance.[19]

It is a mistake, however, to imagine that legal fictions always made for the relaxation of rigidity. If a law became obsolete, the priests in charge of a sacred code would look for new ways of

[19] See J. D. M. Derrett, *Law in the New Testament*, pp. 48-77; and *Studies in the New Testament*, pp. 1-3.

obeying it. The thrice repeated prohibition against boiling a kid in its mother's milk (Exod. 23:19; 34:26; Deut. 14:21) was intended in the two earlier codes to be taken literally as a ban on an objectionable practice in Canaanite religion, for which there is independent evidence in the records of Ras Shamra. But the Deuteronomist transferred it to a new context as a coda to a list of food regulations, with the consequence that it was itself deemed to be a food law, requiring total separation of milk and meat in cooking and at meals, and so constituted a new and arbitrary tyranny to which the orthodox Jewish housewife is subject to this day.

Chapter Eight

Comparative Language I: Simile and Metaphor

'Manna! I have never come across it. What is it like?' 'On the ground it looks like hoarfrost. When you pick it up, it is like coriander seed, and it tastes like honeycake' (Exod. 16:14, 31). 'What sort of creature is a crocodile?' 'His back is row upon row of shields' (Job 41:15). 'How shall I explain to you about the kingdom of God? It is like mustard seed, like yeast' (Mark 4:30). Comparison is one of our most valuable sources of knowledge, the main road leading from the known to the unknown. It comprises a large part of our daily speech and almost all the language of theology. God speaks to man in similitudes (Hos. 12:10), and man has no language but analogy for speaking about God, however inadequate it may be (Isa. 40:18, 25; 46:5). The faculty for perceiving significant, illuminating likenesses is indispensable equipment for teacher, prophet and creative writer alike. It is not the poetic imagination alone that rears its building

> by observation of affinities
> In objects where no brotherhood exists
> To passive minds.[1]

If a comparison is explicit we call it a simile, and it is meant to be taken literally. If it is implicit we call it a metaphor, and it is nonliteral. This distinction does not exhaust the difference between simile and metaphor, which we must explore further at a later stage; but for our immediate purpose it is useful to regard them as interchangeable.[2] All the more complex forms of comparison—

---

[1] W. Wordsworth, *The Prelude* II. 384–6.
[2] Cf. H. W. Fowler, *Modern English Usage*, under Simile: 'every metaphor presupposes a simile, and every simile is compressible or convertible into a metaphor.'

fable, parable, allegory and typology—are elaborations of one or other of these two basic types.

A comparison may fail for one of two reasons. As a means of proceeding from the known to the unknown, it may fail if what the speaker assumes to be known is in fact not known to his audience. The description of manna given in Exodus is informative, provided that you are familiar with coriander seed. We have here a problem which constantly besets readers of the Bible. We do not live in the world of the Old or New Testament, we are unacquainted with what to the contemporaries of Isaiah or Paul were familiar, everyday objects or experiences, and it is therefore easy for us to miss the affinities which imposed themselves on the inward eye of the biblical writers.

> Wer den Dichter will verstehen
> Muss in Dichters Lande gehen.[3]

But the second reason is even more important. When two things are compared, they are not to be considered like in all respects. There is an intended point of comparison on which we are being asked to concentrate to the exclusion of all irrelevant fact; and communication breaks down, with ludicrous and even disastrous effect, if we wrongly identify it. The kingdom of God does not look like mustard seed or taste like yeast, but it acts like both. Human beings are distinguishable from inert clay in the hand of a potter and from sheep in the care of a shepherd, though they have characteristics in common with each (Jer. 18:1–6; Ezek. 34:1–31). When the psalmist tells us that a united family is like oil dripping down Aaron's beard on to the skirts of his robe, he is not trying to persuade us that family unity is messy, greasy or volatile; he is thinking of the all-pervasive fragrance which has so deeply impressed itself on his memory at the anointing of a high priest (Ps. 133:2).

1. Points of comparison

All points of comparison belong to one of four classes: perceptual, synaesthetic, affective and pragmatic. Perceptual comparisons may

---

[3] 'Anyone who wants to understand a poet must go to the poet's country' (J. W. Goethe).

appeal to any of the five senses. The haft of Goliath's spear looked like a weaver's beam (1 Sam. 17:7), what the Israelites saw over the tent of meeting looked like fire (Num. 9:15), in days to come the moon was to look the colour of blood (Joel 2:31). A plague of locusts sounds like the rattle of chariots or fire among the stubble (Joel 2:5), and the laughter of fools sounds like the crackling of thorns under a pot (Eccles. 7:6). A recurrent illness may feel like a spike driven into the body (2 Cor. 12:7), and a constant irritation like a fishhook in the eye (Num. 33:55). Manna tasted like honey-cake (Exod. 16:31), but the decrees of God are sweeter than honey-comb, as indeed are the kisses of a bride (Ps. 19:10; Cant. 4:11). A man's reputation may stink (Gen. 34:30), and love be as fragrant as myrrh or henna blossom (Cant. 1:13). In addition English uses verbs of seeing, hearing, feeling, tasting and scenting metaphoric-ally of intellectual perception or inward experience. In Hebrew seeing and hearing are regularly used in this way, and blindness and deafness are common metaphors for insensitivity or incompre-hension (e.g. Isa. 6:10). Metaphorical uses of touch (1 Sam. 10:26), taste (Ps. 34:8) and scent (Job. 39:25) are rare. The Hebrews knew of course that it is possible to perceive by touch (Gen. 27:12, 22; 31:34, 37), but instead of developing the verb with the double meaning of the English 'feel' they used it of groping helplessly in the dark (Deut. 28:29; Job 5:14; 12:25; cf. Acts 17:27).

Synaesthesia is the use in connexion with one of the senses of terms which are proper to another, as when we speak of sharp words (Isa. 49:2; Acts 15:39; Heb. 4:12). The Israelite officers accused Moses of making them stink in the eyes of Pharaoh (Exod. 5:21). The plague of darkness was thick enough to be felt (Exod. 10:21). Tow may be said to smell the fire (Judg. 16:9), and words may be smooth as butter and slippery as oil (Ps. 55:21). Used as an artificial device synaesthetic metaphor may be ridiculous, and it is easy enough to make fun of it.

> I see a voice; now will I to the chink,
> To spy an I can hear my Thisbe's face.[4]

But synaesthesia itself cannot be laughed away along with the abuses of it. There is considerable evidence that, for some people at least,

[4] W. Shakespeare, *A Midsummer Night's Dream* V.1.190–1.

synaesthetic language is a reasonably accurate transcript of synaesthetic experience. We speak of colour in music, and there are those who actually envisage the different keys as colours. For such people the hybridisation of the senses is integral to their apprehension of reality. Thus, when the editor of the Isaiah corpus introduces an oracle as 'the word which Isaiah the son of Amoz saw' (Isa. 2:1), he is claiming that the verbal message came to the prophet in the form of vision, and not merely as auditory experience in the course of vision.

Affective comparisons are those in which the feel or value, the effect or impression of one thing is compared with that of another. The hearts of Joshua's troops turned to water (Josh. 7:5), i.e. their courage ebbed away. Belshazzar was weighed and found to be substandard (Dan. 5:27). Jeremiah's heartache felt like an incurable wound (Jer. 15:18), and the psalmist's trouble gave him the impression of drowning in a cataract (Ps. 42:7). When John attempts to describe the heavenly figure of his opening vision, he is not giving a visual image which a skilful painter might reproduce (though many have foolishly tried). 'The hair of his head was white as snow-white wool, and his eyes flamed like fire; his feet gleamed like burnished brass refined in a furnace, and his voice was like the sound of rushing waters. In his right hand he held seven stars, and out of his mouth came a sharp two-edged sword; and his face shone like the sun in full strength' (Rev. 1:14–16). He is telling his readers that if, for example, they will think of the feelings they have before a torrent in spate or beneath the brilliance of the midday sun they will have some inkling of the sense of majesty and sublimity which he experienced in the presence of the heavenly Christ.

In pragmatic comparison we compare the activity or result of one thing with that of another. The throats of the wicked gape like an open grave and with the same implication for their victims (Ps. 5:9). Love is more heady than wine (Cant. 1:2). The kingdom works like yeast (Mark 4:30), but so also does the bad example of Pharisees and or Herod (Mark 8:15). As rain descending on parched soil, the ideal king will bring prosperity and hope to his people (Ps. 72:6). The Israelites can as little change their character as the leopard its spots or the Nubian his skin (Jer. 13:23).

A comparison may on occasion fit into more than one of these

four categories. Let us take as an example a passage which
Thorleif Boman has used in an attempt to illustrate the difference
between Hebrew thought and Greek.[5] Boman took Homer to be
typical of Greek thought and contrasted his imagery, in which
everything is externalised and visualised, with that of Canticles.

> Your neck is like David's tower
> which is built with winding courses;
> a thousand bucklers hang upon it,
> and all are warriors' shields
> (Cant. 4:4).

He correctly argued that the point of comparison here is affective;
the simile is designed to give the impression of virginal inaccessibility. What he overlooked is that this impression actually depends
on a perceptual comparison. The girl's neck, encircled by a neck-
lace of overlapping medallions, looks like the unassailable tower
surrounded by the overlapping shields of its defenders. Moreover,
Boman was mistaken in supposing that the affective simile or
metaphor is un-Greek. If instead of contrasting the Hebrew poet
with Homer he had compared him with any of the Greek lyric
poets, he would have found a close kinship of mind. Here is a
fragment of Sappho which, in totally different imagery, expresses
the same notion of inaccessibility.

> Like the sweet apple which reddens upon the topmost bough,
> A-top on the topmost twig,—which the pluckers forgot somehow,—
> Forgot it not, nay, but got it not, for none could get it till now.[6]

This wide range of possibility distinguishes metaphor from
code. In semaphore or the Morse code each symbol has a precise,
unvarying value: _」 \ _」 means P O P, and – · · · – · · · – · means
BBC. If you break a code, you know that you have the correct
answer, since there can be only one; and on this its effectiveness as a
code depends. Mathematical symbols, musical notation, road signs
and knitting patterns are all forms of code; only in the caricature
code of *And Now All This* was *p* the sign for both plain and purl.

---

[5] *Hebrew Thought compared with Greek*, pp. 77–9.
[6] D. G. Rossetti's translation.

But metaphor, like literal language, is capable of multiple meaning. Leaven may be the symbol for good influence or bad (Luke 13:20–21; 1 Cor. 5:6–7), and the birds of the air may signify the Gentile nations or the devil (Mark 4:4, 32). Not surprisingly the most fluid of metaphors is water, which may stand for the source of life (Isa. 55:1), evanescence (Ps. 22:14), cleansing (Matt. 27:24), adultera-tion (Isa. 1:22), trouble (Ps. 46:3), power (Amos 5:24), weakness (Josh. 7:5) or judgment (1 Pet. 3:20). Usually the context tells us which sense is intended. But occasionally a creative writer may play upon the ambiguities with kaleidoscopic effect. The author of Revelation takes Zechariah's vision of Israel as a seven-branched lampstand (Zech. 4:2) and adapts it so that the seven lamps become in turn the seven churches of Asia (1:20), the seven eyes of the Lamb, and the seven spirits of God sent out over all the world (5:6). A single metaphor can even be used in two opposite and contra-dictory senses. The wilderness or desert may be the symbol of desolation, demonic power, everything that has escaped or is resistant to the sovereignty of God (Isa. 13:20–22; 34:13–15; Luke 11:24; Mark 1:13; Lev. 16:7 ff.; Deut. 32:10); but, because of its association with the Exodus, it may also be the symbol of innocence, sincerity, liberation and security under the providential care of God (Exod. 5:1; Jer. 2:1–2; 31:2; Rev. 12:6). But the idea that a word may mean two opposite things should not come amiss to a generation in which stoppage of work is called 'industrial action'.

2. *Visualisation*

The full stock of a book's non-literal language, and more particularly its comparative language, is its imagery. It is a common error to think that imagery means picture language. It includes mental pictures, but a great deal more that is incapable of visualisation. When John tells us that the heavenly Jerusalem is a perfect cube, fifteen hundred miles in length, breadth and height, and that it is constructed of pure gold, transparent like crystal, he obviously does not expect us to visualise it, but is setting out to overwhelm the imagination. Even when a comparison calls up a simple, clearly defined mental picture, it does not follow that the intended comparison is a visual one.

> My love is like a red red rose
> That's newly sprung in June:
> My love is like the melodie
> That's sweetly played in tune.

Burns's parallelism makes it plain that in each case he is comparing one delight with another. In the Bible too parallelism or the juxtaposition of images frequently helps us to locate the point of comparison. This is why so many of the parables of Jesus were told in pairs.

Commenting on Isa. 28:18 ('When the overflowing scourge sweeps by, you shall be trampled underfoot by it'), R. H. Kennett remarked: 'A Hebrew sucked the juice out of each metaphor as he used it, and threw away the skin at once.'[7] He could therefore tolerate a succession of metaphors so rapid as to appear, to some sensibilities, a mixed metaphor. The explanation is that the prophet is not stopping to visualise his metaphors, and Kennett was wrong to suppose that this was a peculiarly Hebrew cast of mind. Shakespeare can do exactly the same.

> Whether 'tis nobler in the mind to suffer
> The slings and arrows of outrageous fortune
> Or to take arms against a sea of troubles,
> And by opposing end them?[8]

When Paul warns his readers 'no longer to be children, tossed by the waves and whirled about by every fresh gust of teaching, dupes of human craftiness (lit. dice-playing)' (Eph. 4:14), we may, if we are so disposed, form a mental picture of a group of children playing dice in an open boat. But the point is that the readers are offered three mutually interpretative metaphors for caprice or arbitrariness: children are easily led, a rudderless boat goes where wind and wave drive it, the roll of a dice is at the mercy of chance. In this instance the three images are relatively undeveloped,[9] two of them consisting of only a single word. But sometimes the successive metaphors are elaborately developed. In 1 Cor. 3:6-17 Paul draws his imagery

---

[7] *In Our Tongues*, p. 8.
[8] *Hamlet* III.1.57-60.
[9] On development, see below, pp. 154-9.

from gardening, building and assaying in such a way that the work of the builder is tested in the assayer's fire. With a similar clash of symbols we are told in Heb. 6:19 that hope is 'an anchor, safe and secure and entering within the veil'.

On occasion we find two metaphors not merely juxtaposed but dovetailed.

> Israel sows the wind and reaps the whirlwind
> (Hos. 8:7).
>
> You shall conceive chaff and bring forth stubble
> (Isa. 33:11).
>
> Their jaws are a grave wide open,
> to devour your harvest and your bread
> (Jer. 5:16).
>
> You it was who fashioned my inward parts;
> You knitted me together in my mother's womb . . .
> You know me through and through:
> My body is no mystery to you,
> How I was secretly kneaded into shape
> And patterned in the depths of the earth
> (Ps. 139:13-15).

In this last remarkable passage the psalmist thinks of himself as an embryo growing in his mother's womb, but superimposes on this the thought of a clay figure taking shape under the kneading hand of the sculptor, and the further mythological notion that all things come from the cosmic womb of Mother Earth.

Such a fusion occurs frequently with metaphors drawn from law court and battlefield. The prophecy of Joel reaches its climax with a summons to the armies of all nations to prepare for war, for a last great battle in the Valley of Jehoshaphat; but the Valley of Jehoshaphat is the Valley of the Lord's Judgment, and the kaleidoscope of imagery rapidly transforms the scene into the Great Assize (Joel 3:9-14). The seer John has a vision of war in heaven between the forces of Michael and those of the Dragon. But what begins as military encounter ends as a legal one; for the Dragon turns out to be Satan, and Satan and Michael are traditionally the prosecuting and the defending counsel in the divine law court. The victory of Michael is the disbarring of Satan: 'the accuser of our

brethren has been cast out' (Rev. 12:7–10). To the theological significance of such passages we must return later. For the present we
are concerned only with the linguistic explanation, which is a
simple one. Law court and battlefield are areas of reciprocal metaphor: it is as natural to describe the courtroom conduct of rival
advocates in terms of battle as it is to speak of submitting a
controversy to the arbitrament of war. In the Old Testament the
Hebrew words which signify a law suit (*rîb, dîn*) are used also of
strife in general, and battles are regarded as the occasion for the
settling of disputes about right and wrong (Gen. 49:6; Judg. 11:27;
1 Sam. 24:12, 15; Isa. 2:4; 2 Chr. 20:12). If military language is
regularly used of literal court cases and forensic language of literal
war, it is easy for the two types of imagery to be fused when both
law suit and battle are metaphorical.

Thus far we have been treating simile and metaphor as variant
forms of a single linguistic phenomenon, but now we must pay
some attention to the differences between them. In metaphor the
two things to be compared are not set side by side; the name of the
one is substituted for the name of the other. To refer to the two
constituent elements of a metaphor Ogden and Richards invented
the useful terms vehicle and tenor: vehicle being the thing to which
the word normally and naturally applies, the thing from which it is
transferred, and tenor the thing to which it is transferred. In a
living metaphor, although both speaker and hearer are aware that
vehicle and tenor are distinct entities, they are not grasped as two
but as one. When we look at an object through a lens, we concentrate on the object and ignore the lens. Metaphor is a lens; it is as
though the speaker were saying, 'Look through this and see what I
have seen, something you would never have noticed without the
lens!'

Not all metaphors, however, are living metaphors. When a creative mind has observed a fresh and illuminating affinity and
captured it in a metaphor, more passive minds will repeat it until it
becomes a stock metaphor. Through constant use it then becomes a
faded or worn metaphor, and finally a dead one. This last stage has
arrived when speaker and hearer are unaware of the duality of
vehicle and tenor, and treat the word as a new literalism. We are
not usually conscious of using a metaphor when we speak of a
needle's eyes, or of using a two-storey metaphor when we speak of a

bottleneck. A dead metaphor may be revived by restoring it to the original context of its vehicle, as happens in children's jokes and riddles ('What has eyes and cannot see?'). Terms such as justification and redemption, for example, have become technical terms of a theological jargon, but may be revitalised by recalling their original setting in law court and slavery.

Metaphor may be employed in the service of any of the five uses of language listed in Chapter One. The lens of metaphor can be both informative and cognitive, an access to fact which would otherwise be unobserved or to truth which would otherwise remain hidden. Many metaphors are commissive. If I call God 'Father', I commit myself to filial dependence and obedience. D. D. Evans (op. cit., pp. 124 ff.) has given the name 'onlook' to this type of metaphor. I look on God as father, king, judge, shepherd, sculptor and commit myself to the attitudes or conduct which any of these implies. Stock metaphors have an important social function in expressing and reinforcing the accepted system of order or belief. For this reason the metaphors of the psalter are for the most part stock metaphors, whereas those of the prophets, who are aiming at cognitive and commissive effect, have a greater freshness.

3. Correspondence and development

Once we have identified the point of comparison intended in a simile or metaphor, the next thing to note is that there are two further ways in which one comparison may differ from another. First, there are varying degrees of correspondence between vehicle and tenor. When family unity is compared with the anointing oil dripping off Aaron's beard, there is a low degree of correspondence: the likeness is restricted to the fragrance and cannot by any stretch of the imagination be pressed further. The comparison of the church with a body, on the other hand, offers a high degree of correspondence: the variety of function in the members contributing to the organic unity of the whole (1 Cor. 12:12–21); the relative importance of the humbler members (1 Cor. 12:22–27); the interdependence of the members (Rom. 12:4); the subordination of the members to the head (Col. 1:18); and the need for steady growth to maturity (Eph. 4:13–16). The distinction between degrees of correspondence has three important applications. It provides one

6

of the criteria for distinguishing the non-literal from the literal (see below, p. 188). It has a vital bearing on the nature of parable and its differentiation from allegory (see below, pp. 163–6). Above all, it provides a useful classification of metaphors which the Bible uses to speak about God. When God is compared to a dry wadi (Jer. 15:18), a festering sore (Hos. 5:12) or a panther mauling its prey (Hos. 5:14), the degree of correspondence is low. It is a little higher when the similitude is drawn from nature in her more beneficent guise: the security of the rock (Ps. 31:2–3), the sun as source of light and life (Ps. 84:11), a bird's care for its nestlings (Deut. 32:11; Luke 13:34). Among anthropomorphic metaphors there is a lower correspondence when the metaphor is drawn from man's dealings with the subhuman world (potter, woodsman, shepherd), and a higher correspondence with those drawn from human relationships (judge, king, father). As father God is the source of life (Deut. 32:6), of parental care (Matt. 7:9–11) and affection (Hos. 11:3–4), of discipline (Heb. 12:9) and authority (Mal. 1:6), of family unity (Eph. 3:14) and mutual love (John 15:9–12); and on those who claim to be his children he lays the obligation to take after their father (Matt. 5:45).

Correspondence belongs to language, but development to speech. The development of a simile or metaphor is the extent to which in any given instance elements of the vehicle are exploited by the user. High development may be employed even where correspondence is low, as regularly happens with the Homeric simile.

> Many a fire before them blazed;
> As when in heaven the stars about the moon
> Look beautiful, when all the winds are laid,
> And every height comes out, and jutting peak
> And valley, and the immeasurable heavens
> Break open to their highest, and all the stars
> Shine, and the shepherd gladdens in his heart.[10]

Not content with comparing the many fires in the Trojan camp, as they feast and wait for dawn, with the many stars in the night sky, Homer fills out the picture, partly to establish a mood of light-heartedness, partly from the sheer delight he takes in description.

[10] Homer, *Iliad* 8. 554–9, translated by A. E. Tennyson.

Occasionally a Hebrew poet will do the same, though usually on a smaller scale.

> Your teeth are like a flock of ewes just shorn
> Which have come up fresh from the dipping;
> Each ewe has twins and none has cast a lamb (Cant. 4:2).

More commonly, however, high development goes with high correspondence. When Isaiah compares Israel with a vineyard, the fertility of the ground, the care taken in the planting, the protective wall and tower, and the disappointment at the poor crop all have their counterpart in the application (Isa. 5:1–7). The metaphors of judge and father may be used to express one simple idea (Gen. 18:25; Mal. 1:6), but the one may be elaborated into a full assize (Isa. 1:2–23; Zech. 3:1–5), the other into a family history (Hos. 11:1–4).

A comparison of low correspondence relies for its effect on freshness, surprise, and even shock. The likeness of God to a festering sore was not one that would naturally have occurred to the ordinary pious Israelite, and Hosea uses it to stab the consciences of the complacent. Comparisons of high correspondence are more obvious, more popular, and therefore more prone to become stock or faded metaphors; so they generally depend for their effectiveness on the vividness of their development.

Some metaphors readily lend themselves to high development because they belong to a metaphor system, i.e. a group of metaphors linked together by their common origin in a single area of human observation, experience or activity, which has generated its own peculiar sublanguage or jargon. Farming, commerce, law, warfare, family, weather, love, health, nature, sport—each of these has a recognisable language of its own, and any metaphor drawn from any one of these areas invites embellishment by the addition of others. Paul in particular has a way of piling up analogies from agriculture (1 Cor. 9:7–12), from the athletic stadium (1 Cor. 9:23–27), from book-keeping (Phil. 3:7–9), and from the experience of darkness and light (1 Thess. 5:1–8); and this same characteristic is also in evidence in the extended military metaphor of Eph. 6:10–17.

To the metaphor systems which are common to all cultures the

Bible adds one or two of its own. By far the most important and extensive of these is the metaphorical use of Exodus language. The Exodus from Egypt marked the beginning of Israel's nationhood, and was commemorated by successive generations as the ground of their faith. Their God was distinguished from the gods of other nations as 'Yahweh your God who brought you out of Egypt, out of the land of slavery' (Exod. 20:1). Thus Egypt became the symbol for any enslavement to tyranny: to become vassals to Assyria was to return to Egypt (Hos. 11:5). Yahweh was an out-of-Egypt-bringing God, who could be trusted to rescue Israel from affliction and sin.

> For in the Lord is love unfailing,
> And great is his power to set men free.
> He alone will set Israel free
> from all their sins   (Ps. 130:7–8).

When the Israelites looked forward to a new age, they envisaged it as a new Exodus (Isa. 11:12–16; 43:16–20). Thus a whole language was ready-made for the early Christians, as they strove to expound the significance of the life and death of Christ, and Exodus imagery abounds in almost every book of the New Testament. 'He rescued us from the domain of darkness and brought us into the kingdom of his dear Son' (Col. 1:13). 'Therefore gird up the loins of your mind' (1 Pet. 1:13). 'Moses and Elijah . . . appeared in glory and spoke of the exodus he was to fulfil in Jerusalem' (Luke 9:30–31). 'The truth is, not that Moses gave you the bread from heaven, but my Father gives you the real bread from heaven' (John 6:32). 'They all drank from the supernatural rock that accompanied their travels—and that rock was Christ' (1 Cor. 10:4). 'I saw what seemed a sea of glass shot with fire, and beside the sea of glass . . . they were singing the song of Moses, the servant of God, and the song of the Lamb' (Rev. 15:2–3). When the New Testament writers speak of 'redemption' (e.g. Luke 1:68; 2:38; 21:28; Rom. 3:24; Eph. 1:14; 1 Pet. 1:19), they are using a metaphor drawn from slavery, but they are using it at one remove; for them the surface significance of the term is that it belongs to Exodus language.

Another important biblical metaphor system is derived from the ritual of the temple, and especially from sacrifice. In connexion with the evolution of the priesthood (see pp. 69–72), we have already taken note of the spiritualisation of sacrifice in the Old Testament. But this phenomenon could equally well be described as metaphor, the transfer of sacrificial terms from their original referents, the lambs, bulls, pigeons and meal-offering of the levitical code, to new referents such as loyalty, obedience and thanksgiving. In a somewhat different fashion the language of sacrifice is metaphorical when used of the death of Christ. Literally the death of Christ was no sacrifice, but a criminal execution, regarded by the one side as a political necessity and by the other as a miscarriage of justice. But because Christ himself chose to regard his death as a sacrifice, and by his words at the Last Supper taught his disciples so to do, he transformed its tragedy into something he could offer to God to be used in the service of his purpose. To regard a violent death as sacrifice is a metaphor of the kind we have called 'onlook'; and since this particular onlook has manifestly changed the shape of history, it serves as a rebuke to those who talk carelessly of 'mere metaphor'. Similarly Paul looks on his apostleship as 'the priestly service . . . of offering the Gentiles to God as an acceptable sacrifice' (Rom. 15:16); and he looks on his own expected martyrdom as 'a libation to crown that sacrifice which is the offering of your faith' (Phil. 2:18).

There is one metaphor system which is not peculiar to the Bible, but which deserves special mention because of its frequent and varied use there. To the modern ear the biblical writers seem inordinately fond of law-court language. Often God is the judge who condemns the wicked and upholds the cause of the weak and helpless (1 Sam. 24:15; Ps. 9:4; 43:1; 140:12; Lam. 3:58; Mic. 7:9). The sentences passed in a human court may be reversed in God's court of appeal (Prov. 22:22–23). But sometimes instead God appears in court as advocate, the guardian of orphans (Prov. 23:11), or as the defending counsel pleading Israel's cause against her aggressors (Ps. 119:154; Isa. 50:8–9; 51:22; Jer. 50:34; 51:36). On other occasions God is himself the litigant, pressing his case against injustice (Ps. 74:22), against the gods of Babylon (Isa. 41:21; 43:9), against all nations (Jer. 25:9), and above all against the rebellious Israel (Ps. 103:9; Isa. 3:13–15; Jer. 2:9; Hos. 4:1–4; 12:2; Mic. 6:1–5). Job constantly returns to the idea that his predicament is to be regarded as a lawsuit between himself and God: he demands that God should state the grounds of his complaint

(10:2), rebukes his friends for thinking that God's case needs the support of their dishonest arguments (13:6–8), laments that he cannot meet God face to face and settle with him out of court (23:3–6), takes a solemn oath of innocence (31:5–40), and finally insists that his accuser ought to have put the indictment in writing (31:35). In an ancient court of law the primary aim of a litigant was not to convince judge and jury, but to convince the adversary, so that he would withdraw his own case and acknowledge defeat by placing a finger on his lips; and this Job does when God's voice has questioned him out of the whirlwind (40:4).

The reason for this frequent recourse to forensic metaphor was not that the Israelites were excessively litigious, nor that law was their religion, but simply that the law-court was the only context in which they experienced a systematic quest for truth governed by rules of procedure. Truth, like justice, was for them something to be discovered and maintained in court. It was natural for them, therefore, to see through the lens of legal metaphor any attempt to arrive at religious truth. Today, when we talk about verification, we are inclined to think in terms of scientific method, even if we hear scientists speaking of evidence, probably unaware that they are using a metaphor taken from the processes of law. But most of the truths that Israel was interested in had to rest on the testimony of witnesses; and the law laid down that 'a charge must be established on the evidence of two or three witnesses' (Deut. 19:15).

When the early Christians began to argue the case for their new faith, they took the law of dual witness very seriously. 'We are witnesses to all this, and so is the Holy Spirit given by God to those who are obedient to him' (Acts 5:32). The apostles were claiming that the truth of the gospel was guaranteed by their testimony to what they had seen and heard, confirmed by the supporting evidence of the works of power which the Spirit had enabled them to do. 'This deliverance was first announced through the lips of the Lord himself; those who heard him confirmed it to us, and God added his testimony by signs, by miracles, by manifold works of power, and by distributing the gifts of the Holy Spirit at his will' (Heb. 2:3–4). In the Revelation the two witnesses are symbolic figures, cast in the mould of Moses and Elijah, but representing the whole vast throng of martyrs, who by their death recapitulate the death and victory of the slaughtered Lamb (Rev. 11:3–12). How deeply the law of evidence had impressed itself on the minds of the early church can be seen from Paul's appeal to it in connexion with his visits to Corinth: 'this will be my third visit to you; and all facts must be established by the evidence of two or three witnesses' (2 Cor. 13:1).

It is in the Fourth Gospel, however, that we find the most elaborate use of forensic metaphor. For one of the strands which John weaves into his rich tapestry is the Old Testament theme of God's lawsuit: he presents to us the case of God v. the world. The first witness to be called is John the Baptist (1:6–7). Then comes the testimony of Jesus: 'he who comes from heaven bears witness to what he has seen and heard, yet no one accepts his witness' (3:31). But after all, no man can expect to be believed on his own unsupported evidence. 'If I testify on my own behalf, that testimony does not hold good. There is another who bears witness for me, and I know that his testimony holds ... I rely on a testimony higher than John's. There is enough to testify that the Father has sent me, in the works my Father gave me to do and to finish—the very works I have in hand. This testimony was given me by the Father who sent me' (5:31–37). Finally, there is the evidence of the Scriptures, with Moses acting as prosecutor in the case against the Jewish nation (5:39–45). As the debate continues, Jesus applies to himself the law of evidence: 'in your own law it is written that the testimony of two witnesses is valid. Here am I, a witness in my own cause, and my other witness is the Father who sent me' (8:17–18). The climax comes with the death of Jesus, when Satan, representing the world of which he is prince, loses his case because he has no hold over Jesus, and incidentally loses his hold over the world for which Jesus dies (12:31–32; 14:30). Yet, even so, the case is not closed, for the world is not yet aware that its case is lost. The truth of the gospel still needs to be maintained, and at this point the dual witness passes to the apostles and the Advocate, the Spirit of Truth. 'When the Advocate has come ... he will bear witness to me. And you also are my witnesses, because you have been with me from the first' (15:26–27). The function of the Advocate, speaking through the mouths of the apostles, is to convince the world that it has been wrong in bringing Jesus to trial and execution, wrong about the meaning of sin, wrong about the meaning of righteousness, wrong about the meaning of judgment (16:8–11).

Chapter Nine

Comparative Language II:
Special Forms

Simile and metaphor between them exhaust the possibilities of comparison. But there are some forms of simile and metaphor which appear to be distinguished from the rest and from each other by possessing labels of their own: fable, myth, parable and allegory.[1] Fable will not detain us long; for this term is best reserved for a story in which animals, plants and even inanimate objects assume human motives and passions, and Jotham's fable about the trees choosing a king is the only such story in the Bible (Judg. 9:8–15). A fable may be used either to make a general observation about human nature or, as in Jotham's case, to expose the realities of a particular situation. In either of these technical senses it may be appropriate to discuss the truth value of a fable, notwithstanding the confusion caused by the derogatory use of the word to connote a story not founded on fact (e.g. 1 Tim. 4:7; 2 Pet. 1:16). The word 'myth' has suffered even more acutely from pejorative use, and the fog which surrounds it is now so dense that it must be set aside for separate study in Part Three.

The problems presented by parable and allegory are quite different, arising largely from over-zealous definition. People with tidy minds are inclined to believe that, if classificatory terms exist, there must also exist distinct classes of objects to which they refer. A story with a hidden meaning, therefore, must be either a parable or an allegory, and we must so define the terms as to render them mutually exclusive. Jesus told parables, not allegories. If, then, we find in the Gospels a story which falls within our definition of allegory (e.g. the story of the Wicked Tenants in Mark 12:1–9), it

[1] The OED defines allegory as 'an extended metaphor', and might reasonably have used exactly the same definition for any of the other three terms.

cannot be authentic. But we have only to examine this argument closely to see that every single step in it contains a logical fallacy. The distinction between parable and allegory is not as easy as that. H. W. Fowler in *Modern English Usage* went so far as to say that 'allegory (uttering things otherwise) and parable (putting side by side) are almost exchangeable terms', and that the distinction between them was only a matter of idiomatic usage. If, as we shall see, he too was overstating his case, at least he was erring on the right side.

The natural but mistaken tendency to look for clear-cut definitions received vigorous encouragement from the immense authority of Adolf Jülicher, whose two-volume work, *Die Gleichnisreden Jesu*, has dominated the study of the Gospel parables for nearly a century. Jülicher was a pioneer who enabled New Testament scholarship to break once and for all with the centuries-long tradition of allegorical interpretation. But he had an obsessive preoccupation with literal speech (*eigentliche Rede*), and he relied far too heavily on Greek and Latin authors who gave him the impression that simile and metaphor, like other figures of speech, were optional rhetorical ornaments. He recognised that both simile and metaphor were forms of comparison, and that the one might readily be converted into the other; yet he believed that the differences between them outweighed any superficial similarity. Simile was honest, literal speech, carrying its plain meaning on the surface for all to see, whereas metaphor wrapped things in mystery and needed to be decoded. Parable, properly understood, was extended simile; allegory was 'many metaphors' (cf. Cicero, *Or.* xxvii.94). Mark made the mistake of turning the parables of Jesus into allegories (particularly the Sower), and it is therefore hardly surprising that he held the view that they were intended to mystify. The other difference between parable and allegory was that a parable has only one point of comparison, while an allegory has many. When Jülicher applied these principles to the exposition of the parables of Jesus, the one point always turned out to be a moral platitude.

Jülicher's house of cards has had a long stand,[2] chiefly because his dictum that a parable has only one point of comparison appealed

---

[2] That only a puff was needed to bring it down has been demonstrated in the brief but adequate critique of *The Mysterious Parable* by Madeleine Boucher, pp. 3–5 (1977).

to the current mood of scholarship: it seemed integral to his refutation of allegorism, and it was congenial to the atomic theory of Form Criticism. C. H. Dodd,[3] for example, followed by J. Jeremias,[4] rejected Jülicher's moralistic interpretations in favour of the now generally accepted thesis that the parables had a particular reference to the ministry of Jesus and the crisis it inaugurated; yet he accepted without question the single correspondence hypothesis. Jülicher's argument needs correction in fact at no fewer than six points. (1) Because simile is an explicit comparison and metaphor an implicit one, it does not follow that the one is clear and the other mysterious. The understanding of both figures depends on our correctly identifying the point of comparison, and this may be as hard with a simile as with a metaphor (e.g. the simile of Aaron's beard, see p. 145). (2) It is an error of classification to identify parable with simile and allegory with metaphor. (3) The Ciceronian description of allegory as many metaphors is inaccurate, since allegory frequently consists of a single, extended metaphor; even the lengthy allegory of *Pilgrim's Progress* has as its unifying plot the one metaphor of a journey. (4) We have seen in the last chapter that similes and metaphors vary in their degree of correspondence, and the same variation is to be seen in parables. (5) The parables of Jesus are not merely expressions of general religious or moral truth, but were intended to have, in the first instance at least, a specific reference to particular situations. (6) Jülicher failed to draw the important distinction between allegory and allegorism (see below).

The Gospel writers give the name 'parable' to sayings of Jesus which are of five different types:

1. Simple simile: e.g. 'the kingdom of God is like yeast, which a woman took and mixed with half a hundredweight of flour till it was all leavened' (Matt. 13:33; Luke 13:20–21).

2. Simple metaphors: e.g. 'do not throw your pearls to the pigs; they will only trample on them, and turn and tear you to pieces' (Matt. 7:6).

3. Simile story: e.g. the Labourers in the Vineyard (Matt. 20:1–16).

4. Metaphor story: e.g. the Prodigal Son (Luke 15:11 -32).

[3] *The Parables of the Kingdom* (first ed. 1935).
[4] *The Parables of Jesus* (first ed. 1947).

5. Example story: the Good Samaritan, the Rich Fool, Dives and Lazarus, the Pharisee and the Publican (Luke 10:30–37; 12:17–21; 16:19–31; 18:9–14).

Jülicher correctly observed that, although Luke calls all the four stories in the fifth class 'parables', they are unlike the others in that they contain no comparison, but only an example of conduct to be followed or avoided. They are the exceptions to the rule that parables are either metaphors and similes or extensions of metaphor and simile.[5] When Fowler declared that parable and allegory are 'almost exchangeable terms', he was obviously thinking only of classes 3 and 4, to the exclusion of classes 1, 2 and 5; for an allegory is always a story, though it need not be as long as Spenser's *Faërie Queene* or Bunyan's *Pilgrim's Progress*.

Let us then concentrate on the parables in story form and ask what, if anything, distinguishes them from allegories. The generally accepted view has been that of Jülicher, that a parable has only one point of comparison, whereas in allegory every detail is significant. Now the strength of this position is that *some* of the parables are what in the last chapter we have called metaphors (or similes) of low correspondence and high development. In the two Lucan parables of the Unjust Steward and the Unjust Judge, for example, we must not identify God either with the employer in his worldly-wise reaction to the ingenuity of his dismissed agent, or with the judge who had no sense of obligation to God or man. But it does not necessarily follow that this limiting principle will hold good for all parables. We have seen that simile and metaphor vary both in correspondence and in development, and we should expect this to be true of parables as well. Sure enough, the simplest example in our list above, 'do not give pearls to pigs', turns out to have two points: the gift will be unappreciated and may be dangerous to the donor. So, when we find the longest and most elaborate of story parables beginning 'A man had two sons', it is reasonable to expect that it will have at least two points. But once we have thrown off the tyranny of the one-point dogma, there is no good reason for denying the name of parable to the story of the Wicked Tenants, which has several points of contact between vehicle and tenor.

---

[5] Against Jülicher's addiction to literality Dr Boucher makes the point that the example story is an extended synecdoche (op. cit., p. 22).

Another possible distinction is that a parable asks for a decision, while allegory is designed only to instruct. In his parable of the Ewe Lamb, Nathan asks David for a verdict on a fictitious legal case, with the intention of applying the same verdict to David's own misdemeanour: 'You are the man' (2 Sam. 12:1–7). Many of the parables of Jesus are cast in the form of a question (e.g. Luke 15:3–4). But it is interesting to note that the one which in this respect comes closest to the Nathan pattern is the Wicked Tenants: 'What will the owner of the vineyard do?' (Mark 12:9). And Mark's comment is that the authorities recognised that the parable was aimed at them, but rejected its implications. On the other hand, the parables of the kingdom, the largest group with a common theme, are purely instructive, asking only for acceptance of the kingdom as Jesus understood it.

A third possibility is that a parable is always true to daily life, while the details of an allegory are dictated by the interpretation and make no proper sense until they are decoded. No real householder orders one servant to throw water on the fire and another to keep it alight with a supply of oil from behind, as Bunyan's Interpreter does; we are as mystified as Christian was, until the water and oil are translated into the spiritual realities they symbolise. The parables of Jesus, on the other hand, have been brilliantly used by C. H. Dodd to reconstruct the daily life of a Palestinian village; and when we read Matthew's version of the Great Banquet, where the dinner is still ready after the host has mounted a military expedition to destroy the city of the guests who murdered his messengers, we are justified in feeling that the story has suffered in the course of transmission (Matt. 22:1–10); and a comparison with Luke's version supports this inference (Luke 14:16–24). Yet in the end this distinction too lets us down. Some at least of the parables of Jesus rely for their effect on a startling departure from normal procedure. A king does not normally allow a servant to incur a debt running into millions (Matt. 18:24). It is unusual for a whole roomful of guests to go back on their initial acceptance of an invitation (Luke 14:18). Workmen do not commonly expect to be paid at the same rate for one hour as for the whole day; like the early workers in the parable, they insist on their differentials (Matt. 20:9).

As one criterion after another fails us, it begins to look as if we should be wise to refrain from drawing hard and fast lines. Nevertheless, several generations of scholars have made strenuous attempts to do so, and the reason lies in their revolt against the long accepted practice of allegorical interpretation. Dodd quotes as a cautionary example Augustine's allegorisation of the Good Samaritan, in which the man is Adam, Jerusalem the heavenly city, Jericho the moon—the symbol of mortality; the thieves are the devil and his angels, who strip the man of immortality by persuading him to sin and so leave him (spiritually) half dead; the priest and levite represent the Old Testament, the Samaritan Christ, the beast his flesh which he assumed at the Incarnation; the inn is the church and the innkeeper the apostle Paul.[6] Most modern readers would agree with Dodd that this farrago bears no relationship to the real meaning of the parable. But the point to bear in mind is that there is a world of difference between allegorisation and allegory. An allegory is a story intended by the author to convey a hidden meaning, and it is correctly interpreted when that intended meaning is perceived. To allegorise is to impose on a story hidden meanings which the original author neither intended nor envisaged; it is to treat as allegory that which was not intended as allegory. Here, as in all questions of meaning, the intention of author or speaker is paramount.[7] An adverse judgment on allegorism no more entails a repudiation of allegory than a refusal to treat poetry as prose entails a rejection of prose. If Jesus in fact composed similitudes with more than one point of comparison, it makes little difference to our understanding of them whether we call them parables or allegories, so long as we recognise that to identify intended points is not to allegorise.

There are two interesting test cases in the parables of the Sower (Mark 4:3–8) and the Weeds (Matt. 13:24–30), each supplied with an interpretation which commentators have generally called allegorical, and have therefore dismissed as secondary. Secondary they may indeed be; for a parable that needs to be explained is about as effective as an explained joke, and we have no good reason for thinking that the disciples to whom the explanations are said to have been given were markedly more obtuse than the crowd who

---

[6] *The Parables of the Kingdom*, pp. 11–12; cf. Augustine, *Quaestiones Evangeliorum* II.19.

[7] Even this rule, however, is no secure protection against the determined allegorist. Philo allegorises the Pentateuch, and is confident that in so doing he is faithfully interpreting the mind of Moses.

heard only the parables. But the question is whether the allegorical nature of the explanations is *in itself* an adequate reason for regarding them as churchly accretions. The parable of the Sower, so we have been told, was intended by Jesus to assure the discouraged disciples that, in spite of initial hindrances and frustrations, the gospel would have large ultimate success; and the interpretation moralises the parable by concentrating attention on human responsibility. But why should not both points have been intended? Why should Jesus have been at pains to describe four kinds of soil if he did not think that it mattered on what human soil the seed of his preaching fell? We have the parable of the Two Houses to prove that he regarded the reception of his message as of crucial importance (Matt. 7:24–27). Whether the interpretation of the Sower comes from Jesus or from the church, only a doctrinaire addiction to the one-point theory could persuade us that it is not what Jesus meant.

With the parable of the Weeds the one-point theory does not arise. If by allegory we mean a story with several points of correspondence, then this is an allegory. Furthermore, at least one of the points has been dictated by the application: a farmer who finds weeds among his wheat does not normally look round suspiciously at his neighbours to see which of them hates him enough to collect a large quantity of darnel seed and scatter it on his land. But since Isaiah's highly developed metaphor of the vineyard (Isa. 5:1–7) may equally well be called allegory, there is no a priori reason why Jesus should not on occasion have resorted to this form of instruction.[8]

There are, however, three parables in which there can be little doubt that allegorical embellishment has occurred, since in each case we can compare the embellished form with a simpler form in another Gospel. In Mark's version of the Wicked Tenants, the son's body is flung out of the vineyard after he is killed, but in Matthew and Luke he is killed outside the vineyard. Here we can see a double influence at work: the fact that Golgotha was outside the walls of Jerusalem, and the ancient law that the carcase of the sin-offering must be burnt 'outside the camp' (Exod. 29:14; Heb. 13:11–13). In Matthew's version of the Great Banquet, the

---

[8] See M. Black, 'The parables as allegory', *BJRL* 42 (1959–60), pp. 273–87.

preparations are interrupted by a punitive expedition which has no counterpart in Luke; and, even if the hybrid form is due to the conflation of two parables, this was undoubtedly occasioned by the destruction of Jerusalem in A.D. 70. In Luke's version of the Money in Trust, the employer is a nobleman going abroad to be appointed king by a foreign power in the face of a strong resistance movement at home, and a comparison with Matthew shows that here too current affairs have insinuated themselves into the story (Luke 19:11–27; cf. Matt. 25:14–30).

Parable and allegory, then, are partial synonyms, and it is less important to distinguish between them than it is to distinguish between allegory, which the author intended, and allegorical embellishment or interpretation, which he did not. But allegorical interpretation (or allegorism) is itself an ambiguous term, covering at least five different types of exegesis.

1. Rationalist allegorism

Among the Greeks the poems of Homer and Hesiod were regarded as sacred texts, yet they contained much that to the rationalist spirit of Greek philosophy was offensive or absurd. Xenophanes had complained that Homer and Hesiod ascribed to the gods everything that is reckoned shameful among men,[9] and Plato had argued for expurgation: 'We must beg Homer not to be angry if we delete such passages' (*Rep.* ii. 387B). An alternative method, said to have been invented in the sixth century B.C. by Theagenes of Rhegium,[10] but further developed by Democritus and Empedocles and brought to full popularity by Zeno and Cleanthes, was to sterilise the suspect material by the allegorical method and to elicit from it general philosophical truths. Philo of Alexandria in his allegorical treatment of the Jewish laws occasionally discloses just such a rationalist streak. It is foolish to think that the world was literally created in six days (*L.A.* I.ii.2), mythical nonsense to speak of God planting a garden (*L.A.* I.xiv.43); and the idea that Cain built a city 'runs counter to reason itself' (*Post.* xiv.50). It is undignified that Jacob should send Joseph to inspect his brothers when he had plenty of servants to send (*Det.* v.13), and contrary to

[9] Clement, *Strom.* 5.110.
[10] See Tatian, *Adv. Graecos* 31.

reason that the Israelites should have lamented at the death of Pharaoh (*Det.* xxv.94–5). Yet he insisted that allegorism had its limits. Just as the Palestinian rabbis distinguished between *halakah* (the strict interpretation of commandments as a rule of life) and *haggadah* (the free, imaginative treatment of the text as a means of instruction or as an aid to devotion), so Philo insisted that commandments were to be understood and obeyed literally (*Mig.* xvi.89–93). He was, however, prepared to allow reason some say in deciding what was and what was not a commandment. The law, for example, forbids a creditor to keep a debtor's cloak in pawn overnight, 'since this is the only covering he has to keep him decent' (Exod. 22:27); and, after pouring ridicule on those who would enforce this as a literal commandment, Philo explains that rational discourse is the only cloak a man has to cover the nakedness of his soul, and regards this as a refutation of the literalists who will not clothe in the garment of allegory a text which without it would appear ridiculous (*Somn.* I.xvii.102–4).

2. *Moralist allegorism*

More frequently Philo uses his allegorical method, following the order of the biblical text after the manner of a rabbinical midrash, to prove that Moses anticipated all that is best in Greek ethical teaching. The foundation of the Stoic moral philosophy, which Zeno had adopted from Heraclitus, was the doctrine that the *logos* or rational faculty in man has affinities with the logos or rational quality of the universe, and that morality consists in allowing the inner *logos* to live in harmony with the universal *logos*. Philo discovers this doctrine in the biblical teaching that the earthly temple is a copy of the heavenly (cf. Exod. 25:40): 'it is evident that there are two temples of God, one being the universe in which the high priest is his own son, the divine logos, and the other being the rational soul' (*Somn.* I.xxxvii.215). The four rivers of Eden represent the four cardinal virtues (*L.A.* I.xix.63), and the human characters of the biblical story are transformed into the cast of a morality play. Adam and Eve stand for mind and sense perception (*L.A.* I.xxx.92; II.xi.38), Sarah and Hagar for virtue and education (*Cong.* v.23), Jacob and Esau for prudence and folly (*Ebr.* ii.9–10), though Jacob frequently appears also as *Asketes*, the Practiser (e.g.

Somn. I.viii.46). Joseph is the Common Man, a prey to vainglory, often found wandering, easily led; and Potiphar's wife is pleasure (*L.A.* III.lxxxiv.237). Much of this is achieved by fanciful etymology of proper names, for which there was ample precedent in the biblical text.

3. Atomic allegorism

This is Moore's name for the allegorical method of the rabbis, 'which interprets sentences, clauses, phrases, and even single words, independently of the context or the historical occasion, as divine oracles'.[11] It differs from the method of Philo in that its object is almost always to discover allusions to the Torah in passages which would otherwise be obscure or devoid of edification.

4. Exegetical allegorism

The author of Hebrews offers a brief allegorical treatment of Melchizedek (7:1–3), which was once thought to be evidence of his dependence on Philo.[12] But a closer examination of his argument reveals that he is not engaging in allegorism on his own account. He is not embarrassed by the nakedness of Scripture, nor does he discover in it any moral commonplace. His starting point is Ps. 110:4, and he is asking the very modern exegetical question: 'why does the psalmist fix on Melchizedek as the symbolic representative of a new and eternal priesthood?' For an answer he turns to Gen. 14, the only other mention of Melchizedek in the Old Testament, and there he discovers that Melchizedek is the first priest to be mentioned in Genesis,[13] and that, unlike other characters in Genesis, he appears on the scene without genealogy and without mention of his birth or death. He therefore deduces that this was what prompted the psalmist to think of Melchizedek as eternal, and it is more than likely that his deduction was correct. That is to say, he

[11] G. F. Moore, *Judaism*, vol. I, p. 248.
[12] See the commentaries of J. Moffatt (ICC) and C. Spicq. For the refutation of this position, see C. K. Barrett, 'The eschatology of the Epistle to the Hebrews' in *The Background to the New Testament and its Eschatology*, ed. W. D. Davies and D. Daube, pp. 363–93, and R. Williamson, *Philo and the Epistle to the Hebrews.*
[13] See F. L. Horton, *The Melchizedek Tradition*, pp. 152–60.

was attributing the allegorical method to the psalmist rather than using it as a tool of his own biblical interpretation.

5. Polemical allegorism

Before Paul became a Christian, he was a Pharisee with rabbinic training, and when he appears to have recourse to allegory, he is usually diverting to Christian ends a conceit from his rabbinic past. One of the favourite devices of the rabbis was to discover in the Scriptures hidden references to the Torah, and for Torah Paul substitutes Christ. It did not require a vivid imagination to identify with the Torah the spring which Moses and the leaders of the people opened up in the wilderness (Numb. 21:16–18). But around this interpretation there had grown up a curious legend that the spring became a rock which rolled along behind the Israelites on their desert wanderings, an idea which would not have appeared at all bizarre to the most sophisticated rabbi, since he would have his mind on the decoded version.[14] It is plain, then, that Paul was not originating a new allegorism but adapting a familiar one when he wrote to Corinth: 'they all drank from the supernatural rock that accompanied their travels—and that rock was Christ' (1 Cor. 10:4).

A close parallel to this is the use made of Ps. 68:18 in Eph. 4:8: 'He ascended into the heights with captives in his train; he gave gifts to men.' The rabbis had taken this to refer to Moses ascending Mount Sinai and returning to give the Torah to Israel. The author of Ephesians, his mind working singularly like the mind of Paul, says, in effect: 'not Moses and the Torah, but Christ and the gifts of the Spirit.' But in this instance there is a new factor to be taken into consideration. The reason why the rabbis discovered an allusion to Moses in Ps. 68 is that this psalm had long been one of the appointed psalms for use at Pentecost; and Pentecost, in addition to being a harvest festival, had become the commemoration of the giving of the Torah. Unfortunately we do not know enough about Jewish liturgy or lectionaries to be able to document in any detail their influence on the interpretation of the Old Testament, but this example by itself is enough to suggest that liturgy may have been of some importance in the development of allegorism. The author

[14] On the origin of this legend see G. B. Caird, 'The descent of Christ in Ephesians 4, 7–11', *Studia Evangelica* II, pp. 535 ff.

of the epistle certainly appears to be arguing that Ps. 68 is to be used in the celebration of the Christian and not the Jewish Pentecost.

Once only, in his handling of the story of Sarah and Hagar, does Paul explicitly call his use of the Old Testament allegorical (Gal. 4:21–31). This passage too is polemical, though in a different way from the two just cited. The underlying debate is whether Jews or Christians have the better claim to be called children of Abraham and heirs to his inheritance. The Jewish case rests on physical descent traced through the free-born wife, with the implication that the repudiated son of the slave-woman represents the Gentiles. Paul's answer is that by physical descent Ishmael is just as much a son of Abraham as Isaac, and that those who rely on physical descent, and the legalistic interpretation of the Old Testament that goes with it, symbolised by Mount Sinai, might just as well be the slave-woman's children, since they are in fact in bondage. The real difference between Isaac and Ishmael is that Isaac was the son of God's promise, so that those who live by faith in that promise are the true children of Abraham and his free-born wife. But the ideas come bubbling up in great profusion, more by free association than by logical argument. On the one hand we have the sequence Hagar—slave-woman—Ishmael–-Arabia—Sinai—legalism—the present Jerusalem; and on the other hand Sarah—free woman—Isaac—promise—Spirit—freedom—the heavenly Jerusalem. What at first sight seems an arid, academic exercise turns out to be more akin to poetry than to prose.

Philo takes this same story of Abraham's two wives and moralises it. 'Sarah, virtue, bears the same relation to Hagar, education, as the mistress to the servant maid, or the lawful wife to the concubine, and so naturally the mind which aspires to study and to gain knowledge, the mind we call Abraham, will have Sarah, virtue, for his wife, and Hagar, the whole range of school culture, for his concubine' (*Cong.* 23). Thus the story and the use of the allegorical method are the only two points which Philo and Paul have in common. Philo is interested in universal symbols and superimposes on the biblical story a platitude of hellenistic moral philosophy. Paul addresses himself to the unfolding of God's purposes in the history of the Jewish people, and it is essential to him that Abraham was a real historic person, whatever symbolic value he may have in addition.

Chapter Ten

Anthropomorphism

The earliest recorded attack on anthropomorphism was made by Xenophanes at Elea in southern Italy in the latter half of the sixth century B.C. 'If oxen or lions had hands to write or to make works of art like men, horses would represent the gods in the likeness of horses, oxen in the likeness of oxen; they would provide them with a bodily form similar to their own.'[1] This remark was apparently prompted by the observation that 'the Ethiopians endow their gods with snub noses and black skins, the Thracians theirs with grey eyes and red hair'.[2] But Xenophanes was less concerned with the physical attributes of the gods than with the tendency of Homer and Hesiod to attribute to them attitudes and actions which among mankind are considered shameful.

Purists, especially those addicted to etymology, will insist on distinguishing between anthropomorphism, i.e. the representation or imagination of God or gods in human shape, and anthropopathism, i.e. the attribution to God or gods of human passions, feelings and attitudes. But in a broader sense anthropomorphism is commonly used to cover any attribution of human characteristics to that which is not human. For the theologian, as for the linguist. there are two good reasons for preferring the broader definition. The first is that anthropomorphism narrowly defined and anthropopathism do not together exhaust all the metaphors which are drawn from human life and applied to God; there are also metaphors of activity and relationship. The second is that problems of theological language look very different as soon as we recognise that anthropomorphism is not confined to religion.

In all languages a considerable proportion of the word stock of

---

[1] See Clement, *Strom.* 5.110.
[2] Ibid. 7.22.

daily speech is supplied by the metaphorical use of words which literally connote parts of the human body: the eye of a needle, a tongue of land, the mouth of a river, the neck of a bottle, the shoulder of a road, the belly of a ship, the foot of a mountain.[3] Only captious pedantry or childish humour will find it necessary to remark that the eye of a needle cannot see or a tongue of land speak. In fable, myth and strip cartoon animals are portrayed acting as though they were human beings (cf. Dan. 8:3 ff.; 2 Esdr. 11:1 ff.; Rev. 5:6 ff.). By what might seem to be a converse process, the names of animals may be applied as a description of character to human beings—lion (2 Tim. 4:17), fox (Luke 13:32), pig (2 Pet. 2:22), snake (Gen. 3:1; Matt. 10:16); but, since the animals in question rarely possess the assumed qualities, this may be more plausibly understood as another example of the projection of human characteristics on to animals.[4] The personification of the inanimate (e.g. Gen. 37:9; Isa. 10:15) and of the abstract (e.g. Wisd. 18:14 ff.; Prov. 8:1 ff.) belong in this category, as does the personification of Nature, commonly but misleadingly called 'the pathetic fallacy'.

The waters saw you, O God, they saw you and writhed;
The ocean was troubled to its depth   (Ps. 77:16).

Let the heavens rejoice and the earth exult,
Let the sea roar and all the creatures in it,
Let the fields exult and all that is in them,
Then let all the trees of the forest shout for joy
(Ps. 96:11–12).

Thus anthropomorphism in all its variety is the commonest source of metaphor, and in it we can observe both the cognitive and the expressive aspects of language at work. The human body, senses and personality are the objects with which we have the most direct, first-hand acquaintance, and the cognitive principle of proceeding from the known to the unknown makes it natural for human beings

[3] Such idiomatic phrases occur also in Hebrew and Greek, but with variations: where we say 'face of the land', Hebrew says 'eye of the land' (Exod. 10:5); where we say 'tongue of land', Hebrew says 'tongue of sea' (Isa. 11:15); and for 'edge of the sword' Hebrew uses 'mouth of the sword' (Numb. 21:24).

[4] By a strange corruption of language distinctively human activities are sometimes described as 'bestial'.

to see the rest of the world in the light of that experience.[5] But the continuing popularity of such usage is undoubtedly due to its vividness and the power of its appeal to the imagination.

The same two principles govern the use of anthropomorphic imagery in reference to God. We have no other language besides metaphor with which to speak about God. Abstract terms, such as 'righteousness', appear to be an exception to this rule, but on closer examination they are found to be abstracted from metaphors. The only choice open to us, therefore, is whether we derive our metaphors from the human realm or from the non-human, and it is important to note that the biblical writers use both kinds. There are frequent images drawn from inanimate nature. God is a sun (Ps. 84:11; cf. Rev. 1:16), his voice like a mighty torrent (Ezek. 43:2; cf. Rev. 1:16) or like thunder (Ps. 29:3; cf. Rev. 14:2), his spirit like the wind (John 3:8), his justice like the deep ocean (Ps. 36:6), his wisdom like an irrigating river (Ecclus. 24:25–29). He is a rock (Deut. 32:15), a spring (Jer. 2:13), a devouring fire (Deut. 4:24). Somewhat less frequently we find animal imagery. God descends on Israel like a lion, panther, leopard or bear (Hos. 5:14; 13:7–8; Lam. 3:10), but also carries them on eagle's wings (Exod. 19:6) or protects them like nestlings (Ps. 17:8; Luke 13:34). Such imagery provides a useful corrective to anthropomorphic metaphor, which always tends by its homely analogies to domesticate the remote, the mysterious and the uncontrollable. It is nature that supplies our imagination with the sensuous language which gives content to the notions of the glorious and the sublime. 'Nature never taught me that there exists a God of glory and of infinite majesty. I had to learn that in other ways. But nature gave the word *glory* a meaning for me. I still do not know where else I could have found one. I do not see how the "fear" of God could have ever meant to me anything but the lowest prudential efforts to be safe, if I had never seen certain ominous ravines and unapproachable crags.'[6]

For all that, by far the greater proportion of the biblical language which refers to God is anthropomorphic. At the simplest level God is said to have head, face, eyes, eyelids, ears, nostrils, mouth, voice, arm, hand, palm, fingers, foot, heart, bosom, bowels.

---

[5] Cf. S. Ullmann, op. cit., p. 214.
[6] C. S. Lewis, *The Four Loves*, p. 29; cf. E. Bevan, *Symbolism and Belief*, pp. 140 ff.

Much of this can of course be discounted. Some of the words occur in prepositional phrases which are purely formal: 'to the face of' = 'before'; 'in the eyes of' = 'in the estimation of'; 'by the mouth of' = 'by order of'. Many of the other instances are either synecdoche (part = person) or metonomy (e.g. 'nostrils' = 'anger'; 'bowels' = 'compassion'). Here as always we must remember that vividness of expression is not the same as literality. There are explicit denials that God has a body of flesh (Isa. 31:3), even though he is envisaged as having one. On the occasions when Israel lapsed into idolatry, the idols they made were not human (Exod. 32:4; 1 Kings 12:28). On the contrary, anthropomorphic imagery is used only very sparingly in descriptions of theophany. Moses is told that he cannot see God's face, only his back (Exod. 33:23). Isaiah sees the Lord enthroned, but does not venture on any description beyond the skirts of his robe (Isa. 6:1). Ezekiel sees a human form, fire from the waist up and fire from the waist down, which, with a triple guard against literality, he calls 'the likeness of the appearance of the glory of the Lord' (Ezek. 1:26–28). Moreover, in all the prophetic attacks on idolatry there is a recognition that the possession of eyes, ears, hands and feet is no guarantee of an ability to see, hear, and act. The God who carries Israel is unlike the idol which 'cannot stir from its place' unless carried in procession by man or beast (Isa. 46:1–7; cf. 45:20).

Far more important is the terminology of divine actions and attitudes, of which it would be difficult, if not impossible, to provide a complete catalogue. God sees and hears, speaks and answers, calls and whistles, punishes and rewards, wounds and heals, opposes and supports, fights, preserves and rescues, guides and guards, makes and unmakes, plans and fulfils, appoints and sends. He displays love, pity, patience, generosity, justice, mercy, jealousy, anger, regret, hatred, pleasure and scorn. He is potter, builder, farmer, shepherd, hero, warrior, doctor, judge, king, husband and father. Whatever may have been the case with their hearers or readers, the biblical writers at least were alert to the possible abuses of such language and at pains to guard against them. God is not like mankind, subject to vacillation and weakness (1 Sam. 15:29; Isa. 55:8; Hos. 11:9; Mal. 3:6). Human judges may be corruptible (1 Sam. 8:3), but it is axiomatic that the judge of all the earth shall do right (Gen. 18:25). Human parents may falter in love for their children, but God's love does not fail (Isa. 49:15). Israel's loyalty disperses like a morning mist (Hos. 6:4), but God's loyalty is everlasting (Ps. 100:5).

It was once supposed that the avoidance of anthropomorphism was bound to go hand in hand with the emergence of 'spiritual religion'; but there is singularly little evidence in the Bible to support such a thesis; and it is in any case a gross error to identify 'spiritual' with 'abstract'. F. Michaeli in 1948 argued that a comparison between 2 Samuel and 1 Chronicles showed a spiritualising tendency at work in the later book,[7] but most of his comparisons involved textual problems, and the tendency he thought he detected would be contradicted by the parallel passages in the still later Septuagint translation.[8] The one place where there was certainly a deliberate avoidance of theological embarrassment was 1 Chron. 21:1, but there the substitution of Satan for God as the instigator of David's census has nothing to do with anthropomorphism. There was indeed a tendency, which began at least as early as the seventh century B.C., to avoid any statements considered derogatory to God, and particularly those which implied that he could literally be seen, and to speak of the divine transcendence with enhanced reverence (see Chapters Three and Six). But neither Deutero-Isaiah, who was vigorous in the denunciation of idolatry and believed in *creatio ex nihilo*, nor Philo at the height of his allegorism, considered it right to abandon anthropomorphic imagery; and the New Testament is full of it.

The simplest defence of anthropomorphism in our language about God is that it is indispensable, and that its limitations are no greater than those which we take in our stride in any secular use of metaphor. But there is also a strong positive case to be made for its retention. Belief in God depends to a small extent on rational argument, and to a larger extent on our ability to frame images to capture, commemorate and convey our experiences of transcendence. Rudolf Otto in *The Idea of the Holy*, a book now justly regarded as a religious classic, argued that man's sense of the numinous, of a haunting presence, such as that which abashed

---

[7] *Dieu à l'image de l'homme.* He compared 2 Sam 5:17 ff. with 1 Chron. 14:8 ff.; 2 Sam. 6:1 ff. with 1 Chron. 15:1 ff.; 2 Sam. 7 with 1 Chron. 17; and 2 Sam. 24:1 with 1 Chron. 21:1.

[8] See esp. the LXX of 1 Chron. 17:5.

Jacob at Bethel (Gen. 28:17), that which gave Eliphaz goose pimples (Job. 4:12–17), that which left the youthful Wordsworth obsessed by 'unknown modes of being' (*Prel.* I 357–400), is *sui generis* and irreducible to other forms of experience; and that the numinous is to be identified with the holy, the 'wholly other', the transcendent. Granted that the numinous is *sui generis*, it is probably more accurate to say that, like the beautiful, the glorious and the sublime, it provides an occasion for the experience of transcendence. For the transcendent does not come to finite creatures unmediated, but always under cover of something else; and many, who have a lively appreciation of the beautiful and the sublime, fail to penetrate its incognito. Otto argued that the numinous (holy) came in the course of time to be moralised, illustrating how in the Old Testament this was brought about by the prophets; and he has been criticised for supposing that there was ever a time in the religious history of mankind when the holy was experienced apart from the sacred, the sense of binding obligation, however vestigial and inarticulate. But neither Otto nor his critics would deny that maturity of religion may be measured by the degree to which the holy and the sacred coincide. Man's sense of obligation to God, though by no means identical with his human loyalties and relationships, is inseparably bound up with them. The two commandments of love to God and love to neighbour belong together (Mark 12:28–34). 'If a man says, "I love God", while hating his brother, he is a liar' (1 John 4:20). Thus the language of human relationships furnishes not only the natural vocabulary for talking about obligation to God, but the indispensable vehicle for experiencing it.

In the Bible the five metaphors in most common use to express God's relationship with his worshippers are king/subject, judge/litigant, husband/wife, father/child, master/servant. In Chapter One we have seen some illustrations of the linguistic mechanism by which these metaphors operate in the service of religious and moral growth. A cynic has remarked that, when God made man in his own image, man hastened to return the compliment; and students of religious history can no doubt adduce much evidence in his support. But for the linguist the actual course of events is the exact converse. Man begins with the familiar situations of home and community and derives from them metaphors to illuminate the activity of God; but the application of these terms to God establishes ideal and absolute standards which can be used as instruments for the remaking of man in God's likeness. Man is created to become like God, and the ultimate justification of anthropomorphic imagery lies in the contribution it makes to the attainment of that goal.

The biblical history of kingship, human and divine, admirably illustrates this two-way traffic in ideas. The mental picture which the ancient Israelite had of divine sovereignty was an offprint from his experience of human sovereignty and had a parallel growth. The story begins with Saul holding court at Gibeah, 'sitting under the tamarisk-tree on the hill-top with his spear in his hand and all his retainers standing about him' (1 Sam. 22:6). The accession of David and Solomon brought some slight elaboration to this simple scene: the open-air court moved into a palace, and the military bodyguard gave place to a permanent council of advisers and secretaries, but otherwise the picture remained substantially unchanged. Before just such a court Micaiah ben Imlah was summoned by Ahab and delivered his prophecy of doom. 'I saw the Lord seated on his throne, with all the host of heaven in attendance on his right hand and on his left. The Lord said, "Who will entice Ahab to attack Ramoth Gilead and fall there?" One said one thing and another said another; then a spirit came forward and stood before the Lord and said, "I will entice him." "How?" said the Lord. "I will go out," he said, "and be a lying spirit in the mouth of all his prophets." "You shall entice him," said the Lord, "and you shall succeed; go and do it" ' (1 Kings 22:19–22). This imaginative picture of God as King, discussing matters of state with his heavenly councillors, was to have a long and influential history (see pp. 232–42). Two and a half centuries later Jeremiah offered as one of the criteria for distinguishing the true prophet from the false that the true prophet 'has stood in the council of the Lord' (23:18), i.e. has been admitted to the press gallery of the council chamber, in order that he may report to God's servant Israel what is demanded of her by God's decrees of policy.

But already in the reign of Ahab Israel had received at the battle of Karkar a foretaste of eastern imperialism, and the successive empires of Assyria, Babylon and Persia were radically to modify her concept of kingship. For in an empire each province is ruled by a viceregal governor, locally supreme, but responsible to the king of kings, and the privy council consists of 'satraps, prefects, viceroys, counsellors, treasurers, judges, chief constables, and all the governors of provinces' (Dan. 3:2). Politically Israel regarded her subjection to foreign despotism as disaster, but linguistically and theologically it was an enlargement of her horizons. It is still under dispute at what date Israel's religion can properly be called mono-theism, but there can be no doubt that complete monotheism can be *envisaged* only through the imagery of world empire.

> When the Most High parcelled out the nations,
> When he dispersed all mankind,
> He laid down the boundaries of every people
> According to the number of the sons of God;
> But the Lord's share was his own people,
> Jacob was his allotted portion
>
> (Deut. 32:8-9).

The sons of God are angels, and the writer is claiming that, in dividing up his world empire into provinces, God appointed angels to be governors or satraps of each of the pagan nations, but decided to govern Israel himself by direct rule. This device enabled the Israelite theologian to assert the world-wide sovereignty of God, and at the same time to draw a distinction between the operations of that sovereignty in Israel, where it was recognised, and in pagan nations, where it was not. It also enabled him to do justice to the political power of the pagan gods without admitting their divinity; for the pagan nations had mistakenly worshipped as gods those viceroys who wielded a genuine but derivative authority. Both the heavenly and the earthly representative of a nation would be held responsible for offences committed under their rule.

> On that day the Lord will punish
> The host of heaven in heaven and on earth the kings of the earth . . .
> The moon shall grow pale and the sun hide its face in shame;
> For the Lord of hosts has become king
> On Mount Zion and in Jerusalem   (Isa. 24:21-23).

A further development of imagery is found in Paul's letter to the Philippians: 'we are citizens of heaven' (3:20). Paul was by birth a

Roman citizen, and Philippi was a Roman colony, i.e. a city situated in one of the provinces, but with the full rights of Roman citizenship (Acts 16:12, 37; 22:25–28). Citizenship of Rome had first been extended to the whole of Italy, and then, under the Empire, had been granted to cities in the provinces where veterans from the army were settled, and occasionally to individuals distinguished in public service. The purpose of this policy was that the colonies should be centres of Roman culture, law and influence through which eventually the provinces would become thoroughly Roman; and so successful was it that even in the course of the first century A.D. many of the most distinguished figures in Roman public life were of provincial extraction. With this model in mind Paul depicts Christians as holders of the citizenship of heaven and each church as a colony of heaven, established in the provinces of God's empire as the means by which the whole might be brought within the influence of his reign.

In these ways the metaphor of kingship provided the imagery adequate to sustain an enlarging belief in divine sovereignty. But already in the earliest stage the process of retrojection had begun, the idealisation of human kingship in order to make it conform to the standards of divine sovereignty. The Lord's Anointed, the reigning monarch of the house of David, was God's earthly representative, appointed to sonship and to world-wide suzerainty, with the authority, if need be, to enforce his benign rule on recalcitrant nations.

> Of me he says, 'I have enthroned my king
> On Zion my holy mountain.'
> I will repeat the Lord's decree:
> 'You are my son,' he said;
> This day I become your father.
> Ask of me what you will:
> I give you nations as your inheritance,
> The ends of the earth as your possession.
> You may break them with a rod of iron,
> You may shatter them like a clay pot.'   (Ps. 2:6–9).

His reign is to be characterised by justice and rewarded with prosperity.

In his days righteousness shall flourish,
Prosperity abound until the moon is no more . . .
For he shall rescue the needy from their rich oppressors,
The distressed who have no protector.
He shall have pity on the needy and the poor,
And deliver the poor from death;
He shall redeem them from oppression and violence,
And precious shall their blood be in his eyes (Ps. 72:7, 12–14).

Inspired by God, he would bring in the golden age of peace (Isa. 11:1–9), when every member of society would be held at his true value (Isa. 32:1–8). So completely is the ideal Davidic king identified with the purposes of God that he can be dignified with the titles of God himself.

He shall be called
Wonderful Counsellor, Mighty God,
Father Eternal, Prince of Peace.
Great shall the dominion be
And boundless the peace
Bestowed on David's throne and on his kingdom
To establish it and sustain it
With justice and righteousness
From now and for evermore.
The zeal of the Lord of hosts shall do this (Isa. 9:6–7). [9]

At whatever dates such passages were composed, there could have been no doubt in the minds of the authors or their contemporaries that they were examples of hyperbole. For in each case the referent, explicit or implicit, is the dynasty of David; and it must have been obvious to all concerned, as it is to modern readers of the Books of Kings, that the actual incumbents of the throne of David fell short of the ideal. The wonder is that the ideal was ever accepted as the norm by which the conduct of the actual kings must be judged, and that it survived the extinction of the Davidic line, which began with the deposition of Jehoiachin (2 Kings 24:12) and culminated in the

[9] Cf. 2 Esdr. 5:43, 56, where God's spokesman, the angel Uriel, is questioned by Ezra as though he were both Creator and Judge. Ezra uses the same style of address to Uriel ('my lord, my master') as he uses in direct petition to God. This practice of treating the agent as though he were the principal is of the greatest importance for New Testament Christology.

disappearance of his grandson Zerubbabel, in whom there had been a momentary hope of its restoration (Hag. 2:20–23; Zech. 3:9). So strong was the belief that God had promised to David an unending dynasty (2 Sam. 7:13; Ps. 89:4), that the ideal was projected into the future and messianism was born. From then on the ideal king was freed from empirical human limitations and progressively more closely assimilated to God.

Thus anthropomorphism is something more than the imposing of man's preconceived and limited images on the divine. There is something that answers back in perpetual dialogue and criticism.

Chapter Eleven

Linguistic Awareness

In an earlier chapter the rule was laid down that the meaning of a sentence is that which the author intends to convey or express by it. If we are to remain faithful to that rule, as I believe we must, it poses a special problem for the study of non-literal language. It is not enough for us to show that a certain locution is a figure of speech by the standards of modern grammar; we must also be satisfied that the author so intended it. There are, as we shall see below, some simple tests by which an author's intention may be ascertained. But before we discuss them, it will be well to dispose of three red herrings.

The technical terms which we use for the figures of speech listed in Chapter Seven have been inherited from Aristotle and the Greek rhetoricians. Classical Hebrew possessed no such elaborate grammatical jargon, but used one term, *mashal*, to cover a variety of kindred forms. The terms parable, allegory and similitude are found in the New Testament, but without any suggestion that the writers who use them had received any formal training in the schools of rhetoric. Eric Auerbach has rightly emphasised the difference in ethos between the New Testament and works written in the rhetorical tradition. 'Surely, the New Testament writings are extremely effective; the tradition of the prophets and the Psalms is alive in them, and in some of them—those written by authors of more or less pronounced Hellenistic culture—we can trace the use of Greek figures of speech. But the spirit of rhetoric—a spirit which classified subjects in genera, and invested every subject with a specific form of style as the one garment becoming it in virtue of its nature—could not extend its dominion to them.'[1] With the substance of this we may agree, but Auerbach is surely inaccurate in

[1] Op. cit., pp. 39 f.

calling the figures Greek; it is only their artificial cultivation and their nomenclature that are peculiarly Greek, for the figures themselves are universal. One does not need to know the name of a thing in order to use it. M. Jourdain discovered to his delight that he had been speaking prose for more than forty years without knowing it.[2] Children regularly indulge in hyperbole long before they learn the word, and equally ignorant parents have been known to accuse them of fibbing. When Michal spoke sarcastically to David, she succeeded in alienating him, although neither of them had a word for 'irony' (2 Sam. 6:20).

For words to be intended in a non-literal sense it is not even necessary that the speaker should be familiar with the distinction between literal and non-literal. It is well known that a person speaking his mother tongue is normally unconscious of grammar. Speech is for the most part a spontaneous and unselfconscious act, and only when we stand back from our own acts of speech to examine them analytically do we begin to ask about them the sort of questions raised in this book. The creative act of imagination in which a poet gives birth to a metaphor, and the appreciative act of the reader who lays himself open to the resultant poem, allowing it to make its own impact on his mind, are both distinct from the act of the scholar who subjects the poem to critical study. Thus, even if it could be proved that an ancient speaker or writer had never stood back at a critical distance from his own speech, it would not follow that he intended his words to be taken literally.

No doubt in any community there will be someone who takes everything literally, someone whose leg you dare not pull for fear that it will come away in your hands. We have already taken note of the frequent use in the Fourth Gospel of dramatic irony, in which the interlocutor takes at their face value words which were intended to be understood metaphorically (pp. 104–5). It is quite likely that some of the difficulties of communication which Paul experienced in his Gentile churches were due to a Greek failure to recognise the figurative vividness of his Semitic speech: for some of his hearers at Thessalonica, like some modern scholars, took literally what he had said to them about eschatology (1 Thess. 5:1–10), and some of his hearers at Corinth took literally what he said about resurrection of

[2] Molière, *Le Bourgeois Gentilhomme* II.iv.

the body (1 Cor. 15:35–50). But we have no grounds whatever for supposing that literalists were commoner in the days of Isaiah and Paul than they are today. Indeed, the converse is more likely. Because the path of biological evolution has led from the simple to the infinitely complex, it is fatally easy to assume that the same must hold good for the evolution of society or of language. Admittedly a word must have been used literally before it could be turned into a metaphor. But it would be wrong to infer from this that there was a literalist period in the history of primitive man which antedated the emergence of metaphor. If there is any correlation between literalism and the evolution of language, the biblical evidence would suggest that literalism came quite late on the scene, the product of that semi-sophistication which is the parent of pedantry. Where we find both a literal and a metaphorical version of a saying or event, it is commonly the literal which is secondary. The earliest traditions of Israel's history were recorded in ballads, and at some time later than the accession of David collections of these were made, of which the names of two have survived: 'The Book of the Wars of Yahweh' (Numb. 21:14) and 'The Book of Yashar' (2 Sam. 1:18). Among the fragments to be preserved out of the second of these is Joshua's prayer at the battle of Aijalon.

> 'Stand still, O Sun, in Gibeon,
> Stand, Moon, in the Vale of Aijalon.'
> So the sun stood still and the moon halted
> Until a nation could take vengeance on its enemies
> (Josh. 10:12 f.).

In his poetic style the bard records a prayer that the day would last long enough to ensure the complete rout of the enemy, and in the same poetic style he describes the granting of the request. It was a later and pedantic prose-writer who transformed the prayer into an unnecessary and improbable miracle: 'the sun stayed in mid heaven and made no haste to set for almost a whole day.' We have seen in Chapter Six how Isaiah in the eighth century B.C. used two vivid metaphors of counterfeit silver and adulterated wine to depict the corruption of the nation's morals, and how more than five centuries later the Septuagint translator took them literally. When Mark tells of the rending of the temple curtain, he leaves little room for doubt that to him this is a figurative description of the effect of

7

the crucifixion, closely parallel to the assertion in Eph. 2:14 that on the cross Jesus demolished the dividing wall between Jew and Gentile, or to the picture drawn in Heb. 10:19 f. of the crucified Jesus opening up a new and living way through the temple curtain into that heavenly presence of which the holy of holies was but a shadowy symbol. The action in Mark's scene never leaves Calvary. 'Jesus uttered a loud cry and breathed his last. The curtain of the temple was torn in two, from top to bottom; and when the centurion, who stood facing him, saw that he thus breathed his last, he said, "Truly this man was Son of God" ' (Mark 15:37–39). The rending of the veil removes the barrier of incomprehension between man and God, and opens the way for the centurion's declaration of faith, which he makes as spokesman of the Gentile church that is to be. It is the later Matthew who takes the verse literally, links the rending veil with an earthquake and the opening of graves, and makes the earthquake the cause of the centurion's awe.

These three examples will suffice to show that the literal is by no means always the primitive. They can of course be matched by sayings or stories which were meant to be taken literally and subsequently spiritualised or allegorised. There is no one-way traffic between the literal and the metaphorical. Once that is established we can come without prejudice to the tests by which the intention of an author may be determined.

1. Explicit statement

There are four ways in which an author may expressly indicate that he does not intend his words to be taken literally. This test might seem too obvious to be worthy of mention, were it not so often curiously disregarded.

(a) The author may use a descriptive term. The evangelists give the name parable or similitude to many of the stories of Jesus. Paul once warns his readers that he is using allegory (Gal. 4:24), thrice that he is using a figure of speech (Rom. 6:19; 1 Cor. 15:32; Gal. 3:15). In Eph. 5:32–33 the readers are instructed that the metaphorical application (*mysterion*) of Gen. 2:24 to Christ and the church does not cancel the literal obligation of mutual love between husband and wife. John tells us that the great city in whose streets the bodies of the martyrs are to be exposed to the view of all nations is named in allegory 'Sodom and Egypt where also their Lord was crucified' (Rev. 11:8). The world-wide city can be no other than Rome, which inherits the depravity of Sodom, the persecuting despotism of Egypt and the faithlessness of Jerusalem. Yet there are still commentators who ignore John's statement and identify the city with Jerusalem.

(b) Biblical writers frequently draw attention to their use of metaphor by alternating it with simile.

> I am a festering sore to Ephraim
> A cancer to the house of Judah.
> So when Ephraim found that he was sick,
> Judah that he was covered with sores,
> Ephraim went to Assyria,
> He went in haste to the Great King;
> But he has no power to cure you
> Or to heal your sores.
> Yes indeed, I will be fierce as a panther to Ephraim,
> Fierce as a lion to Judah—
> I will maul the prey and go,
> Carry it off beyond hope of rescue—
> I, the Lord   (Hos. 5:12–14; cf. 7:11–12).

Similarly, when Paul says of the church in Corinth, 'You are the body of Christ' (1 Cor. 12:27), there should never have been any doubt that this is a metaphor, since it comes as the climax of fourteen verses of simile.

(c) Sometimes the referent of a metaphor is disclosed by the addition of a defining noun (usually in the genitive): 'the sword of the Spirit' (Eph. 6:17), 'the good fight of faith' (1 Tim. 6:12), 'the unleavened bread of sincerity and truth' (1 Cor. 5:8). The author of Hebrews defines the new and living way which Christ has opened up through the temple curtain as 'the way of his flesh' (Heb. 10:20). Is it not then astonishing that, when we are told that the dividing wall between Jew and Gentile which Christ destroyed by his death was a 'wall of hostility' (Eph. 2:14), some scholars should have argued that the epistle could not have been written until after A.D. 70, when the literal wall, the parapet in the outer court of the temple beyond which Gentiles were forbidden to go, was destroyed by the armies of Titus?

(d) Many metaphors are marked by the addition of a qualifying adjective: 'heavenly father' (Matt. 6:14); 'the true bread' (John 6:32); 'a circumcision not done by human hands' (Col. 2:11); 'come to him, our living stone . . . let yourselves be built, as living stones, into a spiritual temple; become a holy priesthood, to offer spiritual sacrifices acceptable to God through Jesus Christ' (1 Pet. 2:4–5).

2. *Impossible literality*

When Matthew tells us (3:5) that 'Jerusalem and all Judaea and the whole Jordan valley' responded to the summons of John the Baptist, we take it for granted that he is thinking metonymically of the inhabitants; it does not occur to us that he might be thinking literally of buildings or terrain. Amos too leaves no foothold for the literalist in his warning to Israel to abandon hope of escape from the coming judgment.

> If they dig down to Sheol,
> Thence shall my hand take them;
> If they climb up to heaven,
> Thence will I bring them down.
> If they hide on the top of Carmel,
> There will I search out and take them;
> If they conceal themselves from me in the depths of the sea,
> There will I bid the sea-serpent bite them   (Amos 9:2–3).

3. *Low correspondence*

In an earlier generation scholars of the greatest eminence held that in primitive society anthropomorphic imagery was taken literally. 'The old anthropomorphic language continued to be used as symbolic imagery long after the belief in the literal truth had disappeared, and the change in idea took place invisibly below the apparent uniformity of the language. Christians and Jews today habitually speak of the Hand and Eyes of God, and of God's throne in the heavens, and so on. No doubt the process by which what was once understood literally came to be understood symbolically was a gradual one, with many confused intermediate stages in which the idea hovered between the literal and symbolical . . . We can be pretty sure that the Hebrew who first put into writing the story of Babel . . . understood it quite literally, and that the later Hebrew who incorporated these old documents in the book of Genesis understood them as figures.'[3] We have already seen that there is no a priori reason why we should regard this as an accurate account of linguistic origins, and later in this chapter we must discuss the evidence which has been advanced to support it. The point which concerns us for the moment is that Bevan could not have written such a paragraph except about images with a high degree of correspondence. Where the degree of correspondence is low, literalism cannot arise. Bevan would not have wished to argue that there was a time in the dawn of Israel's history when God was literally conceived as a lion (Amos 3:8), as a spring (Jer. 2:13) or as a bird-catcher (Hos. 7:12).

4. High development

There is no surer index of the linguistic awareness of an author than the degree to which he exploits imaginatively the ramifications of his own imagery.

> When Israel was a boy, I loved him;
> I called my son out of Egypt . . .
> It was I who taught Ephraim to walk,
> I who had taken them in my arms;
> But they did not know that I harnessed them in leading-strings
> And led them with bonds of love—
> That I had lifted them like a little child to my cheek
> (Hos. 11:1–4).

With less pathos, but no less vigour, a later prophet explores what is entailed in calling God Father, Lord and Creator.

> A son honours his father, and a slave goes in fear of his master. If I am a father, where is the honour due to me? If I am a master, where is the fear due to me? . . . Have we not all one father? Did not one God create us? Why do we violate the covenant of our forefathers by being faithless to one another? . . . The Lord has borne witness against you on behalf of the wife of your youth. You have been unfaithful to her,

---

[3] E. Bevan, *Symbolism and Belief*, p. 44.

though she is your partner and your wife by solemn covenant. Did not the one God make her, both flesh and spirit?

(Mal. 1:6; 2:10, 14).

5. *Juxtaposition of images*

A single vivid image might in isolation beguile the hearer into supposing that it was intended literally. But the piling up of images, which we have seen to be characteristic of the Hebraic style, is an effective antidote.

> What you conceive and bring to birth is chaff and stubble;
> A wind like fire shall devour you   (Isa. 33:11).

In the passage from Malachi quoted in the previous paragraph the parallel ideas of fatherhood and creation are mutually explanatory. So too the psalmist guards against a misunderstanding of the royal ideology by linking the metaphor of sonship with that of appointment.

> He will say to me, 'You are my father,
> My God, my rock and my safe refuge.'
> I will appoint him my first-born,
> High above the kings of the earth   (Ps. 89:26–27).

The New Testament writers who take over this ideology and adapt it to Christ are well aware of the nature of the language they have inherited. 'On the human level he was born of David's stock, but on the level of spirit, the Spirit of holiness, he was appointed Son of God with full power through his resurrection from death' (Rom. 1:3–4). 'He is the image of the invisible God, first-born over all creation' (Col. 1:15). 'In this final age he has spoken to us in a Son, whom he appointed heir to the whole universe' (Heb. 1:2). 'He did not confer upon himself the glory of becoming high priest; it was granted by God, who said to him, "You are my Son; today I have begotten you".' (Heb. 5:5). In this last passage the author of Hebrews has correctly interpreted Ps. 2:7 as a declaration of appointment, not of parentage.

6. *Originality*

All words are liable to fatigue and exhaustion through overuse, and metaphors are particularly susceptible. When a metaphor comes fresh from the creative mind of poet or prophet, no listener is likely to mistake it for literal speech. But metaphors wear out and die, and a dead metaphor is a new literalism. When a metaphor is very familiar, the hearer may cease to be aware of its dual reference to both vehicle and tenor and take it to refer literally to the tenor alone. Those scholars whom we criticised in Chapter Seven for denying that 'the body of Christ' was a metaphor presumably took the word 'body' to *mean* 'the visible, organised form which an entity assumes'. They could then argue that, since the church is the outward, organic form of Christ's presence in the world, it is literally the body of Christ. What they failed to see is that the English word 'body', in this etiolated sense, is a dead metaphor, a victim of linguistic senescence which had not begun to overtake the Greek word *sôma* in Paul's day, when the metaphor was still vivid and fresh.

We may use these tests, singly or in combination, to rule out the literal interpretation of a passage, and still find ourselves left with a tantalising choice of figures, as is the case with the notorious crux of 1 Cor. 2:6–8.

> I speak wisdom among those who have reached maturity, yet not a wisdom belonging to this age, or to the rulers of this age in their waning power. I speak God's hidden wisdom, his secret purpose framed before all ages to bring us to glory, wisdom which none of the rulers of this age knew, since if they had known it they would not have crucified the Lord of glory.

The general drift of Paul's argument is not in dispute. He has heard that there are divisions in the church at Corinth, each party claiming that one or other of the apostles is the sole fount of wisdom; and his reply is that any 'wisdom' which divides the one church of Christ is inspired by 'the spirit of the world' (2:12), by the ethos of 'the existing order' (1:28), which accords a high value to prestige and rank, especially when they are based on knowledge, wealth or birth, and which God by the crucifixion has declared obsolescent. But who are the rulers? We have seen in the last chapter that, according to the Old Testament theology of politics, a nation was conceived as being under the dual control of the earthly monarch and the angelic prince or guardian; and ever since the second century opinion has been divided as to which of the two Paul had in mind in the passage now under discussion. Now the only rulers who could be said *literally* to have had responsibility for the crucifixion were Caiaphas and the Sanhedrin, Herod and Pilate (cf. Acts. 4:25–28), and they are excluded by the test of impossible literality, since by the time 1 Corinthians was written (*c.* A.D. 56) they were all dead, and so could scarcely have been described as 'waning in power' or 'declining to their end'. It is, however, possible that Paul was referring to these same persons figuratively (i.e. by synecdoche) as typical representatives of the old world order to which he accuses the quarrelsome Corinthians of still belonging, when they ought to belong to the new world inaugurated by Christ and inspired by the Spirit of God.[4] If this is so, his intended meaning is closely parallel to that of the Fourth Evangelist when he says, 'he was in the world . . . but the world did not recognise him' (John 1:10): the failure of the whole is implied in the failure of the typical and representative part. The other possibility is that Paul is using the word 'rulers' metaphorically of the angelic principalities and powers which stand invisible behind the thrones of earthly princes. In that case the rulers would be identical with the 'angels' of 6:1–3, where, in dealing with a report that the Corinthians are taking their disputes into the public, pagan law-courts, Paul reminds them that, according to Dan. 7:22, 'the saints of the Most High' are destined to be the judges when the world is on trial, and he adds for good measure that 'the world' includes those angelic authorities to whom he alludes in almost every letter. But now that the choice is clear before us we can recognise how trivial it turns out to be. The path of synecdoche and the path of metaphor lead to the same destination of meaning: in each case the referent is the same, the governing powers of the old order; and the only point that remains in doubt is whether, in this particular instance, Paul envisaged those governing powers in his mind's eye as vested in representative human beings or in symbolic angels. It is as though we were to

---

[4] This view was first proposed by J. B. Lightfoot, *Notes on the Epistles of St. Paul*, p. 174, though without any identification of the figure of speech which this interpretation assumes.

debate whether the Battle of Britain was won by 'the few' and George VI and Winston Churchill, or by John Bull, Britannia, St. George and the British lion.

There is, then, an accumulation of evidence that the biblical writers were not only skilful handlers of words (which is obvious), but were also well aware of the nature of their tools. Yet this conclusion would have been challenged by many Old and New Testament scholars who, whatever their differences of approach, were agreed about one thing: that biblical man was prescientific and therefore naive, that he inhabited a mythical world, and that his intellectual development was at the stage which some of them have designated 'the mythopoeic mind'. This was the presupposition which prompted, for example, Bultmann's influential essay on demythologising. In the opening paragraphs he summarised 'the cosmology of the New Testament', the pictorial framework within which men tried to make sense of their existence and history. The world is envisaged as a three-story house, in which mankind lives on the ground floor, God and his angels on the floor above, and some much less desirable tenants in the basement. So far from being his castle, man's home is constantly being invaded by the occupants of the other two storeys. History 'is set in motion and controlled by these supernatural powers. This aeon is held in bondage by Satan, sin, and death . . . and hastens towards its end. That end will come very soon, and will take the form of cosmic catastrophe . . . All this is the language of mythology . . . To this extent the kerygma is incredible to modern man, for he is convinced that the mythical view of the world is obsolete.'[5] Bultmann's thesis contained two enormous and unargued assumptions: that the mythical creature he called 'modern man' would be more comfortable among the abstractions of existentialist philosophy than with the picture language of the Bible; and that biblical man took that picture language as flat statement of fact. It also employed three conflicting definitions of myth. The complexities and ambiguities of the word 'myth' are the theme of Chapter Thirteen. For the moment we are concerned only with the supposed naiveté of biblical man, and on this there are four points that need to be made:

1. Just as words are not identical with their referents, so

[5] *Kerygma and Myth*, pp. 3 ff.

7*

linguistic statements (i.e. statements about words) are not to be confused with metaphysical statements (i.e. statements about reality).
If I say that the words 'king' and 'father' when applied to God are
metaphors, that is a linguistic statement. If I say that God is the
archetypal king and father, from whom all human kingship and
fatherhood are derived, that is a metaphysical statement; and the
second does not invalidate the first. Consider then the following two
quotations from a book by S. Mowinckel. 'At the "enthronement
festival" . . . ancient Israel witnessed Yahweh's arrival as king,
when he literally founded his kingdom.' 'The concept of Yahweh as
king would hardly be adopted by the Israelites until they themselves had got a king, and, with him, an obvious occasion to bestow
on Yahweh this highest title of honour.'[6] Mowinckel believed that
there was an annual festival in Israel which was at one and the same
time the enthronement of the divine king and of his human
representative, the Davidic king. He was undoubtedly correct in
attributing to the ancient Israelites the belief that the divine kingship was primary and the human derivative, and also in recognising
that to bestow the title of king on God is to use a metaphor; yet
somehow he seems to have managed to confuse these two types of
statement. Could any ancient Israelite have been so simple as to
think that Yahweh actually became king for the first time at the
moment when his worshippers first addressed him by that title?
When they sang the psalms which begin with the words 'Yahweh
is king', they could have believed that this was the occasion 'when
he literally founded his kingdom', but only if they also believed that
he was not king the day before; and since, ex hypothesi, the festival
was an annual one, this is absurd.

2. From the surrounding culture of the ancient Near East and
from periods earlier than the dawn of Israelite history there comes
ample evidence of sophistication in the handling of mythical ideas.
Let us take, for example, the widespread belief that the king is
Son of God. The commissive aspect of this is plain enough. When a
subject said, 'May the king live for ever' (Neh. 2:3; cf. 1 Kings
1:31; Dan. 2:4) or addressed the king as 'God' (Ps. 45:6; Acts
12:22), he was not merely indulging in formal court flattery, but
committing himself to a belief in the sacredness of the king's office

---

[6] *The Psalms in Israel's Worship*, pp. 113, 125.

and the inviolacy of his person. This is illustrated in Israel's history by the episode in which David has the sleeping Saul at his mercy and says, 'God forbid that I should lift a finger against the Lord's anointed' (1 Sam. 26:11; cf. 24:6). But the royal ideology had also an important function in ancient law. 'Every living king was Horus, and every dead king was Osiris, for Osiris was the good king, who had been murdered by his evil brother Seth, but whose throne had eventually been assigned to his son Horus as the result of a lawsuit before the gods themselves. The foundation of the kingship was not merely that the king was divine and descended from the gods who had founded the earth, it was also the legal fact that the king had been vindicated in a divine law-court'.[7] If the king was divine, there might seem to be a prima facie case for saying that his successor was literally the divine son of his divine father. But it is common knowledge that early Egyptian history is divided up into twenty-six dynasties; and a change of dynasty occurs precisely when it is acknowledged that the successor is not literally the son of his predecessor. As Fairman goes on to show, even usurpers regarded previous dynasties as their ancestors, and the rite of sacred marriage was used as a legal fiction to validate the succession (p. 77). O. R. Gurney is equally emphatic that in Mesopotamia 'the fiction of a divine birth' was a legal device designed to secure the legitimation of the king, and that among the Hittites 'the usage may have been introduced from Syria or Egypt and have been adopted by the Hittites as little moie than a form of words'.[8] When Alexander the Great defeated the Persians and annexed Egypt, he took over from the Pharaohs the practice of ruler-worship. The historian of his conquests, Arrian, after recording the honours paid to him, comments: 'As to his claiming descent from a god, this too seems to me no great fault, but only a device to impress his subjects' (*Anabasis* vii.29). Subsequently, in the assembly at Athens Demosthenes argued that, if Alexander wished, he should be regarded as the son both of Zeus and of Poseidon,[9] and this remark was probably intended as a cynical reductio ad absurdum.

---

[7] H. W. Fairman, 'The kingship rituals of Egypt', in *Myth, Ritual and Kingship*, ed. S. H. Hooke, pp. 75 f.

[8] In the essay on 'Hittite Kingship' in the same volume. Cf. R. Labat, *La Caractère religieux de la royaume assyrio-babylienne*, ch. iii.

[9] Hyperides, *In Demosthenem*, fr. 8.

Later, in New Testament times, the emperor Augustus permitted emperor-worship in the eastern provinces, where it had been the long accepted custom. In Rome itself only the three paranoiacs, Caligula, Nero and Domitian, demanded divine honours during their lifetime. For the rest deification was granted or withheld on death by the Senate and carried the legal corollary that the decrees of the deified emperor remained on the statute book, while those of the others lapsed. How seriously they themselves took this legal fiction may be judged by the whimsical words of the dying Claudius, 'I think I am becoming a god.' No doubt in all these cultures deification had the effect of making the monarchy a sacred office, but sacredness is not synonymous with godhead.

3. 'The mythopoeic mind' is supposed, by those who favour the expression, to be characteristic of primitive man. The primitive, they tell us, does not analyse his experience into word and object, symbol and thing symbolised, but grasps all in a unitary act of perception. One example of this is that the early Greek would say 'Zeus is raining' (ὕει Ζεύς), not meaning that Zeus is sending rain or picturing Zeus as an old man in the sky with a watering-can, but identifying Zeus with the rain. Just as Zeus descended on Danae in a shower of golden rain to make her the mother of Perseus, so Zeus-rain descends on mother earth to fertilise her. This example admirably illustrates what is meant by 'mythopoeic mind' and 'unitary perception', but in all other respects it is a somewhat unfortunate choice. If Zeus was conceptually indistinguishable from the rain, watery or golden, what are we to make of the stories that he came upon Antiope as a satyr, on Leda as a swan, and on Europa as a bull? The phrase 'Zeus is raining' is in fact a quotation from Homer (*Il.* xii.25), and since in another passage Homer depicts Zeus sitting in heaven with two cauldrons beside him, one of good fortune and the other of bad, impartially ladling them out over the earth, we might suppose that the mental image of the old man with the watering-can would not have come amiss to him. By the time of Aristophanes (*Nub.* 368) the conventional expression had become a joke:

Socrates: There is no Zeus.
Strepsiades: Then who's raining?

Unitary perception is, to be sure, a well-attested phenomenon, but it is characteristic not of the primitive but of the creative mind in all ages. It appears to be primitive only because in all cultures poetry has developed before prose.

4. In any case, attempts to reconstruct the mentality of primitive man have very little to do with the understanding of biblical literature. We may leave the anthropologists to decide whether there ever was a period in human intellectual development to which the term mythopoeic could apply. If there was, it already lay far in the past before ever the earliest document of the Old Testament was written. There is nothing primitive about the court history of David or the J narrative of the Pentateuch.

Part Three

HISTORY, MYTH
AND ESCHATOLOGY

Chapter Twelve

Language and History

Much of the Bible consists of historical narrative, and parts at least of the narrative are central to the biblical faith. To the people of the Old Testament God was 'the Lord your God who brought you out of Egypt, out of the land of slavery' (Exod. 20:1), and the gospel of the early church was news about recent events, the activity of God in the life, death and resurrection of Jesus. What is meant by 'the activity of God', and how the contingencies of history can be related to the eternal truths of revelation are two of the perennial problems of the philosopher and the theologian. Ours is the preliminary and more modest task of observing the types of language in which the biblical writers record their history and express their involvement in it. Two of these linguistic forms, myth and eschatology, require special treatment and will be the subjects of the next two chapters. But much of what needs to be said about historical language will be a recapitulation of what has already been said about language in general, since it exhibits the same varieties of use and abuse, the same complexities of meaning, the same kinds of semantic change, the same ambiguities and the same figures of speech.

A narrative is not properly called history unless it has genuine historical referents, persons and objects that really existed and events that really happened. The events must be adequately attested, and it is well to recall that the ancient Israelite had in his legal system ample acquaintance with the notion of sufficient attestation (see pp. 157–9). The primary duty of the historian then is to discover 'what actually happened' (*was eigentlich geschehen ist*). But we shall find that this concept is far more complex than has commonly been supposed by those who have quoted this phrase of Leopold von Ranke. In linguistic terms it is a particular application of the general principle of identifying the referent. Yet no historical statement is purely referential.[1] Most of the events which make up the lives of men and nations have not been thought worthy of record. Out of what is available to him (because it has seemed significant to others), the historian selects what he judges to be significant to him and his readers. Bare facts are never significant in themselves, but only when they are brought into relation with a social tradition and are thus seen in a framework of interpretation; and such traditions and frameworks are themselves built of interpreted events. Historiography thus inevitably brings into play the cohesive and commissive aspects of language as well as the referential, as may be most clearly seen in two forms of historical record, the commemorative festival and the celebratory monument.

The lexical distinction between 'historical' and 'historic' is by no means absolute; but by and large usage has decreed that 'historical' places the emphasis on the actuality of events, 'historic' on their significance and seismic effect. A historic event is one which is believed to have changed the course of history, and so has become a symbol or emblem of the interpretative tradition within which it is recorded. In English history one such emblematic event is the signing of the Magna Carta, since this feudal document came in the course of time to be regarded as the foundation of constitutional government and of the legal rights and liberties of the subject. This process entailed some considerable recasting of history. But, as Butterfield has pointed out, 'it was to prove of the greatest moment to us that by the early seventeenth century our antiquarians had formulated our history as the history of liberty.'[2] By his interpretation of the past the historian helps to determine the future. He is in effect saying to his people, 'This is the way which your tradition has marked out for you to follow.'

The past, moreover, is not accessible to us by direct scrutiny, but only through the interrogation of witnesses. History has a factual content, but it comes to the historian not as fact but as evidence, emanating from persons with whom he must engage in conversation. The possibility of such conversation depends on the historian's ability to 'speak the same language' as his source. Just as Odysseus found on his visit to Hades that the dead seer Teiresias could not

[1] 'Antiquities are history defaced, or some remnants of history which have casually escaped the shipwreck of time.' F. Bacon, *Advancement of Learning* II.ii.1.
[2] H. Butterfield, *Man on his Past*, p. 27.

speak to him until his inarticulate ghost had been brought to life by the blood of a sacrifice, so from the life-blood of his own sympathy the historian gives a blood transfusion to the ghosts of the past. Sources are sources only in virtue of the questions which the historian addresses to them, and he to some extent creates his own past by his choice of questions.[3] Thus at one point after another value judgments are involved, and responsible and objective historiography cannot and ought not to ignore or evade this element of subjectivity.

In our study of the biblical narratives there is a further important consideration. The biblical writers believed in dual causation: at one level events could be explained as the effects of earthly causes, while at another level they were believed to be acts of God. Some analogy to their way of thinking is provided by drama. In Shakespeare's *Macbeth*, we may discuss the contribution made by Macbeth himself, by Lady Macbeth, by the witches, by Malcolm, by the force of circumstance etc., to the ultimate downfall of the central character. But there is another sense in which everything that happens in the play is caused by Shakespeare; the course of events is what it is because that is the way he wrote it. The external responsibility of the author does not detract from the internal independence of his characters, nor are his attitudes and purposes to be confused with theirs.[4] In the story of Joseph, the human actors are fully responsible for events at one level, the divine author at another: 'You intended evil against me, but God meant it for good' (Gen. 50:20). Jesus too can say of his approaching death, 'The Son of man goes the way that is written of him, but alas for the man by whom the Son of man is betrayed' (Mark 14:21). He acts out the drama in which he has been cast in the central role, but within the drama Judas and the other actors are the responsible causes of events. Now the modern historian restricts his interest to action within the drama, and does not consider that he has performed his task unless he can trace the sequence of cause and effect in the human affairs he is studying. He is likely to regard some of the biblical narratives as unhistorical on the ground that their

---

[3] 'It has been said that though God cannot alter the past, historians can; it is perhaps because they can be useful to Him in this respect that He tolerates their existence.' Samuel Butler, *Erewhon Revisited*, ch. 14.

[4] See D. L. Sayers, *The Mind of the Maker*, ch. 5.

predominant interest in the playwright has led to the omission of information without which the sequence of cause and effect cannot be reconstructed. But the fact that they are unhistorical in this narrow sense does not logically entail the conclusion that they are unhistorical in the wider sense, i.e. that they do not have for their referents persons who really existed and events that actually happened.[5]

In most of the Old Testament narratives the factual element is sufficiently to the fore to justify their use as reliable sources for the writing of a history of Israel. But they are unashamedly one-sided. Events are seen not merely through Jewish eyes, but through the eyes of the victorious faction within Israel. We do not have an Egyptian account of the Exodus, or Ahab's version of his struggle with Elijah, in which each was honestly convinced that the other was rocking the national boat. ' "Is that you, you troubler of Israel?" "I am not the troubler of Israel, but you and your father's family" ' (1 Kings 18:17–18). Antiochus Epiphanes is given no chance to state his case against the nationalist fanaticism of the Maccabees. But exactly the same would have to be said about the records of Greek and Roman history, not to mention the early history of the Christian church.

The interplay of the factors we have observed is well illustrated by a variety of other biblical narratives which are all too often regarded as the antithesis or negation of history: saga, legend, novel and pseudepigraph.

1. Saga is the name we give to historical memories which antedate written records; and, since in Israel the keeping of written records began with the reigns of David and Solomon,[6] it is correctly applied to all the earlier parts of the Israelite tradition. Much of it must have been preserved in ballad form (Numb. 21:14, 27), of which the Song of Deborah (Judg. 5) is the best surviving example. The primary purpose was celebration, and the language poetic, allusive and imaginative. From such evidence it may be difficult to reconstruct a clear description of the historical referent, and we need to remind ourselves that the most accurate knowledge

[5] See C. F. Evans, *Explorations in Theology* II, pp. 18–33.
[6] The Book of Yashar (1 Sam. 1:18; cf. Josh. 10:13) included a poem by David and therefore cannot have been compiled earlier. The earliest prose work mentioned is the Annals of Solomon (1 Kings 11:41).

of fact does not guarantee a valid interpretation of an event, nor does some degree of error or vagueness of detail necessarily vitiate its emblematic power.

2. Legend is the embellishment of the story of genuine persons and events with anecdotes or details supposed to be illustrative of their character or significance. As long as we concentrate on the referential aspect of history, we shall dismiss legend as unhistorical. Yet the growth of a legend is itself a fact of history. Moses, David and Solomon were historical figures, whose real existence it would be folly to doubt, even though the quest of the historical Moses, David and Solomon is gravely impeded by the accretion of legend. Yet the legend cannot be ignored, since it is testimony to the emblematic status which these three held in their people's history. Moses undoubtedly had something to do with the origins of Israelite law, for which his name became a metonym; but legend ascribed to him not only the authorship of the whole written Torah, but also the oral tradition of rabbinical interpretation (*Pirke Aboth* 1:1). Many no doubt took the legend at its face value, but it must have been obvious to some that it contained an element of legal fiction, since some statutes were known to have been promulgated at a later date (1 Sam. 30:25), and the rabbinic tradition preserved the names of the rabbis from whom its dicta had originated. David was undoubtedly a musician and poet; but legend made him author of the psalms, although the Psalter included psalms explicitly derived from other sources; and the Chronicler transformed him into the architect of the temple and organiser of its priesthood and liturgy, in spite of the earlier record that a prophetic oracle of Nathan had forbidden all this (2 Sam. 7:1–16). Behind this development we can detect at least three influences at work: the use of the name David as a dynastic title ('the psalms of David' were probably in the first instance a collection for use in the royal chapel), the idealisation of the monarchy, and the claim of the post-exilic priesthood, at a time when the Davidic dynasty was discontinued, that the temple worship of their own day was the true perpetuation of the Davidic tradition. There was undoubtedly some foundation to Solomon's reputation for wisdom (foolish though he proved to be in economic administration); but legend made him not only the author of Proverbs, but a repository of universal knowledge (Wisd. 7:15–22; 8:7–8). These three emblematic figures play the

same part in Israel's history as Magna Carta has done in the history of England. It was of the greatest moment for Israel that her historians saw her history as the arena for the implementation of divine law, for the ordering of daily life by divine wisdom, and for the organisation of society around a divinely ordained worship.

3. Although a novel is an overtly fictitious narrative, it may nevertheless be of great value to the historian. *Chamber's Biographical Dictionary* says of James I of England that 'perhaps the best estimate of the man is Scott's representation of him in *The Fortunes of Nigel*'. In the biblical literature there are several works which we might classify as novels (e.g. Ruth, Esther, Jonah, Susanna), but the one which most openly asserts its fictional character is Judith. It opens with a garbling of history too ostentatious to be other than deliberate: Nebuchadnezzar is said to be reigning over the Assyrians from his capital Nineveh, and to be a contemporary of Arphaxad (Gen. 11:10) and Arioch (Gen. 14:1); and at a later point one of the characters relates a brief history of Israel down to a date many years later than the death of the real Nebuchadnezzar (5:19). Judith is not meant to be a historical character at all. Her name means 'Jewess', and she is intended by the author, writing at the time of the Maccabaean war of liberation, to be the ideal Jewish heroine for a period of national crisis. The book has therefore some of the attributes of parable, since it is ostensibly about one period but actually about another; and, once this is recognised, it tells us a great deal about second-century attitudes and aspirations, in which patriotism had become synonymous with religion.

4. There is a similar parabolic quality about a pseudepigraph, which is a work purporting to be written by a well-known figure of antiquity about the critical conditions of his day, but actually concerned with an analogous crisis in the time of the real author. During the three hundred years from 167 B.C. to A.D. 135, when Jewish nationalism was under real or imagined threat from foreign persecution, this was the established convention of resistance movement literature, and works were attributed to such worthies as Lamech, Enoch, Baruch and Ezra. The book variously known as 2 Esdras or 4 Ezra, for example, claims to record the visions of Shealtiel, son of Jeconiah and father of Zerubbabel, thirty years after the destruction of Jerusalem by the Babylonians in 587

B.C.;[7] and it is generally agreed that its actual date of composition was thirty years after the destruction of Jerusalem in A.D. 70 by the Romans, and that the author was grappling with the implications of that catastrophe for the Jewish religion. The one representative of this genre in the Old Testament is Daniel, written ostensibly about persecution of the Jewish religion in sixth-century Babylon, but actually to encourage resistance to the persecutions of Antiochus Epiphanes four centuries later.

All historical statements contain, then, implicitly or explicitly, elements other than referential, but some of them are more frankly, perhaps more intentionally, evaluative than others. Let us consider the following three statements about a less remote past.

A   Charles I was decapitated.
B   Charles I was executed.
C   Charles I was martyred.

There is no problem about identifying the referent, which in each case is the same: Charles lost his head. But the event was one over which sides were taken and passions roused, and its seismic effect is still felt to this day. Statement A appears to be purely referential, but only because the speaker has not disclosed his reasons for thinking this event to be of greater interest and importance than the death of 'some village Hampden', recorded only on a tombstone in a country churchyard. B and C are overtly interpretative: each speaker commits himself not only to a value judgment about the event of 1649, but also to the corresponding religious tradition and political stance. B is shorthand for: 'the advocates of parliamentary democracy, of whom I am one, hold that Charles presented such a threat to constitutional government that he was deservedly arraigned on a capital charge.' C is shorthand for: 'in the opinion of High Church Tories, with which I concur, Charles was entitled to uphold his rights as anointed monarch and died in so noble a cause that he must be enrolled in the army of martyrs.'

We expect the historian to be interested in the commissive statements as well as the referential. 'Erudition and acumen alone

---

[7] By a curious telescoping of history Shealtiel is identified with Ezra, who lived two centuries later.

will not suffice to answer the modest questions whether a statesman has, or has not, breathed the breath of life into the programme of his party, or a statute or tariff moulded the destiny of a society. Yet these questions are precisely those we ask our historians to answer for us, and the study of history would not long retain its high place as a chief instrument in liberal education if we seriously thought the historian could present us with nothing more satisfactory as an answer than a series of brilliant but wilful and contradictory "personal impressions".[8]

Nevertheless, as we saw earlier (p. 21), commissive statements cannot be true or false in quite the same way as referential statements (or the referential parts of statements) can be true or false; but they may be null because of what Austin called 'infelicities'. If then I assert that Charles I was martyred, you ought not to say that my statement is false, unless you mean simply that you disagree with it. But you may reasonably accuse me of hypocrisy, if you are sure that I do not actually hold the religious and political views such a statement entails, that I do not subscribe to the divine right of kings and would not vote for the restoration of absolute monarchy. It was just such an infelicity that Jesus detected in some of his fellow countrymen. 'You build the tombs of the prophets whom your fathers murdered, and so testify that you approve of the deeds your fathers did; they committed the murders and you provide the tombs' (Luke 11:47–48; cf. Matt. 23:29–32). The ostensible purpose of a tomb is to honour and perpetuate the memory of the dead. But a refusal to listen to a living prophet renders spurious any veneration paid to dead prophets. Those who reject Jesus and would like to dispose of him show that in reality they have sided not with the prophets but with those who killed them. They venerate only dead prophets, and the heavy tombs they build are designed to ensure that they shall never return to trouble the living.

The hostility between roundhead and cavalier was particularly bitter because they shared a common past which each interpreted differently. The antagonism between Christian and Jew reflected in the New Testament was a kind of civil war, because they too shared a common past. Paul recalls that in his former life as a

[8] A. E. Taylor, *The Faith of a Moralist* II, p. 132.

Pharisee 'I was outstripping many of my Jewish contemporaries in my boundless devotion to the traditions of my ancestors' (Gal. 1:14). But his conversion persuaded him that he and his fellow Jews had radically misunderstood their own history, failing to recognise that the true son of Abraham is he who shares Abraham's faith (Rom. 4:11–12; Gal. 3:7), that 'the true Jew is he who is such inwardly, and the true circumcision is of the heart, directed not by written precepts but by the Spirit' (Rom. 2:29), and that to identify religion with patriotism and national privilege is to deny the central affirmation of the Old Testament faith, that God is one (Rom. 3:29–30; cf. Deut. 6:4).

The historical tradition to which both Jew and Christian appeal has its root in the Exodus, and much can be learnt from the variety of descriptions of this event in the Old Testament.

A The Lord drove the sea back all night with a strong east wind, and turned the sea bed into dry land (Exod. 14:21).

B At the blast of your nostrils the sea piled up:
The waters stood up like a bank:
Out at sea the great deep congealed (Exod. 15:8).

C Awake, awake, put on your strength, O arm of the Lord,
Awake as you did long ago, in days gone by.
Was it not you who hacked Rahab in pieces and ran the dragon through?
Was it not you who dried up the sea, the waters of the great abyss,
And made the ocean depths a path for the ransomed?
(Isa. 51:9–10).

D Moses stretched out his hand over the sea . . . The waters were torn apart, and the Israelites went through the sea on dry ground, while the waters made a wall for them to right and to left (Exod. 14:21–22).

E On that day you shall tell your son, 'This commemorates what the Lord did for me when I came out of Egypt' (Exod. 13:8).

What actually happened to enable the Israelites to cross the sea and to prevent the Egyptian army from overtaking them? We have no means of telling. There is no description of the event in neutral terms. It was not first experienced as bare fact and later interpreted; it was experienced at the time as a divine deliverance.

Indeed, we can go further. The Israelites would never have set out from Egypt if they had not first been persuaded by Moses to expect a divine deliverance. In this way the interpretation was part of the actuality of the event, part of the chain of causation which led to its occurrence. The two earliest descriptions (A and B), one in prose and the other in poetry, are both theological, since both ascribe the effect to an act of God. They regard the event as miracle, but the miracle consists in a divine use of natural forces, not in the suspension of natural law. C comes from at least three centuries later and is couched in the language of myth. In the creation myth, which occurs in many forms throughout the ancient Near East, God defeated the primaeval ocean, the monster of many names (Rahab, Tiamat, Leviathan), cut it in two and created heaven and earth out of the two halves of its body. The prophet declares his conviction that this initial cosmic victory over the forces of chaos, darkness and evil was repeated at the Exodus, when the waters of the sea were cut in two to provide Israel with a path to safety; and he calls on God to do the same again by leading the Jewish exiles in Babylon in a new Exodus. He is of course well aware that for them the literal barrier to be crossed was sand, not water; yet this does not deter him from a vigorous use of the traditional imagery. D comes from the late, priestly strand of the Pentateuch, and several explanations of it are possible. We could say that Moses waving his wand over the sea represents a recrudescence of magic. We could say that the author was using B as his source and taking its poetic language literally. Or we could see in the two solid walls of water the influence of the creation myth, as in C. Whichever view we adopt, the important point to note is that the development is not *from* the magical, literalistic or mythical to a later rationalism. The early accounts are either naturalistic or poetical.

E stands outside this series and is a simple expression of commitment. The speaker is the head of a household celebrating the Passover, the annual commemoration of the Exodus, and he identifies himself with the generation which experienced it. For him the Exodus is a historic event precisely because it lives on into the present and lays claim to his allegiance. He repeats the story of Israel's deliverance in the stereotyped cadences of inherited ritual, yet there is a sense in which he understands 'what actually happened' better than any of the companions of Moses who on the day looked back in wonder at the turbulent waters. Important events do not disclose their full significance to the participants at the time of their occurrence. A couple celebrating their Golden Wedding may have only a hazy memory of the details of their wedding day and be unable to put a name to half the faces in a photograph of the guests; yet they have a knowledge of 'what actually happened' which was inaccessible to them as bride and groom. We cannot write a history of our own times.

An even greater variety of linguistic style may be observed in the New Testament descriptions of the death of Jesus:

A Then Jesus gave a loud cry and died (Mark 15:37).

B You used heathen men to crucify and kill him (Acts 2:23).

C Christ died for our sins (1 Cor. 15:3).

D For even the Son of Man did not come to be served but to serve, and to surrender his life as a ransom for many (Mark 10:45).

E He did not spare his own Son, but surrendered him for us all (Rom. 8:32).

F He was counted among the outlaws (Luke 22:37).

G For Christ, our paschal lamb, has been sacrificed (1 Cor. 5:7).

H The price was paid in precious blood, as it were of a lamb without mark or blemish—the blood of Christ. He was predestined before the foundation of the world, and in this last period of time he was made manifest for your sake (1 Pet. 1:19 f.).

I He despoiled the cosmic powers and authorities, and boldly made a spectacle of them, leading them as captives in his triumphal procession (Col. 2:15).

J My present bodily life is lived by faith in the Son of God who loved me and sacrificed himself for me (Gal. 2:20).

We have here exemplified ten different ways of speaking about a single event. A is a bare and neutral statement, apparently devoid of interpretation, presenting only the actuality of the event. B is an accusation with an implied value judgment. C, D, and E belong together: the first sentence gives a theological interpretation to the crucifixion, the second adds that this significance was not just read into the story by the church but was foreseen and intended by Jesus, and the third goes further by asserting that this meaning was put into the event by God. F describes one aspect of the cross by using the words of an Old Testament prophecy. G is a typological statement, H an eschatological one and I a mythological one. J is a personal confession of faith, gratitude and allegiance.

These ten statements, in spite of the differences between them, are all forms of historical record. We cannot say that where there is more interpretation there is less history, because the referent is in each case the same. Certainly the earliest mentions of Jesus in Greek and Latin literature show no higher degree of objectivity. Lucian calls Jesus 'that gibbeted sophist'[9] and Tacitus explains that Christian 'hatred of the human race' had its origin in Palestine, where Christ was executed as a trouble-maker by order of Pontius Pilate.[10]

With this list before us we may firmly rebut the facile depreciation of the historical element in Christianity by those who have argued that the evangelists and those who before them transmitted the gospel tradition were preachers, not historians. This may be a true description of their purpose, but not of their method; their purpose was to elicit faith in Christ, but their method was to tell a story. The faith they sought as preachers to elicit was a commitment to a particular interpretation of recent events which they claimed to be the expected outcome of their whole national history (F and G). They claimed furthermore that this interpretation, the idea that in the life, death and resurrection of Jesus God had fulfilled his promises to Israel and the purpose inaugurated with the call of Abraham, was not a theological hypothesis which had occurred to them for the first time when in a moment of tranquillity they recollected the stirring experiences of the past days. Although the events had not been fully understood at the time, they had been experienced when they happened as acts of God. It was from Jesus himself that they had learnt to see the hand of God in his life and theirs. Jesus had acted and spoken as he did at the prompting of a sense of divine vocation. The theological

[9] *De Morte Peregrini* 13.
[10] *Annals* xv.44.

interpretation of his ministry was accordingly no mere epipheno-menon superimposed on a series of bare events: it had produced the events.

This does not mean, however, that all the statements made in the apostolic testimony can be treated as if they were on a single level. Where so many varieties of language are used, it is of the utmost importance that we should recognise which sort of statement we are dealing with. In the quotation I above we are told that God (or Christ) won a victory over the cosmic powers and, like a successful Roman general, made a public display of their defeat in a triumph. But when and where are this victory and this triumph supposed to have taken place? One answer might be that for Paul and his con-temporaries the spirit world existed in its own right, quite indepen-dently of earthly existence and history, so that the victory must be thought of as a purely mythological victory over purely mytho-logical powers. But even a cursory glance at the context in Colos-sians shows this to be nonsense. Paul is talking about the cross, and the only victory he is interested in is the victory won there in the midst of what by worldly standards seemed to be defeat. It follows that the 'powers and authorities' must be personifications of those structures of power—political, social and religious, Roman and Jewish—which brought about the crucifixion. As in quotation C in the descriptions of the Exodus, mythological language is being used with a historical referent.[11]

A similar question must be asked about Mark's account of the death of Jesus. 'Then Jesus gave a loud cry and died. And the curtain of the temple was torn in two from top to bottom. And when the centurion who was standing opposite him saw how he died, he said, "Truly, this man was son of God" ' (Mark 15:37–39). What is the referent in the second sentence of this passage? Are we to take the splitting of the curtain as a physical event, taking place simultaneously with the death of Jesus but in a different location, or as a psychological event, a metaphorical description of the effect of Jesus' death on a Gentile onlooker? Mark's arrangement of his material strongly suggests that he intended it to be taken figura-tively: Jesus died, the curtain was split, the centurion saw and confessed him son of God. Yet this is not the way Matthew and Luke

---

[11] See also above, pp. 114–7.

have interpreted Mark's narrative, for both have detached the rending of the curtain from the centurion's confession and have linked it instead, the one with an earthquake, the other with an eclipse. It would appear that what began as a figurative statement has ended as a literal one: interpretation has been taken as actuality. A similar result is produced in at least one passage where the Scripture is said to be fulfilled, and the Old Testament passage is taken as a literal description of a New Testament event. Mark tells us that the soldiers at the crucifixion offered Jesus wine mixed with myrrh. Matthew, because he regards Ps. 69 as a prophetic description of the sufferings of Christ, and has the words of the psalm running in his mind, changes this to 'wine mixed with gall'. The compassionate offer of a narcotic drug has become an additional piece of derision and cruelty.[12]

In each of these two examples Mark's Gospel provides documentary evidence by which the historicity of the later writings may be tested. But having before us two such cases, we cannot help wondering whether the same process may not have been at work in other instances where no trustworthy control is available. Did John disagree with Mark's dating of the Last Supper and place the crucifixion on the afternoon before the Passover because he, like Paul, was accustomed to speak of Jesus as the paschal lamb, and so assumed that he had died at the time when the lambs were being sacrificed for the feast (John 18:28; 19:14, 36)? Are the stories of the virgin birth of Jesus the result of converting into historic actuality what began as theological interpretation of an Old Testament prophecy? Did the story of the flight into Egypt have any basis other than the prophecy of Hosea it was said to fulfil? It is not easy to give definitive answers to such questions. But it must, I think, be granted that at certain points the Gospel tradition has been embellished with new detail and even new events, because statements originally intended as theological or interpretative comment came to be taken as statements of fact. Yet such an admission does not commit us to a gradual whittling away of the main tradition, until we are left with theological comment on non-existent facts, like the bodiless grin of the Cheshire Cat. For it presupposes an earlier stage in which the various forms of impres-

[12] See B. Lindars, *New Testament Apologetic*, p. 101.

sive symbolic language listed above were used to describe actual events, and at that stage there is good reason to suppose that the memory of eye-witnesses remained in control. C. H. Dodd has pointed out that the New Testament writers did not draw on the whole corpus of messianic prediction. 'There has been some principle of selection at work, by which certain sides of the Messianic idea are held to be fulfilled, and others are set aside. What was the principle of selection? Surely the simplest explanation is that a true historical memory controlled the selection of prophecies. Those were held to have been fulfilled which were in general consonant with the memory of what Jesus had been, had said, had done, and had suffered.'[13] An interesting point to note is that we do not find a higher degree of literalness the nearer we get to the event.

On the other hand, the New Testament lays great emphasis on the actuality of the events it records. 'We cannot possibly give up speaking of the things we have seen and heard' (Acts 4:20). 'This is vouched for by an eyewitness, whose evidence is to be trusted' (John 19:35). The man born blind is held up as an example of the honesty which will not allow dogmatism to prevail over simple fact: 'All I know is this: once I was blind, now I can see' (John 9:25). Luke claims that in writing his Gospel he was 'following the traditions handed down to us by the original eyewitnesses' (Luke 1:2). Eyewitness was one of the qualifications for apostleship (Acts 1:21–2). The apostles were sent out to preach; but both words used for preaching in New Testament Greek connote the proclamation of news. This emphasis is naturally strongest in 1 John, written with one eye on a schismatical group who have denied the genuine humanity of Jesus. According to John there is no Christianity apart from the solid reality of the earthly life of Jesus as recorded in the apostolic tradition. 'It was there from the beginning; we have heard it; we have seen it with our own eyes; we looked upon it, and felt it with our own hands; and it is of this we tell. Our theme is the word of life. This life was made visible; we have seen it and bear our testimony' (1 John 1:1–2). Eternal life remains an unsubstantial dream unless in one man's life it has become earthly reality. 'God is love' is a statement void of real meaning, until we

[13] *History and the Gospel*, pp. 61 f.

see it translated into human and ethical terms in the ministry of Jesus (1 John 3:16; 4:7–12). 'To deny the Son is to be without the Father: to acknowledge the Son is to have the Father too' (1 John 2:23). Without the Jesus of history we know neither the Christ of faith nor the God he came to reveal.

Special importance attaches to the language used in the apostolic testimony about the resurrection (Acts 1:22; 2:32; 3:15; 10:40–41; 13:33; 1 Cor. 9:1; 15:3–8). It will help forward our argument to recognise that within what we have called the actuality of history there are three subdivisions—the public, the semi-public and the private. By public events I mean those in which both the outward occurrence and its eventfulness could have been observed by any-body who happened to be present (in this sense an event may be public even if there is in fact only one witness). By semi-public events I mean those in which there is an outward occurrence perceptible by all, but not all are in a position to recognise to the full the eventfulness of the occasion. According to Acts the con-version of Paul comes within this category, since his companions knew that something remarkable was happening to Paul without actually being able to share his experience. If there had been a third person at the well of Sychar, he could have reported the conversa-tion between Jesus and the Samaritan woman, but a proper appreciation of what happened depended on testimony which only the woman could give: 'Come and see a man who has told me everything I ever did' (John 4:29). A private event is one like the vision of Isaiah or the illumination of Gautama under the bo tree, and it can take place either in solitude or in a crowd. Semi-public and private events, for which only one person's testimony is available, must be allowed to have historical actuality in view of their indisputably historical effects, though this does not necessarily mean that the explanation given by those who experienced them is sound.

R. Bultmann has argued that the resurrection, because it is unique and cannot be proved to the satisfaction of a sceptic to have happened, can have had actuality only of the third and private kind. 'If the event of Easter Day is in any sense an historical event additional to the event of the cross, it is nothing else than the rise of faith in the risen Lord, since it was this faith which led to the apostolic preaching. The resurrection itself is not an event of past history. All that historical criticism can establish is the fact that the first disciples came to believe in the resurrection.'[14] I submit that historical criticism can and must establish something rather different. The first disciples did not come to believe in the resurrection as an event which happened to themselves, comparable with Gautama's illumination, but as an event which happened to Jesus.

I trust that it will be clear that I am not at this point trying to prove the historicity of the resurrection. This is a book about words, and our only concern with the resurrection is to ask whether we can discern the meaning of the words which the New Testament writers use about it. Bultmann has argued in effect that the New Testament statements about the resurrection have no historical referent other than the crucifixion, that they are theological interpretations of the death of Jesus exactly on a par with the ten listed above. Since I have suggested that something of the sort may be the case with the rending of the temple veil, I am bound to admit that his thesis is plausible. But it has been laid down in an earlier chapter than the meaning and reference of words are those intended by the speaker. Now the biblical accounts leave little room for doubt that those who first spoke about the resurrection believed themselves to be speaking about an event which happened two days after the crucifixion. It was not a private, interior illumination which sent them out into the world as preachers of the gospel, but a conviction that they had been witnesses to an event exterior to their own minds, and event which had happened to someone else. They may have been mistaken; they may have misinterpreted their experience; but they claimed to be speaking about a matter of fact.

It is evident from the passages cited above concerning the Exodus and the crucifixion that the most important item in the framework within which the people of biblical times interpreted their history was the conviction that God was lord of history. He uttered his voice and events followed (Isa. 55:11–12). Thus the course of events was itself regarded as a quasi-linguistic system, in which God was disclosing his character and purpose; and this was particularly true of those events which we have called emblematic. The interpretation of God's history-language required the exercise

[14] *Kerygma and Myth*, p. 41.

8

of moral judgment (Jer. 15:19; cf. Heb. 5:14), and it was the task
of the prophet to be the qualified interpreter. He stood in the
council of the Lord (Jer. 23:18), and it was for him to read the
writing on the wall (Dan. 5:5–12) and to discern the signs of
the times (Luke 12:54–57; Matt. 16:2–3). He might of course get the
message wrong. There were false prophets who cried, 'All is well!',
when there was nothing well (Jer. 6:14; 8:11). According to Deuteronomy (13:1–2), God had deliberately left open the possibility of
error to provide a test of his people's loyalty; if they were loyal,
they would be able to distinguish the false prophet from the true.
The prophet thus discharged for his people the kind of responsibility which in this chapter we have been ascribing to the historian.
By his exercise of moral judgment he so moulded their past and
present as to determine the shape of their future, and by their
response he and they would in the end be judged.

Chapter Thirteen

The Language of Myth

The thesis which I shall propound in these last two chapters is that myth and eschatology are used in the Old and New Testaments as metaphor systems for the theological interpretation of historical events. In Chapter Twelve we have already encountered passages which exemplify this usage, where the Exodus, the return from Babylonian exile, and the crucifixion were referred to in mythical or eschatological terms. But I am well aware that I am challenging some of the long-cherished axioms of biblical scholarship, and that such a challenge needs to be supported by a persuasive array of evidence and argument.

Any treatment of myth which is to avoid hopeless ambiguity must begin with an index of the many senses in which this exceedingly slippery term is used. In popular parlance myth is a story with no foundation in fact, a sheer fiction, a falsehood; and one of the hazards which beset the serious student of mythology is that this sense (Myth^F) is always lurking in the background. For the reader of the Bible the hazard is even greater, since this is the only sense the word has in the New Testament (1 Tim. 1:4; 4:7; 2 Tim. 4:4; Tit. 1:14; 2 Pet. 1:16—the AV renders all these by 'fables'). At the other extreme is a regrettable and confusing fashion whereby 'myth' is used to cover the whole range of theological language; any 'God-talk', any sentence containing the word 'God', is myth (Myth^T). In his essay on demythologising Bultmann's third definition of myth was of this sort: 'Mythology is the use of imagery to express the otherworldly in terms of this world and the divine in terms of human life, the other side in terms of this side.' (op. cit. p. 16). Mythology, he would have us believe, is the theological use of metaphor; and since all theological language is metaphorical, his critics justifiably retorted that demythologising would on this definition reduce theology to silence. I am arguing (a) that myth is a specialised kind of metaphor, and (b) that its use in the Bible in particular is metaphorical; but I do not think that any useful purpose is served by obliterating the distinction between myth and metaphor in general.

Let us then firmly set aside Myth^F and Myth^T. In the discussion that follows we shall assume that myths are stories about the past which embody and express a people's traditional culture. But even with this limitation of reference, the word is used as a technical term in many different disciplines and with a considerable variety of connotation or association of ideas. The main division is between the phenomenologists, who are primarily interested in myth as an element in (primitive) culture, and the symbolists who are primarily interested in it as a vehicle of meaning.

A. PHENOMENOLOGICAL

1. Myth^E (Evolutionary)

The earlier ethnologists, such as Andrew Lang[1] and E. B. Tylor,[2] regarded myth as primitive and therefore obsolete science, a pre-scientific attempt to explain natural phenomena. 'The myths, shaped out of those endless analogies between man and nature which are the soul of all poetry, into those half-human stories so full to us of unfading life and beauty, are the masterpieces of an art belonging rather to the past than to the present. The growth of myth has been checked by science, it is dying of weights and measures, of proportions and specimens—it is not only dying, but half-dead, and students are anatomising it. . . . There is a kind of intellectual frontier within which he must be who will sympathise with myth, while he must be without who will investigate it.'[3] It was this somewhat dated concept of myth that provided Bultmann with the first of his three definitions, and persuaded him that the gospel, couched in traditional terms, 'is incredible to modern man, for he is convinced that the mythical view of the world is obsolete' (op. cit., p. 3). Tylor, more percipient than Bultmann, recognised the affinity between myth and poetry and regarded the

[1] *Myth, Ritual and Religion* (1887).
[2] *Primitive Culture* (1871).
[3] E. B. Tylor, op. cit., 4th ed. (1903), p. 317.

supposed obsolescence of myth with regret. The comparison between science and myth is superficially attractive, since both are systems of explanation; but in science explanation consists in the quest for causes, whereas in myth it consists in the quest for meaning. It is moreover a fallacy that science is hostile to myth. The imagination of our own age has been gripped by the myth of the arrival of explorers from outer space, which owes its wide popularity to the fact that it decks out with the apparatus of sophisticated technology the ancient myth of visitants from another and better world.

2. Myth^R *(Ritualist)*

A very different and more probable view is that myth was intimately related to social structure and grew up as an accompaniment to ritual observance. It was, as the Greeks put it, *ta legomena epi tois drômenois*, the words spoken over the actions. 'In all the antique religions, mythology takes the place of dogma; that is, the sacred lore of priests and people, so far as it does not consist of mere rules for the performance of religious acts, assumes the form of stories about the gods; and these stories afford the only explanation that is offered of the precepts of religion and the prescribed rules of ritual ... What was obligatory or meritorious was the exact performance of certain sacred acts prescribed by the religious tradition ... So far as myths consist of explanations of ritual, their value is altogether secondary ... The myth itself requires to be explained, and every principle of philosophy and common sense demands that the explanation be sought, not in arbitrary allegorical theories, but in the actual facts of ritual or religious custom to which the myth attaches ... Religion was part of the organised social life into which a man was born, and to which he conformed through life in the same unconscious way in which men fall into any habitual practice of the society in which they live.'[4] 'Myth is a constant by-product of living faith, which demands miracles; of sociological status, which demands precedent; or moral rule, which demands sanction.'[5] 'Myth ... in its living primitive form, is not merely a story told but a reality lived. It is not of the nature of

[4] W. Robertson Smith, *The Religion of the Semites*, 3rd ed. (1927), pp. 17–21.
[5] B. Malinowski, *Myth in Primitive Psychology* (1927), p. 92.

fiction . . . but it is a living reality, believed to have once happened in primaeval times, and continuing ever since to influence the world and human destinies.'[6]

3. Myth^P (Pragmatic)

Whereas students of primitive culture, which tends to be static, have regarded myth as a force making for stability, sociologists such as Georges Sorel, whose interest has been in more stirring times, have seen in it an instrument for social manipulation and control, the means with which social movements win support by presenting themselves to the imagination as struggles for an eventually victorious cause.

4. Myth^N (Naturalist)

Just as plants break through the runways of a disused airfield, and the jungle returns to its strength to engulf a dead civilisation, so Henri Bergson envisaged myth as nature's way of breaking through the hard crust by which man has alienated himself from the springs of his true being. This theory has been taken up in some modern accounts of artistic inspiration: when the rational intelligence is quiescent, then out of the abyss through unguarded fissures in the mind primordial images stream in to set the creative powers alight.

B. SYMBOLIC

5. Myth^I (Idealist)

Plato used myths to convey universal truths which could not otherwise be so readily or so vividly expressed; and it has been a widely held view that this is the function of all mythology. The modern counterpart to Platonic philosophy is structuralism, which starts from a belief in the uniformity of the structures of the mind. 'On the one hand, a myth always refers to events alleged to have taken place in time: before the world was, during its first stages—anyway, long ago. But what gives the myth an operative value is that the

---

[6] Ibid., p. 100.

specific pattern described is everlasting; it explains the present and the past as well as the future.'[7]

6. Myth[PS] (Psychological)

Under the influence of Jung's psycho-analytical theory of universal archetypes arising from the collective unconscious, myth has been treated as the expression of deep-seated and permanent human needs, and at the same time as a means of directing the flood of emotion into socially acceptable channels.[8]

7. Myth[L] (Literary)

Literary critics have adapted Myth[PS] by enlarging it to include their own concerns. 'When I use *myth, mythical* . . . I refer to the universal instinct of any human group, large or small, to invest, almost always unconsciously, certain stories or events or places or persons, real or fictional, with an uncommon significance; to turn them into instinctive centres of reference; to make among stories A, B, C, D, all roughly having the same theme or moral, *one*, and only one, the type. Made thus typical, the story becomes a communal possession, the agreed and classic embodiment of some way of thinking or feeling.'[9] The lectures introduced by this definition give a series of examples from literature, including the mediaeval myth of the harrowing of hell, the Tudor myth of pedigree which inspired Spenser's *Faërie Queene*, and the Victorian myth of Oliver Twist asking for more. In this definition myth comes near to what in the previous chapter we have called the emblematic.

Faced with this array of opinion, we shall be wise to conclude that myth has a complexity which defies all attempts of the foolhardy to reduce it to a single origin or function. Yet there is no real conflict between the various schools of thought, but rather some impressive areas of agreement. Most of the scholars consulted would agree that myth fulfils all the uses of language which we have listed

---

[7] C. Lévi-Strauss, 'The structural study of myth' in *Myth—A Symposium*, ed. T. A., Sebeck.

[8] See e.g. G. Roheim, *The Riddle of the Sphinx*.

[9] E. M. W. Tillyard, *Myth and the English Mind*, pp. 11–12. Cf. also Northrop Frye, *Anatomy of Criticism*; Maud Bodkin, *Archetypal Patterns in Poetry*; P. Wheelwright, *The Burning Fountain*.

in Chapter One. It is performative, 'a living reality' which commits its adherents to a pattern of life. It is expressive and evocative, appealing to the imagination through a sense of the impressive, the enchanting, the sublime and the mysterious. It is par excellence the language of social cohesion. Above all it is referential in the same fashion as metaphor is referential. It tells a story about the past, but only in order to say something about the present and the future. It has a literal referent in the characters and events of the vehicle story, but its tenor referent is the situation of the user and his audience. Like the user of other forms of metaphor, the user of myth says to his audience, 'Here is a lens which has helped me to understand the world you and I live in; look through it yourselves and see what I have seen.' 'To accept the vehicle in its literal aspect is the way of superstition; to accept its transcendental reference (the tenor) exclusively is the way of allegory. The primitively mytho-religious attitude in its most characteristic forms has tended to settle into some kind of fertile tension between these two extremes without yielding completely to either of them. So far as the mythic storyteller is half-consciously aware of the tension, his narrative may achieve that tone of serious playfulness which characterises so charmingly much early myth.'[10]

It is now time for us to turn to the Old Testament and to see how far the uses of myth in it bear out and are illuminated by the theories of the experts. Let us begin with an unambiguous example.

> How have you fallen from heaven,
> Bright shiner, son of the dawn,
> Felled to earth, sprawling helpless across the nations!
> You thought in your own mind,
> I will scale the heavens;
> I will set my throne high above the stars of God,
> I will sit on the mountain where the gods meet
> In the far recesses of the north.
> I will rise high above the cloud-banks
> And make myself like the Most High.
> Yet you shall be brought down to Sheol,
> To the depths of the abyss   (Isa. 14:12–15).

[10] P. Wheelwright, 'The semantic approach to myth' in *Myth—A Symposium*.

The prophet is making use of a story about the planet known to us as Venus, but to the Hebrews as 'bright shiner' (*Heylel*), which is called 'son of the dawn' or morning star because it rises shortly before the sun.[11] According to the myth Heylel aspired to make himself king by scaling the mountain ramparts of the heavenly city, only to be vanquished by the all-conquering sun.[12] But the biblical context makes it quite clear that the prophet is speaking about the king of Babylon and his aspirations to world dominion. By looking at the contemporary tyrant through the lens of myth he is classifying him with all other rebels against the authority of God, and giving eloquent and forceful expression to his own confidence in Babylon's rapidly ensuing downfall; and his purpose is to reinforce his people's faith in God's lordship over history at a time when the brute facts of international politics shrieked against their creed.

In the same vein Ezekiel draws upon the myth of paradise lost to depict the approaching fall of Tyre (28:13-16).

> You were in God's garden of Eden,
> Adorned with gems of every kind . . .
> Your commerce grew so great,
> Lawlessness filled your heart and you went wrong,
> So I brought you down in disgrace from the mountain of God,
> And the guardian cherub banished you
> From among the stones that flashed like fire.

We have no means of knowing whether Ezekiel believed that human history had begun with a literal fall of the first man and woman, but this passage makes it clear that for him, as later for Paul (Rom.

[11] Heylel was translated *Phôsphoros* in the Septuagint and *Lucifer* in the Vulgate, and at some point became identified with Satan. But his original identity is still plainly visible even in George Meredith's sonnet, 'On a starr'd night Prince Lucifer uprose'.

[12] The city of the gods is in the north because the pole star is the point round which the heavens revolve. The same phrase, 'the recesses of the north', is found in Ps. 48:2, where Jerusalem is identified with the heavenly city where the Great King sits enthroned, and is thus declared to be the hub of the universe. For Jerusalem the north was literally the quarter from which enemy armies could be expected, but the mythical motif is probably present in Jeremiah's predictions of an enemy from the north (1:14; 4:6 etc.), as it undoubtedly is in Ezekiel's predictions about Gog (38:6,15; 39:2), in Daniel's designation of the Seleucids as 'the northern king' (11:6 ff.), and in Joel's paradoxical description of an army of locusts as 'the northern peril' (2:20).

8*

5:12 ff.), the myth owed its power to the fact that Adam's story was the story of Everyman, constantly re-enacted in the subsequent history of men and nations.

The most widespread and influential of all the myths of the ancient Near East was the story of creation. In its most familiar Babylonian guise, by order of a heavenly council which has decreed his destiny, the god Marduk, representing light and order and goodness, goes to battle against the ocean monster Tiamat, representing darkness and chaos and evil, defeats her, cuts her body in two 'like a flat fish', and of the two parts makes heaven and earth. In other versions of the myth the ocean monster is known as Rahab, Leviathan (the seven-headed Lotan of Ras Shamra), or simply the dragon. It need hardly be said that this story was never intended as a scientific account of cosmic origins, the ancient equivalent of the 'Big Bang'. It was a declaration of faith that the world had originated in a victory of order over chaos, a summons to the worshipper to enlist with the army of light in the ongoing battle against the forces of darkness, a confident assertion of the ultimate victory of good over evil. We can detect the presence of this myth in the background of the Creation story of Genesis 1, but it is present in a singularly etiolated form. Tiamat is still recognisable in *T^ehom* (the great deep), and the two parts of her body account for the waters above the firmament and the waters below the earth; but everything else has been transformed by the monotheistic faith of the priestly author. The imposition of order upon chaos is achieved by fiat, not by battle. Brevard Childs has called this 'broken myth', and others have called it 'demythologised'.[13]

There are however other parts of the Old Testament which make use of the myth in the full robustness of its original imagery.

> By your power you cleft the sea-monster in two
> And broke the dragon's heads above the waters;
> You crushed the many-headed Leviathan
> And threw him to the sharks for food.
> You opened channels for spring and torrent;
> You dried up rivers never known to fail.
> The day is yours, and the night is yours also,
> You ordained the light of moon and sun;

[13] B. S. Childs, *Myth and Reality in the Old Testament*, p. 42.

You fixed all the regions of the earth;
Summer and winter, you created them both

(Ps. 74:13–17).

On the face of it this appears to be a simple assertion that the orderliness of nature, the regular succession of day and night and of the seasons, rests upon God's primaeval victory over the chaos monster. But the passage is part of a psalm in which the psalmist laments the destruction of Jerusalem and the exile of her citizens and appeals to God to rescue them from the tyranny of their enemies. The implication is that the primaeval victory can be repeated over the contemporary dragons of political power which are still recalcitrant to the gracious purposes of God.

But the myth is equally applicable to the problems of the individual sufferer. Job protests that God must have mistaken him for the sea-monster if he finds it necessary to crush him so severely (7:12), and declares himself helpless in the presence of him before whom 'the partisans of Rahab lie prostrate' (9:13). The poet thus treats the myth as a symbol of eternal truth (Myth[1]), evoking a sense of wonder before the unfathomable mystery of God's power.

> The pillars of heaven quake
> and are aghast at his rebuke.
> With his strong arm he cleft the sea-monster,
> and struck down the Rahab by his skill.
> At his breath the skies are clear
> and his hand breaks the twisting sea-serpent.
> These are but the fringe of his power;
> and how faint the whisper that we hear of him (26:11–14).

In one of the many oracles in which Isaiah attacks the political party in Jerusalem that is seeking to offset the growing threat of Assyria by alliance with Egypt, he contemptuously dubs Egypt Rahab-Sit-Still (30:7). If you are going to invoke the protection of the dragon, you had better be sure that it is not Dragon Do-nothing. The association of Egypt with the mythical Rahab appears to have been a long-established tradition (Ps. 87:4), probably because Egypt was the first, and therefore the typical, oppressing power from which Israel had needed rescue. Hence in the prophecy of Deutero-Isaiah already quoted on p. 209, the emblematic event of the Exodus has first been interpreted in the light of the myth and then absorbed into it so as to provide the basis for a prediction of a new Exodus from Babylon. And a later member of the Isaiah school depicts in the same imagery God's final deliverance of his people: 'on that day the Lord will punish with his cruel sword, his mighty powerful sword, Leviathan that twisting sea-serpent, that writhing serpent Leviathan, and slay the monster of the deep' (Isa. 27:1).

One of the indispensable features of myth is that its characters must be capable of bearing a contemporary face. The English myth of St. George and the Dragon is a true myth precisely because the cartoonist can give to St. George the face of a contemporary states-man, who is thus proclaimed to be the archetypal Englishman engaged in the chivalrous task of liberating Britannia from some monstrous peril. Similarly, in biblical cartoons, the chaos monster is given the face of Nebuchadnezzar by Jeremiah (51:34), of Pharaoh by Ezekiel (29:3), and of Pompey by the author of the Psalms of Solomon (2:29).

When Daniel in the first of his night visions saw four monsters arising from the sea, which he subsequently identified as symbols for the successive world empires of Babylon, Media,[14] Persia and Greece, we have no difficulty in recognising the sea as the cosmic ocean of the creation myth, from which the monstrous creatures of world power arise to challenge the authority of God. The writer's immediate interest was in the fourth beast, and in particular in its little horn, Antiochus Epiphanes, who at the time of writing (*c.* 167 B.C.) was attempting to eradicate the Jewish religion by systematic persecution. The book was a tract for the encouragement of the resistance movement. In his application of the myth to current affairs the author was heir to the tradition already established by the prophets, but in one respect he showed himself a thinker of creative originality. Whereas the prophets had been content to use mythical motifs for the interpretation of isolated events, he sets the drama of his own day against the backdrop of world history. He has already disclosed in his story of Nebuchadnezzar's dream the connecting thread which he sees running through the epochs.

[14] There never was a Median empire; but the author of Daniel was neither well-informed about nor greatly interested in ancient history.

Nebuchadnezzar is thrice told that he must learn 'that the Most High controls world dominion and grants it to whom he will' (4:17, 25, 32); and because he has governed in defiance of this truth, he is turned into a beast. All imperial power is held by delegation from God, and will be removed by God when it turns bestial, until in the end it is vested in the saints of the Most High, under the symbol of a human figure (one like to a son of man), coming with the clouds of heaven.

So influential was Daniel's vision that it, like the Exodus in the prophecies of an earlier age, was absorbed into the myth; and thereafter no Jewish or Christian writer could use the lens of this myth except as it had been reground by Daniel. The author of Revelation, an even more imaginative and creative artist than the author of Daniel, derives from the myth his glassy sea (4:6) and the seven-headed monster that rises from it (13:1), but the monster exhibits characteristics of all four of Daniel's beasts. For him the current embodiment of the chaos monster is Rome, but he sees Rome as the residual legatee of all the pagan empires of the past. Because he uses the universal language of myth, what he has to say about Rome in the reign of Domitian is equally applicable to totalitarian and tyrannical power at any other period of the world's history.

A Jewish contemporary of John, the author of the Ezra Apocalypse, describes a 'Son of Man' vision which is clearly derivative from Daniel (2 Esdr. 13). It too opens with the sea churned up by the wind, but out of the sea there arises the human figure who is subsequently seen 'flying with the clouds of heaven'. When Ezra asks his angel guide the meaning of these symbols, he is told: 'It is beyond the power of any man to explore the deep sea and discover what is in it; in the same way no one on earth can see my son and his company until the appointed day' (13:52). In other words, the mythical sea, which was understood by all previous users, including Daniel and John, to be a symbol for the mystery of iniquity, has here become a symbol for the mystery of God's inscrutable purpose. The author has inherited the imagery, but has either totally lost touch with, or deliberately repudiated, its original significance.

When we look back over this catena of passages, one striking fact is noticeable: with the exception of Isaiah's sardonic jibe, all these uses of myth belong to the exilic or post-exilic period. Most of them could be classified as Myth[P], since the author is in each case arguing for a particular theological interpretation of current events, and is so attempting to influence the history of his people. They are a remarkable testimony to the vitality of myth beyond the point where it could have had any immediate relationship to the cultus of the Solomonic temple.[15] But it would be rash to conclude that no such relationship ever existed. These later writers must have derived their mythical vocabulary from some tradition; and, whatever foreign influence may have added to their mental furniture, the use of 'Rahab' by Isaiah in the eighth century proves that the tradition was in the main indigenous to Israel. This is confirmed by the presence in Solomon's temple of a huge hemispherical basin, mounted on twelve oxen and called 'the Sea'—undoubtedly a symbol of the cosmic ocean of myth (1 Kings 7:23–26).

In 1922, when ritualist theories of myth were at their height, Sigmund Mowinckel argued in his *Psalmenstudien* that many psalms which had previously been assigned to a late, post-exilic date actually belonged to the monarchy and had their setting in the cultus of the temple. He argued that Israel, like other near-eastern peoples, had a New Year festival, which celebrated the enthronement both of Yahweh and of the Davidic king and re-enacted the myth of Yahweh's victory over his primaeval enemy, the ocean.

> The Lord is king: he is clothed in majesty;
> the Lord clothes himself with might
> and fastens on the belt of his wrath.
> You have fixed the earth unmovable and firm,
> your throne firm from of old;
> from all eternity you are God.
> O Lord, the ocean lifts up, the ocean lifts up its clamour;
> the ocean lifts up its pounding waves.
> The Lord on high is mightier far
> than the noise of great waters,
> mightier than the breakers of the sea   (Ps. 93:1–4).
>
> O Lord God of Hosts, who is like you? . . .
> You rule the surging sea,
> calming the turmoil of its waves.

[15] The cultus of the post-exilic temple is reflected in the Priestly Code of Exodus, Leviticus and Numbers, and is quite devoid of mythical overtones.

You crushed the monster Rahab with a mortal blow
and scattered your enemies with your strong arm　(Ps. 89:8–10).

After nearly thirty years of debate and criticism, Mowinckel restated his case in a more restrained fashion in *The Psalms in Israel's Worship*.[16] The re-enactment of the myth was now restricted to 'the great procession with its dramatic and symbolic character' (p. 130). 'The festal procession of the day is identical with the act of salvation of the past' (p. 173). He even conceded the possibility 'that most of the things "taking place" were presented by means of suggestive symbols' (p. 170). The victory of Yahweh, for example, might have been represented by nothing more than the carrying of the ark (cf. Numb. 10:35). What he now recognised to be of central importance was the historical reference of both myth and cultic act. The ocean over which Yahweh asserts his victory and sovereignty always stands for historical enemies, usually foreign nations seen as a threat to Yahweh's people and therefore to his purpose (p. 245). 'In Yahwism the cult has been made into history, and history has been drawn into the cult' (p. 139).

It is by no means certain that Israel ever had a festival of exactly the kind that Mowinckel envisaged. But it is generally agreed that the royal psalms and those which celebrate the kingship of Yahweh (93, 95–99) had their origin in a cultic setting, and that the mythical allusions they contain were part of an interpretative framework within which Israel endeavoured to make sense of and give direction to her national history. But if this is the case, then the cultic use of myth in the earlier period did not conspicuously differ from its non-cultic use in the later and better attested period with which we began. One at least of Mowinckel's sympathetic but rigorous critics would have wanted to go further. 'I now reject the view that the autumn festival was concerned with the cyclic renewal of the social unit, and argue instead that its orientation was not merely towards the following cycle of twelve months but towards a completely new era. That is to say, if ever it had its roots in a

---

[16] Mowinckel's thesis was taken up enthusiastically in Sweden by G. Widengren and G. Engnell, rather more cautiously in Britain by the so-called 'Myth and Ritual' school, led by S. H. Hooke. See *Myth, Ritual and Kingship* and *The Labyrinth*, both edited by Hooke. The theory of a New Year festival was rejected in toto by N. Snaith in *The Jewish New Year Festival*.

complex of myth and ritual which was primarily concerned with the cycle of the year and an annual attempt along magico-religious lines to secure a renewal of life for a specific social unit, this had been refashioned along morally persuasive lines in terms of Yahweh's eternal kingship and Israel's experience of His activity on the plane of history.'[17] The thought world of myth was not a world of shadow and fantasy in which the ancient Israelite sat enchained, like the prisoners in Plato's cave, unable to escape into the world of reality. It was rather a fund of powerfully emotive language on which creative thinkers could draw 'along morally persuasive lines', to lead their people into ever deepening appreciation of the significance of their national history.

The refashioning of a mythical motif to bring it into line with the realities of historical experience is well illustrated by the development which took place in the myth of the heavenly council; and it is interesting to note how often the imaginative exploitation of ambiguity had a part in the process. The idea that human affairs are controlled by a council of the gods is familiar to readers of Homer, and was widespread in the mythology of other ancient cultures.[18] Some traces of a polytheistic stage survive in the Old Testament in a handful of references to 'gods' or 'sons of God' who surround the throne of Yahweh.[19]

> In the heavens who is there like Yahweh,
> Who is like Yahweh among the sons of Elim,
> Who like God is feared in the assembly of Holy Ones,
> Great and awesome above all who surround him?
> Yahweh God of Hosts, who is like you?   (Ps. 89:6–8).

Even in frankly polytheistic cultures the heavenly council had a president who ranked above its other members, so that the myth was readily adaptable to Israel's emergent monotheism. No doubt the establishment of an earthly monarchy accelerated the change by which the gods were demoted to the status of courtiers in the

[17] A. R. Johnson, 'Hebrew conceptions of kingship' in *Myth, Ritual and Kingship*, p. 234.

[18] For the part played by the council in the victory of Marduk, see p. 226 and for Egypt, see p. 195.

[19] *Bene Elim* or *Elohim*: the *ben* in these phrases is the *ben* of classification, not of paternity.

heavenly court. But the belief persisted that God had a Privy Council with which he discussed affairs of state, the most picturesque examples of which are in the story of the death of Ahab (I Kings 22:19–22) and in the prologue to the Book of Job. According to Jeremiah (23:18) the mark which distinguishes the true prophet from the false is that he, like Micaiah ben Imlah, has 'stood in the council of Yahweh' and has therefore been admitted to the secrets of his policy (cf. Amos 3:7). Even as late as the second century B.C., Jesus ben Sira sets the scene thus for the autobiography of the personified Wisdom:

> Hear the praise of wisdom from her own mouth as she speaks with pride among the people, before the assembly of the Most High and in the presence of the heavenly host (Ecclus. 24:1–2).

In modern usage it is customary to refer to God's entourage as 'angels', but this comprehensive use of 'angel' is later than the Old Testament. The Hebrew *malak*, like the Greek *angelos* means 'messenger', and the word strictly applies only to those sent on an errand.

> You make the winds to carry your messages
> and flames of fire to run your errands (Ps. 104:4).[20]

The 'gods' who surround the throne of Yahweh are 'holy ones' (cf. Deut. 33:2) or 'the host (army) of heaven', since the king's courtiers are also his warriors. But 'the host of heaven' also denotes the stars; and it is here that we meet the first of our fruitful ambiguities. The starry host is also the heavenly council. It is they who celebrated God's triumph at creation,

> When the morning stars sang together
> and all the sons of God shouted for joy (Job. 38:7).

and it is the same heavenly host that praises God at Christ's nativity (Luke 2:13). But they also fight God's battles:

---

[20] The Septuagint reversed the predication:

> He makes his angels winds (or spirits)
> and his ministers a flame of fire;

and this rendering was followed in the AV (cf. Heb. 1:7).

> The stars fought from heaven,
> the stars in their courses fought against Sisera
>
> (Judg. 5:20).

In the battle commemorated in the Song of Deborah the heavenly armies were on the side of Israel, but the lesson was learned at an early date that this was not necessarily so. 'When Joshua came near Jericho he looked up and saw a man standing in front of him with a drawn sword in his hand. Joshua went up to him and said, "Are you for us or for our enemies?" And the man said to him, "No! I am here as captain of the army of the Lord" ' (Josh. 5:13-14).

The earliest definition given of the title *Yahweh S^ebaoth* (Lord of hosts) is 'God of the armies of Israel' (1 Sam. 17:45). But the way was open for a transfer of the reference to the armies of heaven. The full title—Yahweh of hosts enthroned upon the cherubim (1 Sam. 4:4; 2 Sam. 6:2)—appears to have been associated with the ark, and must from the start have had mythical and cosmic significance, since the cherubim were the four winds, the four corners of the earth, the pillars of heaven, the supporters of God's heavenly throne (cf. Ps. 18:10; Ezek. 1:22-26). It is impossible to assign a date to this semantic change, but it had certainly occurred when Ps. 89 was written (see above), and by the time of Amos the armies of Israel have dropped out of the picture. The God of hosts controls all the forces of nature, including the constellations, and Israel's very existence depends on his being on her side (Amos 4:13; 5:8-9,14).

When the Old Testament was translated into Greek by many different hands, there was no unanimity about the rendering of *Yahweh S^ebaoth*. All the translators agreed in translating Yahweh by *Kyrios* (Lord), but some transliterated the second term and produced the outlandish title 'the Lord Sabaoth', which misled Egyptian magicians into thinking that they had discovered the secret name of God; others rendered it by *Pantokratôr* (Omnipotent); others again by *kyrios tôn dynameôn* (Lord of the powers). And through this last version of the title Philo of Alexandria, with considerable help from Greek philosophy, breathed new life into the old myth of God's heavenly council by his elaborate doctrine of powers.[21]

---

[21] For a detailed treatment see H. A. Wolfson, *Philo* II, pp. 217 ff.

In the traditional style of the Old Testament Philo describes the powers as attendant on God (*Spec.* 1.8.45; *Deus* 24, 109); 'on either side of him and nearest to him are the senior powers, the creative and the kingly' (*Abr.* 24, 121). They are co-workers with God (*Opif.* 24, 75). In a more philosophical vein he explains that the powers have three modes of existence: eternally, in the mind of God; as spiritual beings before the creation of the world; and as immanent forces in the universe. In the natural order Philo volunteers that they function somewhat after the manner of the Platonic ideas; 'since they bring form into everything that is, giving order to the disordered, limit to the unlimited, bounds to the unbounded, shape to the shapeless, and in general changing the worse to something better' (*Spec.* 1.8.48). In the life of mankind the powers are of two sorts, according as they mediate God's goodness on the one hand or his authority, rule, law and punishment on the other; and of these two the cherubim are the symbols (*Cher.* 9.27–28). In one passage with charming naiveté Philo remarks that God delegates to the powers of sovereignty the tasks which he finds incompatible with his own essential goodness, namely government and punishment (*Qu. in Ex.* II.68). In particular Philo interprets the first person plural of Gen. 1:26 to mean that the powers participated in the creation of man. 'He employed the powers that are associated with him not only for the reason mentioned, but because, alone among created beings, the soul of man was to be susceptible of conceptions of evil things and good things . . . therefore God deemed it necessary to assign the creation of evil things to other makers, reserving that of good things to himself alone' (*Fug.* 13.70).

Philo's concept of powers is important for biblical studies, not because it is identical with Paul's 'principalities and powers', nor yet because he had any direct influence on Paul, but because Philo and Paul were two highly intelligent thinkers grappling with similar problems on the basis of the same body of Old Testament material. But before we turn to Paul, we must retrace our steps and follow the myth of the heavenly council through the second of its ambiguities.

In the context of Ps. 89 the question 'Who is like Yahweh among the sons of Elim?' is unambiguous. Yahweh has no equal in the court of heaven. But in another context it could be a challenge

thrown out to the pagan world, a claim that Yahweh has no equal
among the gods of the nations; and so it clearly is in the Song of
Moses which celebrates the triumph of the Exodus (Exod. 15:11).
In the cycle of enthronement psalms Yahweh's triumph over the
ocean is at the same time his triumph over the nations and their
gods, and the gods are accordingly summoned to take their place in
his retinue.

> Ascribe to Yahweh, you gods,
> ascribe to Yahweh glory and might.
> Ascribe to Yahweh the glory due to his name;
> bow down to Yahweh in the splendour of holiness . . .
> Yahweh is king above the flood,
> Yahweh has taken his throne as king for ever
> (Ps. 29:1–2,10).

> Yahweh is a great God,
> a great king above all gods   (Ps. 95:3).

> Let all who worship images, who vaunt their idols,
> be put to shame;
> bow down, all gods, before him   (Ps. 97:7).

The psalmist does not deny the existence of those beings whom the
nations worship, but only their deity.

This triumphalism, however, could not long survive without
coming into conflict with the facts of experience. Confronted with
the imperial strength of Assyria, Babylon and Persia, Israel might
deny the divinity of pagan gods, but could not well deny their
power. The unpalatable realities of history must be absorbed into
the myth, and imperial administration supplied a pattern for the
adjustment.

> When the Most High parcelled out the nations,
> when he dispersed all mankind,
> He laid down the boundaries of every people
> according to the number of the sons of God
> (Deut. 32:8).

As the imperial monarch rules his provinces through governors and
satraps, so God governs the nations through the members of his

first going back to fight with the prince of Persia, and, as soon as I have left, the prince of Greece will appear: I have no ally on my side to help me and support me, except Michael your prince' (Dan. 10:20–21). Thus the struggles of the Jewish people for the survival of their religion during the persecutions of Antiochus Epiphanes are reflected in the contest of angel princes in the court of heaven.

This evidence from the Old Testament enables us to identify the referent of a number of terms in the vocabulary of Paul: powers, authorities, sovereignties, thrones and lordships. A preliminary survey of the passages in which these entities are mentioned yields the following information. They are no longer capable of separating the Christian from the love of God (Rom. 8:38), they are destined to be reduced to impotence (1 Cor. 15:24), they were created by God (Col. 1:16), and they were disarmed and defeated by Christ on the cross (Col. 2:15). In the first passage they are associated with angels, and in three out of the four passages they either operate or are capable of operating in opposition to the will of God. In Eph. 6:12 they are further defined as 'the cosmic potentates of this dark world, the superhuman forces of evil in the heavens'; and if this epistle is not by Paul, it is by a brilliant disciple who thoroughly understood Paul's mind. Three possibilities may therefore be dismissed out of hand. (1) Although all the words are in form abstract nouns, connoting structures of power, they do not in these contexts denote abstractions, but personal beings who symbolise, personify, embody or wield power. (2) They are not the human authorities referred to in Rom. 13:1 ff., the emperor and his subordinate magistrates. (3) They are not, as Dionysius the Areopagite supposed, hierarchies of angels attendant on the heavenly throne.

A fourth possibility, that they are denizens of a fantasy world of demons, entirely unrelated to the ordinary affairs of this-worldly existence, requires more extended refutation. The view that members of the early church lived in a demon-ridden world gains some superficial plausibility from the frequent mention of demon-possession in the Gospels, but it must be noted that this phenomenon is never even alluded to in the Pauline epistles. Paul uses the word *daimonion* in one passage only. 'The sacrifices the heathen offer are offered "to demons and to that which is not God"; and I will not have you become partners with demons. You cannot drink the cup of the Lord and the cup of demons. You cannot partake of the Lord's table and the table of demons' (1 Cor. 10:20–21). But Paul is here quoting from Deut. 32:17 (LXX), where 'demons' is simply a disparaging term for other peoples' gods. Thus Paul's one reference to demons is entirely in line with the Old Testament attitude to pagan religion. This passage actually supports a fifth view, to which also the abstract connotation of the five words we are considering strongly points, that in Pauline usage these terms denote heavenly beings who represent the power structures of the old world order which Paul believed to be tottering to its end. The Christian's fight against them 'in the heavens' is not a different battle from his daily struggle to live the new life of faith in the hostile environment of pagan society, just as the contest of Michael and the man clothed in linen against the princes of Persia and Greece was indistinguishable from the earthly struggle of the Jewish people to maintain religious integrity under foreign tyranny and persecution.

In two of his letters Paul uses the expression 'the elements of the world' (*ta stoicheia tou kosmou*) (Gal. 4:3, 9; Col. 2:8). He cannot mean by this the physical elements of the Greek cosmology—earth, water, air and fire. The choice, as we have already seen (Chapter Four), lies between 'elementary teaching characteristic of this world' and 'elemental powers which control the present world order'; and if the second solution should prove to be correct, we should have yet another term to add to those we have been studying. The arguments for 'elementary teaching' are simple and still have their adherents. This sense is in keeping with the comparison of the Christian's former life to a child's minority under the tutelage of trustees and guardians (Gal. 4:1–2), and with the reference to 'human traditions' in Col. 2:8. There is in addition the negative point that the use of *stoicheia* by astrologers to denote the heavenly bodies, conceived as astral powers, is not attested as early as the first century. This last point is not a strong one, since the volume of literature surviving from antiquity is not so large as to preclude the possibility that the New Testament may preserve the earliest example of a well established usage; and the impact of astrology on the Graeco-Roman world began three centuries before Paul. On the other hand, this first explanation is open to two damaging objections. In each letter the context requires a derogatory sense: the *stoicheia* stand for something that constitutes a bondage from which Christians must remain free. Now the English 'elementary' and 'rudimentary' can carry such a derogatory sense, but *stoicheia* (in the usage under consideration) never does: it does not connote naive notions or childish fancies which must be outgrown like a belief in fairies or Santa Claus, but rather the fundamentals of a subject, its axioms or essentials (cf. Heb. 5:12). It is hard to see how anyone could need to be delivered from bondage to the fundamentals of religion. Moreover, 'the fundamentals of the world' would be a very odd phrase indeed, scarcely analogous to 'the fundamentals of mathematics'.

We turn therefore to the other, mythological explanation and find that it admirably fits the data of Galatians.

> We were slaves to the elements of the world, but in due time God sent his own Son, born of a woman, born under law, to purchase freedom for those under law' (4:3–5).

> Formerly, when you did not acknowledge God, you were slaves of beings which in their nature were not gods. But now that you do acknowledge God ... how can you turn back to those mean and beggarly elements and want to be enslaved to them all over again?'
> (4:8–9).

> Tell me, you who are so anxious to be under law . . . (4:21).

The first quotation tells us that, before the coming of Christ, 'we' (all Christians) were in bondage to the elements and therefore to law. The second quotation tells us that for 'you' (Gentile Christians) the elements were the gods of their pagan religion, though they now recognise that they are not really gods; yet they want for some reason to revert to the bondage out of which they have come. The third quotation tells us that what they in fact want is to be under the (Jewish) law. The situation in the Galatian churches appears to be that Paul's Gentile converts have discovered since his departure, whether through the interference of Jewish mentors or by their own reading of the Scriptures, that there is more to the Old Testament than Paul has been letting on. They therefore propose to embellish his instruction with regulations drawn from the Torah, and particularly from its ceremonial portions. Paul's reply is that to do this would be to return to the very slavery from which they have been emancipated. Now on any showing this is a staggering assertion for a Jew to make, and it raises two questions: if for a Gentile the elements are to be identified with the pagan no-gods, how can Paul say that the Jews have been under a comparable bondage; and secondly, what has made him think of pagan religion as a regime of law?

The answer to the first question is that this is not dispassionate theological discourse, but a highly polemical use of myth (Myth^P). In describing the pagan gods as no-gods, Paul is making an obvious allusion to one form of the Jewish myth of the 'sons of God': the pagan gods are subordinate figures with a delegated authority, and in worshipping them the Gentiles have become slaves to an idolatrous illusion which exalts into absolute and final significance that which is secondary and derivative, that which is not God. But in the previous chapter Paul has already alluded to a different form of the same myth: 'the law was promulgated through angels' (3:19; cf. Acts 7:53; Heb. 2:2). When God gave the law he was attended by the whole host of heaven.

> The Lord came from Sinai
> and shone forth from Seir.
> He showed himself from Mount Paran,
> and with him were myriads of holy ones,
> streaming along at his right hand   (Deut. 33:1–2).

In the Jewish tradition the heavenly retinue was taken to enhance the importance of the Torah; it came not merely from God, but from the God of gods, to whom all the powers of heaven were subject. As a Jew Paul had no doubt been accustomed to use both forms of the myth to express the superiority of the Jewish religion to all others. Now he uses them to turn Jewish disparagement of paganism against the traditions of his own Jewish past. God had never intended the Torah to be his full and final revelation. His eternal purpose was disclosed in his promise to Abraham, to which the law was added as a secondary codicil (Gal. 3:15–18). In exalting the law to absolute significance the Jews had committed a blunder dangerously similar to Gentile idolatry and just as enslaving. The angels of Sinai are the symbols of a derivative and provisional authority, and are therefore in the same category as the sons of God who preside over the destinies of other nations.

But why did Paul think that the Gentiles lived under law? It would not naturally occur to readers of Homer to describe the capricious and often immoral behaviour of the Olympian gods as a rule of law. It is here that the appeal to astrology comes to our aid, if it be allowed. For it was the astrologers who taught the Greeks to give to the planets the Olympian names they still bear, and so to regard the pantheon as 'the army of unalterable law'. This association of ideas would be wholly congenial to a student of the Old Testament, to whom the stars were the sons of God and the armies of heaven.

Paul's powers, then, like those of Philo, are spiritual beings created by God and immanent within the world; but, unlike those of Philo and like the princes of the nations, they frequently act in defiance of God's purpose and to the enslavement of mankind. They stand, as their names imply, for the political, social, economic and religious structures of power, Jewish and pagan, of the old world order which Paul believed to be obsolescent. When therefore he claims that on the cross Christ has disarmed the powers and triumphed over them, he is talking about earthly realities, about the impact of the crucifixion on the corporate life of men and nations. He is using mythical language of great antiquity and continuing vitality to interpret the historic event of the cross. But he is also using history to reinterpret the myth. The historic event is taken up into the myth to transform it: henceforth the victories of God over all the forces in the universe which are resistant to his will are to be won, not by the thunderbolts of coercive might, but by the persuasive constraints of self-sacrificing love.

Chapter Fourteen

The Language of Eschatology

Eschatology is the study of, or the corpus of beliefs held about, the destiny of man and of the world. Unlike myth, which is in the vocabulary of every educated person, it is a term used only by theologians. If you find the Pythagorean belief in life after death, or the Stoic belief that the universe would dissolve into its original flames at the end of a calculable cycle, or the Marxist myth of a classless society called eschatological, you may be sure that the writer is borrowing from the jargon of theology. Now the only defence of jargon is that specialised studies and activities require a clearly defined set of technical terms. Regrettably 'eschatology' no longer has that clarity of definition. If scholars had been content to abide by the broad definition given above, the word would have remained useful and intelligible. But during the last eighty-five years it has been subjected to a series of tactical definitions which have rendered it more useful to those who want to win an argument than to those who aim at exact knowledge; and one recent writer has even suggested that it is overdue for burial.[1]

The word was coined in Germany in the early nineteenth century and subsequently imported into English.[2] In all English dictionaries of the nineteenth century it had the clearly defined sense which is still the only one recognised in the *OED* (1891 and 1933): 'the department of theological science concerned with the four last things, death, judgment, heaven, and hell'. This definition, which we may label Eschatology[I] (Individual) was clearly dictated by the traditional shape of Christian dogmatic theology at a time when the Bible was still regarded as a quarry for evidence in

---

[1] J. Carmignac, 'Les dangers de l'eschatologie', *NTS* 17 (1971), pp. 365–90. See also I. H. Marshall, 'Slippery words I: eschatology', *Expos. Times* lxxxix 9, pp. 264–9.

[2] The first recorded use given in the *OED* is in 1845 in a work by an American author, G. Bush.

support of orthodox doctrine. But during the nineteenth century Biblical scholarship won its emancipation from Dogmatics, and biblical scholars began to redefine the term to bring it into line with the material they were studying. In English works of reference the shift was first recognised in the *Jewish Encyclopaedia* (1903), where Kaufmann Kohler wrote: 'Jewish eschatology deals primarily and principally with the final destiny of the Jewish nation and the world in general, and only secondarily with the future of the individual: the main concern of Hebrew legislator, prophet, and apocalyptic writer being Israel as the people of God and the victory of His truth and justice on earth.'

This enlargement of scope, which we may call Eschatology[H] (Historical), because it deals with the goal of history, was entirely legitimate and proper, and it has been included in the comprehensive definition with which we began. But it brought with it one serious danger of misunderstanding. In the life of the individual death has an obvious finality; whatever he may believe about an after-life, death is simply and literally the end of his earthly existence. Now I shall argue below that the biblical writers did in the same simple and literal sense believe that the world would one day come to an end, just as they believed literally that in the past it had had a beginning. But the expectations which Kohler includes under eschatology do not necessarily, or even normally, have the same sense of literal finality. One characteristic form of Jewish eschatology is the belief in two ages: the present evil age will give place to the coming age of justice and peace, so that the end of the one is the beginning of the other; and in many, if not all, forms of this belief the coming age was conceived as a new and ideal epoch of world history. The danger, then, is that in using the one word eschatology to cover both types of belief we should overlook the fact that we may be using words such as 'last', 'final' and 'end' in different senses.

In this chapter we shall be mainly concerned with Eschatology[H] and the debates to which it has given rise. But something must first be said about Eschatology[I]. During most of the long period covered by the Old Testament the Hebrew people had no belief in an after-life. Sheol, like the Greek Hades, was the abode of the dead, the universal graveyard, and its nature can best be measured by the synonyms with which it is associated in the parallelism of

Hebrew poetry: death, darkness, oblivion, the grave, the pit. Its inhabitants were shades, wraiths, flimsies, mere carbon copies filed away in the record department.[3] The individual lives on only in his good name and in his children. It was the continuance of the holy nation that mattered; and as late as the second century B.C. Jesus ben Sira believed that the heroes of the nation's history are well enough rewarded for their loyalty if 'their children are within the covenants . . . and their name lives for ever' (Ecclus. 44:12–14). Intimations of immortality came slowly and along two lines of development, both of which have left their mark on the language of the New Testament. One of these begins with the dawning recognition of the worth of the individual to God, usually associated with Jeremiah, and culminates in the conviction, expressed in one or two of the later psalms, that it is possible to have communion with God such that death cannot interrupt.

> Whom have I in heaven but you?
> And having you, I desire nothing else on earth.
> Though heart and body fail,
> Yet God is my possession for ever
> (Ps. 73:25–26; cf. 16:8–11; 49:15).

One of these psalms is applied to Jesus by Luke in Peter's Pentecost speech (Acts 2:24–28), where the argument is that belief in the resurrection of Jesus, based no doubt on his appearances to the apostles and on the report of the empty tomb, is credible because Jesus had lived so close to the presence of God that death could not have parted him from it. Thus when the author of the Wisdom of Solomon declares that 'the souls of the just are in God's hand . . . for though in the sight of men they are punished, they have a sure hope of immortality . . . because God tested them and found them worthy to be his' (3:1–5), his terminology may be Greek, but the ideas are inherited from his Hebrew forebears. It is not surprising therefore to find New Testament writers speaking of a heavenly life for the 'soul' or 'spirit' (1 Cor. 5:5; Heb. 12:23; 1 Pet. 3:18; 4:6; Rev. 6:9–11). The last of these passages is particularly interesting

---

[3] Ezekiel actually pictures Sheol as a classified filing room in which the dead are arranged in nations (32:22–30). Cf. also the opening lines of Homer's *Iliad*: 'Sing, Muse, the accursed wrath of Peleus' son Achilles, which consigned the wraiths of many famous heroes to Hades, while they themselves were left as prey for dogs and birds.'

for our purpose. John sees under the heavenly altar the souls of those who have suffered martyrdom for their faith, and hears their appeal for vindication, which receives a double answer. Each is given a white robe, the symbol of life immortal, but they are told that the final victory of the cause for which they died must wait upon the completion of the full tally of those who are to die in God's service. Eschatology[I] is firmly dissociated from Eschatology[H]: the entry of the redeemed into the presence of God and their access 'to the springs of the water of life' (7:17) are not postponed until the final consummation of God's purposes.

The second line of development displays a curious interplay between the metaphorical and the literal. For the language of resurrection was used metaphorically of national recovery from disaster long before Israel had any belief in life after death (Hos. 6:1-2; Ezek. 37:1-14). Centuries later, almost certainly under the impact of persecution and martyrdom, the possibility began to be mooted that this language might have a more literal reference. It was all very well to be confident that the day of deliverance for the nation was certain to come. How fortunate for those who happened to be alive to share in the banquet of the new age (Isa. 25:6-8; cf. 2 Esdr. 5:41). But what about those who in the meantime had died for their faith? Could it be that they too might have a share in the blessings of the brave new world?

> Your dead live, their bodies will rise again,
> They that sleep in the earth will awake and shout for joy . . .
> and earth will bring those long dead to birth again
>
> (Isa. 26:19).

The reason why the risen dead would require their bodies was that at this stage the new life was still being envisaged as a continuation in some idealised form of the present earthly existence. From these tentative beginnings belief in an after-life rapidly matured, until in New Testament times all except the Sadducees accepted it. But even when resurrection language came to signify a transfer to a life of a totally new order, it was never wholly cast adrift from its moorings in the national hope. As so often happens, the imagery outlived the evolution of the referent (see Chapter Three), and this created problems of communication of which we can observe some echoes in the New Testament. When some Sadducees put to Jesus a hypothetical case of a woman who, in obedience to the levirate law (see pp. 141–2), was married to seven brothers in turn, and asked whose wife she would be in the resurrection, Jesus replied that this was a meaningless question since it wrongly assumed that the resurrection life would be a replica of the bodily conditions of earth (Mark 12:18–25). When Paul preached at Corinth the gospel of resurrection, he was apparently quite unprepared for the literalism with which his words were received, and he had to be at great pains to reassure them that the resurrection body would not be a body of flesh and blood (1 Cor. 15:35–50).

The New Testament writers, then, inherited two different styles of language for talking about life after death, which to the pedantic mind appear mutually contradictory. The one implies that entry into the future state is an individual matter and takes place at death (see, e.g., Luke 16:19 ff.), while the other pictures the dead as sleeping in the tomb until all are roused by the last trumpet. Like Lawrence's Arabs, these writers pursue the logic of both forms of language, even in close juxtaposition, without showing any signs of uneasiness at the clash. Luke records the promise of Jesus to the penitent criminal, 'Today you shall be with me in Paradise', (23:43), without any sense of conflict between this and the traditional beliefs, which he too accepted, that Jesus rose on the third day (24:7) and 'that there is to be a resurrection of good and wicked alike' (Acts 24:15).[4] If this example stood alone we might hesitate to draw any firm conclusion. But we find Paul more than once using both forms of language in close contiguity, even in a single letter. His earliest letter contains a vivid description of resurrection at the last day, but this is immediately followed by an assurance that the date of that event is of no consequence to Christians, since they are already 'children of the day' and therefore, awake or asleep (i.e. before or after death) they live in the company of Christ (1 Thess. 4:13—5:10). In his first letter to Corinth his long chapter on the resurrection culminates in a lyrical description of the final victory over death (1 Cor. 15:51–57), yet in his second letter, in a passage full of echoes of his earlier treatment of the theme, he can say: 'We

[4] Some scholars have attempted to resolve the inconsistency by demoting Paradise to the status of a waiting room. But this makes nonsense of the story, which requires that Jesus should promise more, not less, than the man had asked.

know that as long as we are at home in the body we are exiles from the Lord; faith is our guide, we do not see him. We are confident, I repeat, and would rather leave our home in the body and go to live with the Lord' (2 Cor. 5:6–8). Finally, when he is in prison on a capital charge, he can write to his friends in Philippi that he does not know which way the verdict will go, nor which way he would like it to go: 'What I should like is to depart and be with Christ; that is better by far; but for your sake there is greater need for me to stay on in the body' (Phil. 1:23). Yet later in the same letter he can say: 'We . . . are citizens of heaven, and from heaven we expect our deliverer to come, the Lord Jesus Christ, who will transfigure the body belonging to our humble state, and give to it a form like that of his own resplendent body, by the very power which enables him to make all things subject to himself' (Phil. 3:20–21).

Among the tests of linguistic awareness laid down in Chapter Eleven was the test of juxtaposition of images. By that test we may confidently say that Luke and Paul did not expect their language about life after death to be taken with flat-footed literalness. In the case of Paul this conclusion is confirmed by the test of explicit statement. For his two most vivid descriptions of the final resurrection are both introduced with a warning that what follows is in the exalted language of vision or inspired prophecy.[5] Beyond this we are in the realm of conjecture. But these two intelligent men, each with an intimate knowledge of the Old Testament, must surely have been alert to the limitations of language in expressing the relation of time to eternity, of which the Old Testament writers were already aware:

> Before the mountains were brought forth,
> or earth and world were born in travail,
> from age to age everlasting you are God   (Ps. 90:2).

Here is how another writer, a little later than Paul and Luke, grapples with this problem.

---

[5] Paul had the gift of inspired prophecy (Acts 13:1; cf. 1 Cor. 14:1 ff.). In 1 Thess. 4:15 'a word of the Lord' manifestly does not denote a saying of the earthly Jesus, so that Paul must be referring to something that has come to him in a state of inspiration. Similarly 'a mystery' (1 Cor. 15:51) is a prophetic insight into the secret purposes of God (cf. Eph. 3:3–5).

I said, 'But surely, lord, your promise is to those who are alive at the
end. What is to be the fate of those who lived before us, or of ourselves,
or of those who come after us?'
He said to me, 'I will compare the judgement to a circle: the latest will
not be too late, nor the earliest too early.'

(2 Esdr. 5:41–42).

The point of the comparison is that in a circle every point on the
circumference is equidistant from the centre. In the human experience of time the deaths of humankind are strung out in long succession through the ages, but from the other side of the curtain they
are all simultaneous. Every death is equidistant from eternity. This
writer, therefore, would have had no difficulty in believing at one
and the same time that everyone enters the after-life at the moment
of death, and that all rise together in response to the last reveille.

There remains an important question about the linguistic status
of the word 'resurrection' as applied to Jesus. We have seen that
other terms were available to express the conviction that he who
had died was now alive in the presence of God. In Jewish usage
'resurrection' denoted a single event expected at the end of the
present age or, more commonly, at the end of the world. When
therefore the early Christians apply this word to the event of Easter
Day, there is a prima facie case for saying that this is metaphor, the
use of end-of-the-world language to refer to that which is not
literally the end of the world. But we should then have to ask what
justification these early Christians had for looking at this particular event through this lens. This is the linguist's approach to the
debate about eschatology which has occupied so much of the attention of biblical scholars since the beginning of the century; and to
that debate we must now return.

The story begins with two scholars, Johannes Weiss and Albert
Schweitzer, who, apparently in ignorance of one another's work,
came to similar conclusions. Weiss wrote his little book *The Kingdom
of God in the Preaching of Jesus*[6] in revolt against the widely accepted
views of his father-in-law, Albrecht Ritschl, who had interpreted
the kingdom of God in terms of Jesus' moral influence on his
disciples and the subsequent formation of the Christian community. Weiss insisted that Jesus must not be thus modernised, but

---

[6] *Die Predigt Jesu vom Reiche Gottes* (1892).

must be seen in the setting of first century Judaism. He asserted that in contemporary Jewish expectation the kingdom of God was fully eschatological, i.e. its establishment would coincide with the end of the world; and that Jesus' belief in its imminence was the central idea in the light of which all the rest of his teaching must be understood. The kingdom, moreover, was in no sense the work of men: 'it is solely the work of God and therefore in every respect to be left to God' (p. 12). Even Jesus could do nothing to hasten its coming but, like everybody else, could only wait for God to act. Schweitzer went further than Weiss, declaring that Jesus confidently expected the end of the world to come in the course of his own ministry, and that when disillusionment set in he went to the cross in an attempt to force God's hand.[7]

The modern linguist cannot but applaud the demand of Weiss and Schweitzer that the words of Jesus should be interpreted in their historical context, even though with the wisdom of hindsight we can see that their critical tools were singularly blunt and their knowledge of the Jewish context fragmentary. But this is not the place to undertake an evaluation of their work. Our concern is with the effect they had on the definition of eschatology. Their claim was that the eschatology of Jesus and the early church, i.e. their views about the end of the world (Eschatology[H]), consisted in a belief that the end was imminent. But not content with that, they both took it for granted that no other belief could properly be called eschatology. 'We do not share the eschatological mood, namely, that the form of this world is passing away.'[8] 'The term eschatology ought only to be applied when reference is made to the end of the world as expected in the near future.'[9] In this way they built the conclusion of their argument into the meaning of the word 'eschatology', and by this tactical definition effectively disqualified from consideration any evidence in the New Testament or elsewhere which militated against their case. The name they gave to the school they founded was *Konsequente Eschatologie*, and we shall accordingly label this new definition Eschatology[K]. Resort to tactical definition is far too common an occurrence in the history of

---

[7] *Skizze des Lebens Jesu* (1901) and *Vom Reimarus zu Wrede* (1906), Eng. tr. by W. Montgomery, *The Quest of the Historical Jesus* (1910).

[8] J. Weiss, op. cit., p. 67.

[9] A. Schweitzer, *Paul and His Interpreters* (1912), p. 228.

scholarship to cause much surprise. What is astonishing is that the new definition came so rapidly to be accepted as normal even by those who repudiated the conclusions which Weiss and Schweitzer had drawn from it.

I am not for a moment denying that there are passages in the New Testament which give colour to the thesis of these two great scholars, or that they did a service to biblical scholarship by insisting that biblical theology would be out of focus if eschatology were ignored.

> Before you have gone through all the towns of Israel the Son of Man will have come (Matt. 10:23).

> There are some of those standing here who will not taste death before they have seen the kingdom of God come with power (Mark 9:1).

> Like the lightning flash that lights up the earth from end to end will the Son of Man be when his day comes (Luke 17:24).

> It is time for you to wake out of sleep, for deliverance is nearer to us now than it was when first we believed (Rom. 13:11).

> The Lord is near (Phil. 4:7).

> For soon, very soon, he who is to come will come; he will not delay (Heb. 10:37).

> You must be patient and stout-hearted, for the coming of the Lord is near (Jas. 5:8).

> The time has come for the judgment to begin: it is beginning with God's own household (1 Pet. 4:17).

But there were two points which Weiss and Schweitzer overlooked.

The first is that even within the material which appeared to support their view there are incoherences of a kind not unlike those we detected in our study of Eschatology[1]. According to Luke 17:22–37 the coming of the Son of Man is to be unheralded, over-taking people in the midst of their ordinary daily occupations of buying, selling, building, planting, marrying and giving in marriage, just like the flood in Noah's day or the destruction of Sodom and Gomorrah. But according to Mark 13 the Son of Man is to come only after a long series of warnings—wars, famines, earthquakes, persecution, the ravaging of Judaea, the appearance of false prophets and messiahs, and the falling of the stars from heaven; which one might have expected to cause some disruption of daily routine. Nor is this merely a disagreement between evangelists or their sources, for the incoherence is present in Mark 13 itself: after its catalogue of premonitory signs leading up to the final crisis, the chapter ends with a parable in which that crisis is compared to the return of an absent householder who may come at any time of the day or night and catch his servants unawares. To put it bluntly, the great day cannot happen for a long time yet; nevertheless the disciples had better be on the lookout for it now. In the next chapter Mark records Jesus' answer to the high priest at his trial (14:62): 'You shall see the Son of Man seated at the right hand of Power and coming with the clouds of heaven.' Matthew, who shows elsewhere a great interest in the final coming of the Son of Man, repeats Mark's words with the addition of 'from now on'; in other words, the coming of the Son of Man was for him not just an event of the end, but one which was to occur either continuously or repeatedly from the moment of the crucifixion. Paul, writing two letters to Thessalonica at no great interval can remind his converts in the first that the day of the Lord comes like a thief breaking in at night when the householder is saying, 'All is safe and secure'; and can chide them in the second for getting morbidly excited about the day of the Lord when he had been at some pains to explain to them that it could not happen yet (1 Thess. 5:1–3; 2 Thess. 2:1–8). And to all this we may add a few explicit statements that the date of the end is a secret which God keeps entirely to himself, for the very good reason that only he can decide when he will be ready for it (Mark 13:32; Acts 1:8; 2 Pet. 3:3–8).

The second point is associated with the name of C. H. Dodd, since it was he who rescued New Testament scholarship from the cul-de-sac into which Weiss and Schweitzer had directed it. Dodd pointed out[10] that the dominant note in the faith of the New Testament is not expectancy but celebration of the life, death and resurrection of Jesus as the completed work of God (e.g. John 17:4; 2 Cor. 6:2; Heb. 10:12–14; 1 Pet. 1:3); and that Jesus himself had laid the foundation for this by proclaiming that the prophecies of

---

[10] First in a paper delivered to a theological conference in 1927, subsequently in *The Parables of the Kingdom* (1935) and *The Apostolic Preaching and its Development* (1936).

the Old Testament were being fulfilled (Luke 10:23–24), that the day of God had come (Mark 1:15), that the kingdom of God had arrived (Luke 11:20) and was open for all who were prepared to enter it (Matt. 21:31). Dodd argued that the parables of crisis, which in the Gospels have for their referent the future coming of the Son of Man, were originally spoken by Jesus with reference to the crisis of his own ministry, a crisis which entailed death for himself, persecution for his disciples and ruin for the Jewish nation which had rejected in him God's last appeal to them, in all of which he taught his disciples to see the judgment of God. To this dominant emphasis in the teaching of Jesus Dodd gave the name 'realised eschatology' (Eschatology^R): in Christ the *eschaton*, the expected end, had fully entered history. At first he went so far as to say that the presence of the *eschaton* in Jesus was so complete as to leave no remainder, no room for a future coming of the Son of Man; the use of future tenses with regard to the kingdom of God and the Son of Man was only 'an accommodation of language' to the problems of time and eternity. But soon, in response to criticism, he revised this extreme position, and held that New Testament eschatology was well summarised by the Johannine sentence, 'The time is coming and now is.'

Dodd's critics protested with some justification that 'realised eschatology' was a contradiction in terms. Dodd had defined the *eschaton* as 'that beyond which nothing can conceivably happen'; and if that is what fully entered history in A.D. 30, it would seem to follow that succeeding centuries have consisted of non-events. What seems to have escaped notice at the time is that Eschatology^R is metaphor, the application of end-of-the-world language to that which is not literally the end of the world.[11] One of the critics, J. Jeremias, attempted to rescue the literalism of Eschatology^K by offering Dodd an alternative title, 'inaugurated eschatology', the idea being that Jesus had initiated a process destined to work itself out to its culmination of the last day. This idea has a certain attraction, since it does justice to some New Testament expressions, e.g. the description of believers as 'on the way to salvation' (1 Cor. 1:18), or Paul's prayer that 'he who began the good work in you will

---

[11] In 1939 Amos Wilder (who had the advantage of being a poet as well as a scholar) in *Eschatology and Ethics in the Teaching of Jesus* made a plea for the recognition of the poetic nature of eschatological language. Cf. also J. A. T. Robinson, *In the End God*.

complete it against the day of the Lord Jesus (Phil. 1:6). What it leaves out of account is the New Testament consensus that God's work of salvation was accomplished once for all in the representative person of Jesus.

In the meantime, however, Bultmann, a pupil of Weiss, had been grappling with the implications of Eschatology[K] for the modern believer. The common sense approach would have been to say that anyone whose whole outlook was dictated by a belief that the world would end in the middle of the first century A.D. was so catastrophically wrong that he could have no more relevance for modern man than any other fanatic who has predicted the end of the world, and then to abandon either the Christian faith or the hypothesis. Bultmann chose a more elaborate and philosophical escape route, provided for him by the existentialism of Heidegger. Jesus literally expected an imminent end, but what made his expectation fully eschatological was that in it God's future wholly determined the present. Eschatology in fact was a Jewish form of self-understanding. For the modern Christian the teaching of Jesus is eschatological in so far as it reaches out from the past and impels him to an existential decision and thus to an encounter with God. Two comments must be made on Bultmann's Eschatology[E] (Existential). The first is that, if a belief in the temporal imminence of the end has no other function than to express the ultimate and transcendent significance of a present decision, then neither 'imminent' nor 'ultimate' is being used in its literal, temporal sense. The second comment is that, if Bultmann had gone a step further and had defined eschatology as a Jewish understanding of history, the Jew's self-understanding of his involvement in the corporate life of his nation and of mankind, this chapter of mine would not have needed to be written, since he would have given a fair summary of the conclusion to which it is leading. But Bultmann's theology was intensely individualist: only an individual can make an existential decision or experience an existential encounter. He had no place in his thinking for the corporateness which is the very stuff of ordinary historical existence, and even dismissed as 'gnostic' Paul's teaching about the unity of mankind in Adam.[12] For him genuinely

---

[12] 'Adam and Christ according to Romans 5' in *Current Issues in New Testament Interpretation*, ed. W. Klassen and G. F. Snyder, pp. 143-65.

historical existence had a pin-point focus in existential commitment, and he was able to maintain this thesis by exploiting the two German synonyms for history in a way which ran counter to normal German usage. *Historie*, so he argued, is the past in its pastness, the subject matter of historical research. *Geschichte* is the past in its power to reach into the present. The cross, for example, is an event in *Historie* in A.D. 30, but an event in *Geschichte* only at the point where it impels a person to faith or unbelief. Thus 'eschatological' became a synonym for existential and, together with *geschichtlich*, an antonym of *historisch*;[13] and at this point our semantic confusion is almost complete.

All the conflicting definitions we have so far surveyed were produced by New Testament scholars, greatly to the embarrassment of Old Testament studies. The extent and nature of the embarrassment became apparent in 1951, when Mowinckel published his monumental work on the development of messianic belief,[14] in which he stated that the prophets of Israel had no eschatology. It is not difficult to see which definition he was using (see p. 125). He had docilely accepted Eschatology[K], despite the fact that this rendered the term inapplicable to the material he was studying, since, as he correctly observed, when the prophets spoke of an imminent event it was not the end of the world they were referring to. The difficulty is that many of the eschatological passages in the New Testament are couched in language borrowed from the prophets, and we are begging far too many questions if we so define eschatology that it fits the one context and not the other. Accordingly, other Old Testament scholars began to explore the possibility that the constituent element in eschatology is not finality (let alone imminence), but newness[15] or purpose[16]; and so to our already over-burdened list of definitions we add Eschatology[N] and Eschatology[P]. Eschatology[N] is open to the obvious riposte that a term derived from the Greek word for 'last' is a silly word to use for it. But Eschatology[P] is worth exploring further. The prophets

---

[13] The irony is that nobody was likely to experience an existential encounter with God by reading Bultmann's *Die Geschichte der synoptischen Tradition*, which was uncompromisingly *historisch*.

[14] *Han son Kommer*; Eng. tr. *He That Cometh* by G. W. Anderson (1956).

[15] E.g. J. Lindblom, *Prophecy in Ancient Israel*.

[16] E.g. R. E. Clements, *Prophecy and Covenant*.

undoubtedly believed that God was working out a purpose in history, particularly in the history of their own nation, and it is hard to conceive of a purpose apart from the complementary notion of goal. The idea that things are what they are in virtue of their purpose or goal has a long and honourable record under the name of teleology, and the classical exponent of it was Aristotle, who taught that all things have four causes (the efficient cause which brings them into being, the formal cause which is their essential nature, their final cause or purpose, and the matter of which they consist), that the first three are merely different aspects of the same reality, and that even God acts as Prime Mover by reason of being the goal to which all things are drawn.[17] Thus Eschatology[P] would be a Jewish equivalent of teleology, sensitive (as the Greek philosophers were not) to the reality and significance of historical events.

No term can remain long in currency as a valuable medium of exchange unless the users are in general agreement about the value they put on it, and the question therefore arises whether this one has not now been devalued beyond recovery. The loss of it would create an awkward gap in theological vocabulary, and for this reason it is worth while to make some attempt at its rehabilitation. If it is to be rescued, we need a definition more flexible than any we have so far been offered, capable of doing justice to all the valid insights contained in the conflicting theories we have catalogued.

My proposal may be set out in three propositions, and has the advantage of being simple and comprehensive, as well as being in line with all that we have observed about biblical language in the previous chapters of this book:

1. The biblical writers believed literally that the world had had a beginning in the past and would have an end in the future.

2. They regularly used end-of-the-world language metaphorically to refer to that which they well knew was not the end of the world.

3. As with all other uses of metaphor, we have to allow for the likelihood of some literalist misinterpretation on the part of the hearer, and for the possibility of some blurring of the edges between vehicle and tenor on the part of the speaker.

---

[17] κινεῖ ὡς ἐρώμενον. See Arist. *Met.* xii.7.1072[b]3. Cf. also the last line of Dante's *Divine Comedy* (Paradiso xxxiii.145): 'L'amor che muove il sole e l'altre stelle' (The love which moves the sun and the other stars).

Proposition 1 is easily established for the Old Testament. It is implied in such phrases as 'until the moon is no more' (Ps. 72:7) and in the ancient promise to Noah:

> While the earth lasts
> seedtime and harvest, cold and heat,
> summer and winter, day and night,
> shall never cease (Gen. 8:22).

In some passages it is explicitly stated.

> Long ago you laid the foundations of the earth,
> and the heavens were your handiwork.
> They shall pass away, but you endure
> (Ps. 102:25–26; cf. Isa. 51:6; 54:10).

It is no objection that in other passages the earth is said to last for ever (Ps. 78:69; Eccl. 1:4). In comparison with the transitoriness of human existence, the earth will last till the end of time, but it is not everlasting as God is everlasting. When Mowinckel declared that the prophets had no eschatology, it was not Proposition 1 that he was denying. He himself believed that the myth which was enacted in the temple ritual was a complete world view, spanning the whole of time. 'In the cultic festival past, present and future are welded into one.'[18] Yahweh's initial victory at creation, which established him as king over the primaeval flood (Ps. 93), was to be consummated in his final victory when he comes to judge the earth (Ps. 96:13; 97:1–9; 98:9); and beginning and end meet in that moment of demand and opportunity which is called today (Ps. 95:7; cf. Heb. 3:13). Myth and eschatology belong together.

Our first problem arises when we try to decide whether the expressions 'the latter end of the days'[19] and 'the day of the Lord'[20] are eschatological in this plenary sense. For the first of these phrases the Hebrew dictionary of Brown, Driver and Briggs gives the following definition: 'a prophetic phrase denoting the final period

---

[18] *The Psalms in Israel's Worship*, p. 113.

[19] Gen. 49:1; Numb. 24:14; Deut. 4:30; 31:29; Hos. 3:5; Isa. 2:2; Jer. 23:20; 30:24; 48:47; 49:39; Ezek. 38:16; Dan. 2:28; 10:14.

[20] Amos 5:18, 20; Isa. 2:12; 13:6,9; Zeph. 1:7, 14; Jer. 46:10; Ezek. 13:5; 30:3; Obad. 15; Zech. 14:1; Mal. 4:5; Joel 1:15; 2:1,11, 31; 3:14.

of the history so far as the speaker's perspective reaches.' It is thus the equivalent of the English expressions 'in the end' or 'ultimately' when we use them to mean 'sooner or later' or 'in the future'; and it has precisely that vagueness which makes for the blurring of the edges mentioned in Proposition 3. The origins of the phrase 'the day of the Lord' are as yet obscure and conjectural. When it is first used in the eighth century B.C. by Amos, it clearly has a long history behind it. His contemporaries who long for it regard it as a day of Yahweh's victory in which they will share, and Amos warns them that it will be Yahweh's victory over them. What is not in doubt is that the day came to be described in terms of cosmic disaster, as the return of primaeval chaos, and so by imaginative elision to be seen as the end of the world.

In thirteen of the eighteen instances of its occurrence, the day of the Lord is said to be either imminent or present. It is here that Proposition 2 comes to our aid. For when we examine the contexts, we find that in one case the referent is the overthrow of Babylon, in another the annihilation of Edom, in another the ravaging of Judah by a plague of locusts. Now these prophets were not claiming that the contemporary crisis *was* the day of the Lord, in the same sense in which May 24, 1819 (and not August 4, 1914 or the Ides of March 43 B.C.) was Queen Victoria's birthday. None of them would have argued that, because he himself was right, the others must be wrong. Yet neither did they believe in a succession of days of the Lord. The day was his victory, when he would come decisively for salvation and judgment, and they were inviting their hearers to see that day in the current crisis. In other words they were using the term as metaphor.

The prophets looked to the future with bifocal vision. With their near sight they foresaw imminent historical events which would be brought about by familiar human causes; for example, disaster was near for Babylon because Yahweh was stirring up the Medes against them (Isa. 13:17). With their long sight they saw the day of the Lord; and it was in the nature of the prophetic experience that they were able to adjust their focus so as to impose the one image on the other and produce a synthetic picture. Yet they did not thereby lose the ability to distinguish between the two types of vision, any more than the writer of Ps. 23 lost the ability to distinguish between himself and a sheep. To prove the truth of this assertion, there is fortunately a simple test ready to hand in the life story of Jeremiah. At the outset of his ministry (626 B.C.) Jeremiah predicted the destruction of Jerusalem by an enemy from the north (Jer. 1:14–15; 4:6; 6:1, 22; 10:22), and in synthetic vision he saw this as God's judgment, depicting it as the return of chaos and even using the words *tohu wabohu* (waste and void), which occur elsewhere only in the account of creation in Gen. 1:2.[21] The expected attack did not come, and for years Jeremiah had to live with the haunting doubt that he might be a false prophet, guilty under the Deuteronomic law of a capital offence (Deut. 18:20–22). He even accused God of having duped him (Jer. 20:7). But in 605 B.C. he reissued his early prophecies by dictating them to Baruch (Jer. 36:1–4). This time his prediction came true, for Jerusalem was captured in 598 B.C. and reduced to ruins in a further siege eleven years later. But it never occurred to Jeremiah or anybody else that he might still be regarded as a false prophet because the world had not come to an end.

The Book of Joel provides an interesting study in what we might call prophetic camera technique. The book opens with some close-up shots of a locust swarm overrunning the countryside. Then the scene changes to the temple, where priests and elders are instructed to proclaim a national fast in recognition that the calamity is God's judgment.

> Alas! the day is near,
> the day of the Lord: it comes
> a mighty destruction from the Almighty.
> Look! it stares us in the face   (1:15).

The prophet says that the day is 'near', because that is the traditional word to use about the day of the Lord, but what he means by it is that it has arrived. Any possible doubt about this is rapidly dispelled.

> Blow the trumpet in Zion,
> sound the alarm upon my holy hill;

---

[21] Jer. 4:23–26. Cf. Shakespeare's *Othello* III.iii.90–2:

> Perdition catch my soul
> But I do love thee! and when I love thee not
> Chaos is come again.

> let all that live in the land tremble,
> for the day of the Lord has come,
> surely a day of darkness and gloom is upon us   (2:1-2).

But this local manifestation of God's judgment has the power to call the nation to repentance because it is seen as an anticipation and embodiment of the universal judgment to come. So the foreground scene fades into a telephoto panorama of all nations gathered in the Valley of the Lord's Judgment.

> The roar of multitudes, multitudes in the Valley of Decision!
> The day of the Lord is at hand
> in the valley of Decision;
> sun and moon are darkened
> and the stars forebear to shine   (3:14).

Few would hesitate to call this an eschatological vision, yet it is not the end: the effect of this judgment is not to determine the destiny of individuals in some after-life, but to 'reverse the fortunes of Judah and Jerusalem' (3:1), so that afterwards

> there shall be people living in Judah for ever,
> in Jerusalem generation after generation   (3:21).

Thus the nearness of the day is given both a short range and a long range application, and it is of some significance for the interpretation of Mark 1:15 that in the short range 'is near' is synonymous with 'has arrived'.[22] On the other hand the long range vision is introduced by two quite vague indications of time, 'a day will come' (2:28) and 'when that time comes' (3:1), so that the proclamation that the day has now arrived for the multitudes of all nations tells us nothing whatever about its date.

The unconvinced advocates of Eschatology[K] can, however, properly object that I have as yet said nothing about apocalyptic. This name was derived from the title of the Book of Revelation ('The Apocalypse of Jesus Christ') and applied to a range of Jewish

---

[22] Cf. Lam. 4:18: 'Our end has drawn near, our days have run their course (lit. are full), our end has come.' In the vocabulary of the temple a priest was said to bring an offering near, which meant that he presented it at the altar, not that he left it a mile outside the city.

writings which appeared to belong to a similar literary genre, particularly in their use of vivid and sometimes bizarre symbolism.[23] When the term first came into currency, it was generally assumed, largely because of a total lack of sympathy with the poetic and imaginative nature of their language, that the world view of the apocalyptists was drastically different from that of the prophets, not least in their deep pessimism and their consequent preoccupation with the end of the world; and it was this apocalyptic world view that Weiss and Schweitzer believed to be determinative for the interpretation of New Testament eschatology. More recently, however, there has been a swelling chorus of protest against this facile verdict.[24] It would still be agreed that apocalyptic differed from the prophetic writings of an earlier age, but only because of two major changes in historical circumstance. First, the conquests of Alexander the Great had broken down national boundaries, and so had compelled Jewish thinkers, as never before, to see their national history against a backdrop of world history; and this we see happening for the first time in the Book of Daniel. Secondly, the apocalyptic books were all written in the three hundred years between the outbreak of persecution under Antiochus Epiphanes in 167 B.C. and the final destruction of the Jewish nation by Hadrian in A.D. 135. They have their context in a period of intense nationalism, when the Jewish people either were, or at least felt themselves to be, engaged in a desperate struggle for the survival of their national life and their religion. It is hardly surprising therefore that these documents are full of cryptic but easily decodable references to current affairs; or that they evince a pessimistic helplessness on the part of the Jews in the face of world powers over which they have no control. If we miss the note of moral and social concern which is characteristic of the prophets, this is no symptom of spiritual or

[23] The most important of these are Daniel (in the O.T.), 2 Esdras or 4 Ezra (in the Apocrypha), 1 and 2 Enoch, 2 Baruch, Jubilees, the Martyrdom of Isaiah, the Sibylline Oracles and the Testament of the Twelve Patriarchs (all of which may be found in vol. II of *The Apocrypha and Pseudepigrapha of the Old Testament*, ed. R. H. Charles); and to them must now be added one or two of the documents from Qumran.

[24] E.g. H. H. Rowley, *The Relevance of Apocalyptic* (1944); S. B. Frost, *Old Testament Apocalyptic* (1952); D. S. Russell, *The Method and Message of Jewish Apocalyptic* (1964) and *Apocalyptic: Ancient and Modern* (1978); K. Koch, *The Rediscovery of Apocalyptic* (1970; ET 1972); J. Barr, 'Jewish Apocalyptic in recent scholarly study', *Bulletin of the John Rylands Library*, 58.1 (1975); G. B. Caird, 'Eschatology and politics' in *Biblical Studies in Honour of William Barclay* (1976).

intellectual decline. One does not expect a programme of social reform from the liberation front.

When an author writes a book consisting wholly or mainly of symbols, there is a prima facie case for not supposing him to be a literalist; and the case holds even if he should prove to be a slavish imitator using conventional imagery and with little imagination of his own.[25] But this generalisation does not decisively settle the more particular question whether the apocalyptists intended their eschatology to be taken literally. That can be determined only by reading the books.

The Book of Daniel is a pseudepigraph, i.e. a book attributed to someone other than the actual author. The author purports to be Daniel, living in the sixth century B.C., though in fact he lived in the second century and was writing at the outbreak of persecution in about 167 B.C. The stories of the first six chapters are not historical memories of the Babylonian and Persian periods, but parables of what was actually happening under Seleucid rule. There is no evidence of any kind that the Babylonians interfered with the Jewish food regulations (ch. 1) or compelled the Jews to worship their own gods (ch. 3), or that the Persians forbad them to observe the rules of their religion (ch. 6). But we have only to read 1 and 2 Maccabees to see that all this was what Antiochus was doing at the time when Daniel was written. When we come to the visions of chapters 7–11, we find the fictitious Daniel describing in prophetic terms the history of the period between his time and the actual author's with greater wealth of detail as he approaches the real date of writing. The purpose of this curious literary device was to assure the readers that their sufferings had been foreseen, that they were part of a regular pattern and under the control of a divine plan which God was working out on the stage of world history and would bring to a successful conclusion. The visions reach their climax in the setting up of the 'desecrating horror' (abomination of

---

[25] No doubt some of the authors of these books were imitators. I have elsewhere suggested that the nearest modern equivalent to apocalyptic is the political cartoon with its 'bizarre animal symbolism' (lion, eagle, bear, carthorse, bulldog, kangaroo, elephant, donkey etc.), which the humblest reader of the daily paper deciphers more easily than he reads print—see *Expos. Times* lxxiv (1962–3), pp. 13–15, 51–3, 82–4, 103–5. The reception of Daniel into the canon of the Old Testament and of Revelation into the canon of the New was no accident, but was due to public recognition that these two are works of creative originality and power which put them in a different class from the rest.

desolation), the altar to Olympian Zeus which Antiochus had erected on top of the altar of burnt offering in the Jerusalem temple. Thus far the eschatology of the book is Eschatology[R], since what was future to 'Daniel' was past or present to the author and his readers. Insofar as the author looks to the real future, it is to the removal of the 'horror' and the end of persecution. For a moment, indeed, he uses the telephoto lens (12:1–3), but at once he brings us back to the foreground. Daniel asks how long it will be until the end and is given the symbolic figure of 'a time, times and half a time'. But this is only the interval that must elapse before 'the shattering of the holy people ceases' (12:7); the end of the age is further off (12:13).

The same device of pseudepigraphy provides the framework for the Ezra Apocalypse.[26] The author purports to be Shealtiel, father of Zerubbabel, writing in 557 B.C., thirty years after the destruction of Jerusalem by the Babylonians, though with a curious disregard for chronology he is also identified with the fourth century Ezra. It is clear, however, that the actual date of writing is about A.D. 100, thirty years after the destruction of Jerusalem by the Roman Titus, and that the purpose of the book is to wrestle with the immense theological difficulties which that calamity posed for the Jewish people. The first six chapters (3–8) are a debate between Ezra and his angel guide Uriel about the justice of God: why has God destroyed Jerusalem when other nations are manifestly more sinful? When the argument ranges widely over the eternal destiny of individuals and reaches a climax in a detailed description of the last judgment, we begin to wonder whether the author has lost track of his original theme; but he returns to it in three visions, one of a widow (Jerusalem) bereaved of her only son, one of an eagle (Rome) dethroned by a lion (Messiah), and one of a triumphant human figure rising from the sea (9–13). These three visions together contain a promise of national restoration. 'Take courage, Israel; house of Jacob, lay aside your grief. The Most High bears you in mind, and the Mighty One has not for ever forgotten you' (12:46). However idealised the picture may be, what is envisaged is a new epoch of world history. The Messiah who inaugurates it is himself a mortal figure. 'My son the Messiah shall appear with his companions

---

[26] 2 Esdras (4 Ezra) 3–14, chapters 1–2 and 15–16 being later additions.

and bring four hundred years of happiness to all who survive. At the end of that time, my son the Messiah shall die, and so shall all mankind who draw breath. Then the world shall return to its original silence for seven days as at the beginning of creation . . . Then the Most High shall be seen on the judgment seat' (7:28–33). However we interpret the four hundred years, the last judgment is hardly imminent. The author is a bigoted nationalist whose indignant plea is that Israel shall be given the place in the present world which God has promised her. 'You have said that you made this first world for our sake, and that all the rest of the nations descended from Adam are nothing, no better than spittle . . . And yet, Lord, those nations which count for nothing are today ruling over us and devouring us . . . Was the world really made for us? Why then may we not take possession of our world? How much longer shall it be so?' (6:55–59). He finds the answer in an eschatological judgment which is the end of an old world order that has lost its youth (14:10); but it is not the end of the world!

It is of course perfectly possible to give a different description of the phenomena we have examined. Russell, for example, prefers to think in terms of the fluctuation between the transcendental (the end of history) on the one hand and the temporal (the continuation of history) on the other, 'and, at times, a mingling and merging of these two concepts.'[27] But the merging of two concepts, held together in synthetic unity by a single term, is one of the definitions of metaphor. One of the great advantages of describing the apocalyptic merging of concepts as metaphor is that it brings apocalyptic out of the Jewish backwater, to which so much unimaginative scholarship has consigned it, into the main stream of the world's literature; and this, to judge from its influence on art, music and poetry, is where it belongs. We have already observed many examples of fluctuation or two-way traffic between the vehicle and tenor of metaphor. The image of king, judge or father is used to say something about the divine unknown in the light of the human known, but it comes back with a return ticket to dictate how human kings, judges, fathers ought to behave (p. 19). The mythological language of the beginning of time is used to impart significance to an event in time, and the emblematic event is then

[27] *Apocalyptic: Ancient and Modern*, p. 24.

taken up into the myth to furnish it with richer detail (p. 228). Similarly, when the eschatological language of the end of time is used to interpret a historical event, that event can be taken up into the myth of the end. Because Daniel saw the setting up of the 'desecrating horror' and its removal as eschatological events, that term and the symbolic 'time, times and half a time' were absorbed into eschatological vocabulary, to be used by others with reference to the crises of their own age (Mark 13:14; Rev. 12:14), just as his four beasts from the sea contribute new features to the primaeval ocean monster (Rev. 13:1–2).

If Weiss and Schweitzer were correct in thinking that apocalyptic provides the indispensable background for the understanding of the teaching of Jesus, then the one inescapable inference is the one which they and their successors persistently refused to draw: that the gospel of Jesus was directed to Israel as a nation with a summons to abandon the road of aggressive nationalism and return to a true understanding of her historic role as the people of God. There is much in the Gospels to support this view, beginning with John the Baptist. Baptism apart, the one fact known with certainty about John is that he proclaimed the imminence of divine judgment, and the advocates of Eschatology[K] have been content to call his preaching 'eschatological' without bothering to enquire what was its referent. Once this question has been raised, it is self-evident that what John predicted was a judgment on Israel, in which its dead wood was to be cleared away and its grain separated from its chaff, in which it would be useless to claim an impeccable Jewish pedigree, since the verdict would be based on performance alone (Matt. 3:7–12; Luke 3:1–9, 15–17). Israel stood at the parting of the ways and must decide whether to follow the road of national repentance or the road of national ruin. This was the atmosphere of expectancy which Jesus accepted as in inheritance from his forerunner, and it accounts for his repeated warnings that in disregarding his teaching the nation was heading for irretrievable disaster. The cities of Galilee would suffer a fate worse than that of Sodom and Gomorrah (Luke 10:12–15; Matt. 10:15).[28] Jerusalem, having

---

[28] Compare the description of the long agonies of the siege of Jerusalem in Lam. 4:6:

The punishment of my people is worse than the penalty of Sodom,
Which was overthrown in a moment, and no one wrung his hands.

abandoned God in the person of his messenger, would be abandoned by him to her enemies (Matt. 23:37–39; Luke 13:34–35).[29] This generation would have to answer for the cumulative guilt of past ages (Luke 11:49–50).

There can be no doubt that this is how Luke understood the ministry of Jesus. His Gospel opens with a group of pious Jews waiting expectantly for 'the restoration of Israel' (2:25) and 'the liberation of Jerusalem' (2:38), and with songs which celebrate the prospect of a national deliverance. It ends with Jesus reassuring two disciples that their hope 'that he was the man to liberate Israel' had not been misplaced. In between are frequent warnings, couched in language drawn from the prophecies of Jeremiah and Ezekiel, that Jerusalem is to be destroyed by Roman armies, and that this will be the judgment of God, 'because she did not recognise the moment when God was visiting her' with his final offer of peace (19:41–44; 21:20–24; 23:27–31). In the school of Bultmann Luke has been accused of 'historicising' the original eschatological gospel. Is there then any evidence in the other Gospels to show that this accusation is ungrounded and that he, the Gentile, had correctly understood the character of Jewish eschatology?

Mark 13 begins with Jesus predicting the destruction of the temple, and four of his disciples asking when this is to happen. Now according to Eschatology[K], Mark, instead of giving Jesus' answer to this reasonable question, has tacked on an answer to a completely different question: when is the world going to end? But have we any serious justification for supposing Mark to be a fool? The natural assumption is that he regarded the discourse of Jesus as his answer to the question which occasioned it: the disaster to Jerusalem will come within the lifetime of the present generation, and, when it arrives, they are to see in it the coming of the Son of Man to whom God has entrusted the judgment of the nations (Dan. 7:22; cf. John 5:27; 1 Cor. 6:2). The chapter contains a notable self-contradiction. Jesus knows that the Son of Man will come within a generation, but the day and the hour are known only to God (13:30, 32). Literalists are accustomed to explain that Jesus knows roughly the year in which the world will end, but not whether

[29] Before the capture of Jerusalem in 587 B.C. Ezekiel had a vision of God's glory leaving the temple, and so abandoning the city to its fate (Ezek. 8–11).

it will be a Tuesday or a Wednesday, not whether it will be at
10 a.m. or 6 p.m.; and against such bathos it is pointless to argue.
The paratactical Hebrew mind did not need to be told that the two
sayings were at different levels: embodied in the historical event
which Jesus predicted, the day would come within a generation; in
its full final, literal reality its time was known only to God.

The proof that this is the way Mark's mind worked comes in the
parable of the Absent Householder with which the chapter ends:

> Be alert, be wakeful. You do not know when the moment comes. It is
> like a man away from home: he has left his house and put his servants
> in charge, each with his own work to do, and he has ordered the door-
> keeper to stay awake. Keep awake, then, for you do not know when the
> master of the house is coming. Evening or midnight, cock-crow or
> early dawn—if he comes suddenly, he must not find you asleep.

R. H. Lightfoot[30] pointed out that Mark has used these four
watches of the night to punctuate the passion narrative that follows.
Evening is the time of the last supper when Judas is caught
napping (14:17), midnight the hour of Gethsemane when Jesus
finds his three companions asleep and repeats the command to keep
awake (14:32); cock-crow is the time of Peter's denial (14:72); and
dawn is the hour when Jesus is handed over to Pilate (15:1). No
doubt Mark believed in a final day when God the householder would
call his servants to account, but he sees that day anticipated in the
critical moments of his story. Hence the servants must be vigilant
at all times, because the master comes to each of them at an hour
and in a manner that he least expects.

Matthew appears to be less amenable to such treatment. Writing
long after the fall of Jerusalem, he more obviously than the other
evangelists has adapted the traditional material to make it applicable to the church of his own day. He alone of the four uses the
term *parousia* (advent) and the phrase 'the end of the world'.
Parables which, as Dodd demonstrated, had their original referent
in the crisis of Jesus' ministry were universalised by being made to
refer to the final judgment, and Mark's question about the destruction of the temple was recast to include this wider reference: 'When
will this happen? And what will be the signal for your coming

---

[30] *The Gospel Message of St. Mark*, pp. 48–59.

(*parousia*) and the end of the world?' (24:3). Yet Matthew was very far from being committed to a literalist eschatology. As we have seen above, his version of Jesus' reply to the high priest contains the words 'from now on' (26:64). It little matters whether these words are his own editorial insertion or came to him from a traditional source. He was quite capable of deleting anything that did not express his own conviction. And the conviction they unambiguously express is that the coming of the Son of Man on the clouds of heaven would be seen not merely at the end of time but continuously or repeatedly from the moment of Jesus' death. Thus this verse helps us to see that Bultmann's Eschatology[E], though inadequate for the Bible as a whole, comes very near to expressing Matthew's thought. For Matthew's emphasis on the final judgment does not arise out of any preoccupation with the end of the world, but rather from a recognition that the final judgment is for ever pressing upon the present with both offer and demand. How could it be otherwise in a Gospel which begins with the birth of him whose name is Immanuel, God with us, and ends with his promise, 'I am with you to the end of the world'?

Among the early Christians there were of course some who misunderstood. Paul recalls that on his arrival at Thessalonica he had taught his converts to turn from idols to the service of the true God and to wait for his Son from heaven; and he was taken by surprise when some of them, whom he accuses of truancy, gave up earning their living to prepare for the imminent crisis. Luke introduces one of the parables with the remark that Jesus told it to dispel any notion 'that the reign of God might dawn at any moment' (19:11), and it is reasonable to infer that he had some people of the same persuasion among his own acquaintance. Much later the author of 2 Peter cites an ancient Christian prophecy that scoffers would arise in the future, demanding to know what had happened to the promise of Christ's coming. He assumes not only that such people are wrong, but that from the first they have been known to be wrong, since the end will come only when God is ready for it, and the maturing of God's purpose is not reckoned in years: one day or a thousand years makes no difference to the divine patience as it waits for all to come to repentance (2 Pet. 3:2–9).

There are two passages in the Pauline epistles which have been thought fatal to my argument, and we must examine each in turn.

> In all this remember how critical the moment is. It is time for you to wake out of sleep, for deliverance is nearer to us now than it was when first we believed. It is far on in the night; day is near. Let us therefore throw off the deeds of darkness and put on our armour as soldiers of the light. Let us behave with decency as befits the day: no revelling or drunkenness, no debauchery or vice, no quarrels or jealousies! Let Christ himself be the armour you wear; give no more thought to satisfying the bodily appetites (Rom. 13:11–14).

The literalists see in this passage decisive evidence that Paul expected the end to come shortly, perhaps in his own lifetime. Even at his conversion 25 (?) years ago, it had been imminent, only x years away. Now it was $x-25$ years away, appreciably nearer. But observe the disastrous effect of this interpretation on the paragraph as a whole. *Ex hypothesi*, our 'deliverance' or 'salvation' is that which will be achieved at the coming of Christ, an event to be equated with the dawning of day. Until then it will continue to be night, and night is the time for sleep. Since his conversion Paul, along with other Christians, has been comfortably asleep, having set his alarum clock for an hour before dawn. But now the alarum is arousing him and his friends to greet the approaching day. We have only to compare this with what Paul says elsewhere to see how improbable it all is. He believed that Christians were already 'sons of day', 'sons of light', and so did not belong to night or darkness (1 Thess. 5:4–5), and that already at their baptism they had 'put on Christ' (Gal. 3:27). He is not asking the Roman Christians to wake up or throw off the deeds of darkness *for the first time*, but reminding them that watchfulness and resistance to the seductions of paganism are a constant necessity for those who have enlisted as 'soldiers of the light'. What then can Paul mean by saying that 'our deliverance is nearer to us now than it was when first we believed'? There are two possible ways of taking this sentence, either of which yields a tolerable sense. The first is to say that the darkness which is nearly over represents the old, pagan world order which Paul believed to be tottering to its fall, more dangerous than ever before in its death throes. The Christian need not be afraid to undergo hardship and rigorous discipline during this period of pagan hostility, since he knows that it will not last; his deliverance from it is perceptibly nearer. Alternatively we may adopt the more traditional view that 'deliverance' means final salvation, which can come only when God's purposes are complete, when the gospel has been preached to all the world, when all mankind has been given time for repentance, when the church has been built up into the full stature of Christ. In this case Paul will be saying that sufficient progress has already been made to give the Christian soldier the assurance that God's purpose is moving towards its goal and that the campaign against the powers of darkness is worth while.

The other passage is 1 Cor. 7, where it has commonly been held the Paul's ascetic, and strangely un-Jewish, instructions about marriage are dictated by his belief that there is too little time left for such frivolities. There are three verses which give some colour to this view: 'a time of stress like the present' (7:26);[31] 'the critical time will not last long' (7:29); 'the form of this world is passing away' (7:31). Does Paul mean that world history is about to come to an end, or simply that, in a period when the old regime is cracking up, Christians must expect to live under harsh social pressure? Everything depends on the sense we give to 'this world',[32] which is a phrase Paul normally uses of the old order, now rendered obsolete by the coming of Christ. It is curious to observe how half-hearted is Paul's so called asceticism. He has received a letter from Corinth from a tough-minded group who have suggested that everyone ought to follow the splendid example of Paul and renounce marriage so as to be free for the service of the gospel, and he is half inclined to agree with them, though only in the case of those who have the gift of continence. A man who is widowed or divorced ought not to be looking for a wife; but if he does get married, there is nothing wrong in that (7:27–28). A father who has a twelve-year-old daughter and has made up his mind not to arrange a marriage for her is following the better course, always provided that he has not contracted any obligations for her. But if she has reached the advanced age of thirteen (*hyperakmos*) and there is a young man in the offing, and if he thinks the neighbours are beginning to gossip, it is perfectly in order for the couple to get married (7:36–38).[33]

---

[31] In some modern translations this phrase is impudently and inaccurately rendered 'the impending distress', i.e. the woes which herald the end.

[32] See above, Chapter One.

[33] See J. D. M. Derrett, *Studies in the New Testament* I, pp. 184–91.

A slave should not be bothering his head about emancipation, but if a chance comes, he should take it (7:21). The one governing principle is: 'I want you to be free from anxiety' (7:32). It is not just that marriage is a distraction from full-time service. Paul wants to spare his friends the sort of distress which married people are liable to experience in times of emergency (7:28). The one argument he conspicuously fails to use is that they should be ready for the coming of the Lord. 'In saying this I have no wish to keep you on a tight rein. I am thinking simply of your own good, of what is seemly, and of your freedom to serve the Lord without distraction' (7:35).

It appears, then, that Weiss and Schweitzer were right in thinking that eschatology was central to the understanding of biblical thought, but wrong in assuming that the biblical writers had minds as pedestrian as their own; that Bultmann was right in defining eschatology as a Jewish form of self-understanding, but wrong in failing to see that it was above all a Jewish understanding of history; that Dodd was right in describing the beliefs of Jesus and the early church as realised eschatology, but wrong in thinking that this term adequately distinguished the events of the gospel story from other events, both before and after.

I have made no attempt here to show how the notion of myth and eschatology as metaphor helps to make glorious and Christian sense of the Book of Revelation, since I have already done this in another work. But it is John who provides this notion with its full theological justification. Dodd and others have spoken of eschatology as though it were concerned with the *eschaton*, the final event, that beyond which nothing can conceivably happen. About an *eschaton* John has nothing to say. Instead he introduces us to a person who says, 'I am the Alpha and the Omega, the first and the last, the beginning and the end.' Wherever in the course of time men and women come face to face, whether for judgment or for salvation, with him who is the beginning and the end, that event can be adequately viewed only through the lenses of myth and eschatology.

Index

I. BIBLICAL PASSAGES

II. AUTHORS

Index

III. SUBJECTS

(**Bold type** indicates the page(s) on which a definition of the term is found.)